Walking
the dales

mike harding
Walking the dales

foreword by tom stephenson

Michael Joseph – London

First published in Great Britain by Michael Joseph Ltd
27 Wrights Lane, Kensington, London W8 5DZ
1986

Extract from 'Taxes on the Farmer Feeds Us All' by Ry
Cooder reproduced by permission of Chappell Music Limited,
London. Lines from 'Briggflatts' by Basil Bunting from
his *Collected Poems* (1978) reproduced by permission of
Oxford University Press. Extract from 'The Blue Tar Road' by
Liam Weldon reproduced by permission of Mulligan Music Limited.

Harding, Mike
Walking the Dales.
1. Yorkshire Dales National Park (England)
—Guide-books
I. Title
914.28′404858   DA670.Y6

ISBN 0-7181-2701-3

Filmset in Sabon by MS Filmsetting Limited,
Frome, Somerset
Printed and bound in Holland
by L. Van Leer and Co. Ltd, Deventer

contents

FOREWORD

WALKING the Dales – when Mike Harding first came this way they were of course the Yorkshire Dales! Since then the mandarins of Whitehall, who wouldn't know the difference between the Trough of Bowland and the Butter Tubs Pass, have juggled with the boundaries. They have ignored the Biblical injunction, 'Thou shalt not remove thy neighbour's landmark, which they of old time have set in thine inheritance' (Deuteronomy 19:14). Slices of Yorkshire have been taken into Lancashire, Cumbria, and Durham. Our author, though, is not likely to bother about boundaries. He would probably say, with Tom Paine, 'My country is the world.' (I think *Ower t'Tops* would have been a better title, though perhaps less appreciated south of Watford.)

When the fourteen-year-old Mike Harding and his good friend Dave set out on their two-week tour of the Yorkshire Dales, they could not have foreseen that it would lead to this odyssey.

Mike and Dave spent their first night at Stainforth Youth Hostel. I too discovered Stainforth long before there was a youth hostel or even a Mike Harding. At four o'clock on a May morning I had left Whalley and walked up the Ribble valley, via Clitheroe, Sawley, Wigglesworth, Rathmell and Settle and then to the summit of Pen-y-ghent – the dome of which had been my guidemark, for I possessed neither map nor compass. So I came to Stainforth at four o'clock in the afternoon, still twenty-five miles from home. My four pennies stretched to six penny glasses of milk because two farmers' wives refused to take my money.

So from Stainforth, or the more pivotal Pen-y-ghent, Mike and I in different eras have travelled the same ways and to a remarkable extent have found the same favourite places. Among them, not in any order of preference, are the upper reaches of the various dales, the Howgills (in my day, little-known country), particularly Carlingill, Black Force and Cautley Spout, the sources of the Eden and the Ure, Mallerstang Edge faced by the Baugh and Swarth Fells, culminating in the steep-nosed Wild Boar Fell, Dentdale, of course, and the lonely Barbondale.

On a more recent May morning we sat in the garden of Mike's Ribblesdale cottage in bright sunlight. Billowing cumulus clouds were drifting slowly over the summit of Pen-y-ghent, here seen broadside on from the famous stepped profile at the southern end. Against the morning light the stratification was scarcely evident.

A bumble bee buzzed round us, and from the fields came the baa-ing of lambs. A few hundred yards away a wheeling plover warned its young with frantic cries to take cover. Overhead, faint specks in the blue, larks were trilling. Most memorable of all were the eerie bubbling cries of curlews, a sound which does for me more than the jug-jug of a nightingale.

As we sat I remembered it was almost to the day seventy-five years ago that I first climbed Pen-y-ghent. Then I was a trespasser. Today thousands of walkers have worn a broad track up that steep nose, over the plateau, and descended to Horton-in-Ribblesdale. Unfortunately, the marks of their passing are only too evident. So far, no acceptable way has been found to cover their tracks. There are some who would close the paths but that is not practicable today. Townspeople have found the beauty and joys of the countryside and no longer will they be debarred from them.

Beside those vast limestone quarries at Horton, the Pennine Way paths are insignificant scratches. The quarries themselves are huge permanent blots on the landscape. Once-winding lanes between stone walls have been widened and straightened to make room for heavily laden juggernauts. All this could have been avoided if the now threatened Settle–Carlisle Railway had been used to carry away the products of the quarry. This desecration of the landscape has been allowed in an area which is designated a National Park to preserve and enhance its natural beauty and to provide enjoyment for the public.

There is a similar story in Wharfedale, where 100,000 tons of limestone have been taken without planning permission at Coolscar, a quarry which runs behind Kilnsey Crag, that bull-nosed ice-smoothed blunt termination of the ridge. In the Peak District, thousands of tons of limestone are quarried annually and the owners still ask for more. As Mike says, 'The plain and simple reason for the destruction of our National Parks is greed.'

Tom Stephenson,
the creator of the Pennine Way

To turn to a far pleasanter theme, many of your readers, including myself, Mike, will thank you for the reference to Arthur Raistrick, 'Dalesman and the greatest living Dales historian'. He is a kind and gentle man admired by all who have met him. He is a doughty champion of the Dales and all natural beauty. At the age of eighty-nine, only last June (1985) he stood in the cold rain on Malham Moor while you and Barbara Castle and I addressed a crowd of ramblers celebrating the jubilee of the Pennine Way.

You, Mike, a Lancastrian, and still an 'off-comed-un' in the Dales, may have been inspired by the writings of this brilliant self-effacing Yorkshireman. Be that as it may, your book will carry on his message and lead people not only to view the countryside but to care and work for its protection.

Tom Stephenson

introduction

THE northern Pennine Dales of Yorkshire and south Cumbria contain within their boundaries some of the most beautiful country in mainland Britain. Not as sweepingly majestic as the Highlands of Scotland nor as ruggedly grand as the Lakes, they are more rounded, more welcoming, perhaps (as is the nature of the folk of these dales) more friendly. There are few peaks much above 2000 feet and few areas where a walker is liable to find himself in any difficulty. Somebody once called them 'The Striding Dales' and that seems to me an apt description, for seen from the summit of

Pen-y-ghent

ABOVE: *A chicken in a barn-loft door, Gawthrop, Dentdale* LEFT: *Enid and Brenda Mason clipping sheep at Hill Top Farm, Deepdale. Enid is using hand shears*

any of the major hills such as Ingleborough, Whernside, Great Shunner Fell, Wild Boar Fell or the Calf, the Dales seem to spread out across the landscape in great giant strides.

I came to the Dales first as a lad of fourteen when, with a good friend called Dave, I cycled out of Manchester to spend a fortnight of our summer holidays cycling and walking and staying in youth hostels. We had very little money and even less idea of where we were eventually going to end up. With the optimism of adolescence, we just looked at the map and decided to make for Stainforth on the first day and let whimsy decide where we should go from there. Dave had a brand new Dawes Lincoln Imp bicycle with ten-speed derailleur gears and alloy drop handlebars with drinking bottles fastened to them. I had a

basic sit-up-and-beg bike that had been converted to a 'sports model' by the addition of a pair of chrome steel drop handlebars; but where Dave's had cotton tape wound round the bars like a true racing bicycle, mine had had the rubber hand grips off my old straight bars forced on with plenty of Fairy soap. It didn't look right somehow. It was like a Reliant Robin with a Rolls-Royce radiator. Even worse – on the road it was like pedalling an iron bedstead.

We left Manchester on a hot sunny July afternoon and pedalled northwards through Bury and on to Burnley. In those days, although the cotton industry was in decline, there were still many working mills. In Burnley it was 'Wakes Week', the time of the annual cotton holidays, and the entire town had closed and

ABOVE: *Sheepdogs watching the Masons clipping* RIGHT: *Scout Special northbound at Selside*

gone to Blackpool. The only moving things were the hands on the town-hall clock. At any minute I half expected tumbleweed to come rolling down the streets or a saloon door to bang in the hot dusty breeze.

On out of Burnley, over the hills above Barrowford and on through Gisburn we pedalled, in real countryside now where fat cows looked at us over stone walls, some with the eyes of Sunday School teachers, others with the eyes of rude girls. At the road's edge butterbur grew thickly and everywhere I looked the hay meadows were clotted with the flowers of high summer. I knew the names of none of them save the buttercup but I was drunk on the sun, the green fields and the whole new world that was opening before me.

I had been in the country before, but that was with the Boy Scouts at camp or on walks with relatives when the words 'Behave', 'Don't get dirty', and 'Don't touch that' had drowned out the birdsong. Now I was free! There were no adults around to say yea or nay, no red-brick terraced streets, no school bell, no paper round, no homework, just the open road, the sun above and the sound of our wheels on the hot tarmac. I felt just like the mole in *Wind in the Willows* as he throws his whitewash brush away and runs through the fields to the riverbank.

The only drawback was that we had something like two pounds each to last us a fortnight. It did last us a fortnight, but only because we lived on a basic diet of toast and Sunny Spread (the brand name of something made from eighty per cent water, fifteen per cent sugar and five per cent honey). We had Sunny Spread on toast for breakfast, Sunny Spread sandwiches for lunch, and skinless sausage sandwiches followed by Sunny Spread on bread for our dinner.

We spent all of the first day getting to Stainforth and the second day walking around Catrigg Force and Victoria Cave and swimming and diving in Stainforth Force. On the third day we walked up Pen-y-ghent. It was a cloudless summer's day.

Dotted all over the Dales are disused lime kilns like this one. Limestone was burnt in the kilns to make lime which was spread on the land to sweeten it.

Insects I didn't recognise were diving in and out of flowers I didn't know the names of. On we went in the midsummer heat, up Long Lane to Churn Milk Hole and then on and up, scrambling and drenched with sweat over the nab end of the hill, to the summit.

We crossed the wall at the trig point and sat on the edge of the cliffs of the south-west face. Two girls were sitting close by us. They were about fifteen or so years old, were wearing the best walking gear available and were carrying two expensive rucksacks. They had the well-fed, well-groomed look of the rich. We were wearing pumps and carrying a carrier bag and had the scruffy rag-and-tag look of the not rich. We said hello to them, they looked around puzzledly as though the very stones had spoken, then suddenly they noticed us. 'Oh, hello,' they said, then as though the ground had opened beneath us and devoured us, they ignored our existence completely. We opened our carrier bag and took out a bottle of water and four rounds of bread and Sunny Spread. They opened their rucksacks and took out chicken legs, slices of ham, tomatoes, buttered rolls, a big bottle of pop and two Mars bars. We watched them scoff the lot. I've never come so close to pushing anybody off a mountain in my life.

We spent the rest of the fortnight walking, cycling, climbing and swimming all over the Dales – we scrambled in caves and up rock faces, swam in Semer Water and in the Wharfe under the bridge at Kettlewell, and cycled through sleepy villages like West Burton, Thorpe and Arncliffe until our time was up, our money was all gone and, sworn off Sunny Spread for life, we pedalled back to Manchester.

It was a holiday that lodged itself neatly in my mind high up on the shelf marked 'Good Times' and when, years later, in 1971, I moved into a house in the Dales, I continued a love affair with the area that had begun when I was a boy of fourteen.

This book began simply as a collection of photographs that I amassed from 1971 to 1984. Living in the Dales I'd taken photographs of everything from sheepdog trials to the purple saxifrage on Pen-y-ghent. My camera had gone with me on every walk that I had done. Over the years the idea of writing a book on the Dales began to nudge at me and hustle me along. Like many of my ideas, I thought I was having it when it was really having me. The idea became an obsession, and in 1985 I finally started to knock into some sort of order the feelings and photographs that had been building up inside and outside me.

I decided to write it as a series of walks, as though the person reading this book were there at my side as I was walking. It isn't an A to Z book telling you where to walk in the Dales and it isn't a topographical book telling you all about the history and geology of the Dales. I'm afraid I wouldn't be much good at writing either of those sort of books. The sort of travel books I like most are those that are written by real enthusiasts who love the territory or people they're describing with an intense, almost spiritual love. Eric Newby's *Short Walk in the Hindu Kush*, the late and much-loved Pete Boardman's *Sacred Summits* and Harry Rée's *Three Peaks of Yorkshire* are amongst my favourite books of all time because the authors convey a sense of place and a love of that place that includes me, armchair traveller that I am, in their travels.

This is no walk in the Hindu Kush, nor is it a trek in the high Himalayas; there are not even any Munroes to bag, so there are no high-level adventures and no strange natives except the occasional gamekeeper. It is instead a book of some of my favourite walks, some walked alone, some with friends, in rain, sun, snow and mist, and although they may not have been as adventurous as a journey to the source of the Amazon, I didn't get bitten by snakes and I was always home in time for tea.

Mike Harding
Dentdale, November 1985

ABOVE: *Typical limestone formations in Ibbeth Peril Cave, Dentdale. Ibbeth Peril is said to have been the home of a witch, Ibby, although on the day I crawled inside it there was nothing more frightening there than a dead sheep* BELOW: *Sunset, Dentdale*

the yorkshire dales

BOUNDED to the north by the Stainmore Gap and the Brough–Appleby road, to the west by the Craven Fault and the Kendal–Skipton road and to the east by the Plain of York and the beginnings of industrial Yorkshire, the Yorkshire Dales are a vaguely wedge-shaped core of upland peaks and valleys lying largely within that area now designated as the Yorkshire Dales National Park. They possess a beauty and a majesty found nowhere else in Britain. Stark hills rise up above valleys patterned with intake fields and villages; rivers, sometimes peaceful, at other times raging in flood, thread the

FACING PAGE: *Bringing down the 'yowes' for dipping near Combe Scar, Dentdale. In the far distance are the Howgill Fells*
BELOW: *Tan Hill Inn, the loneliest pub in England and haven for thousands of walkers. It is seen here in March, just before the thaw*

dale floors; thickly wooded gills rise up from the valley bottoms to the very edges of the fell, and everywhere, in the dry-stone walls, the Iron Age circles, Roman roads, lead-mine spoils, railway viaducts and clustered hamlets, there is the evidence of man in the Dales.

Seen from above, the landscape has a certain regularity. The major peaks all have their summits within a hundred feet or so of each other and many of the dale sides have a terracing or stepping pattern. This is because the character of the landscape was formed in the main by the sedimentary rocks that were laid down in the warm seas of the earth's creation, when the only forms of life were minute marine animals. Limestone, formed from the crushed and compounded bodies of these creatures, lay on sandstone, and in its turn sandstone, formed from eroded grits washed into the seas by the rivers, lay again on the limestone. Alternate layers of sandstone and limestone followed one on top of another like the layers of a great cake. There was a massive upheaval of the earth's crust, in which the bed of the sea became land and what is now the Yorkshire Dales was thrust up in one massive block. Faulting occurred so that the land slipped and formed complex fractures, which were further complicated by the Ice Age and the coming of the glaciers.

During the Ice Age great rivers of ice ground their way slowly down from the heights, tearing the landscape as they travelled, so that V-shaped valleys became U-shaped valleys, and when the glaciers melted, great mounds of debris that had been carried along by them as though on a conveyor belt were dumped, forming moraines, some of which were cone-shaped and earned the name drumlins, and some of which lay across the

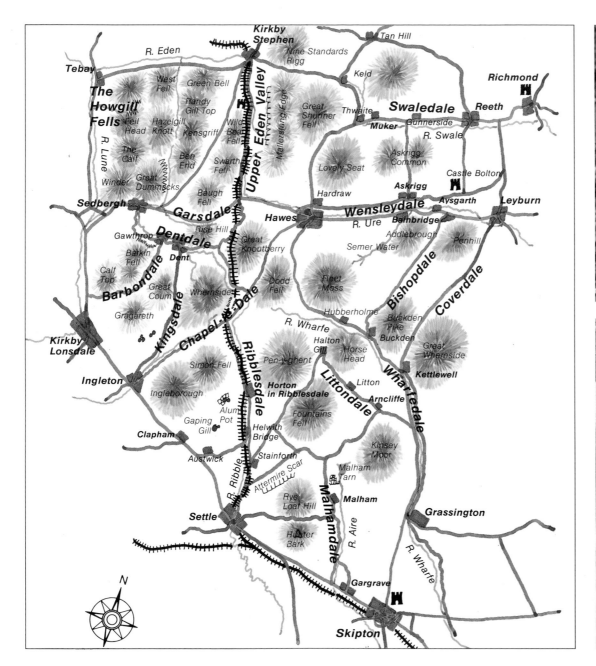

LEFT: *Bird's-eye primula*
BOTTOM LEFT: *(bottom) Hart's-tongue-fern growing safe from sheep's tongues in a gryke in a limestone pavement near Colt Park, Ribblesdale*
RIGHT: *Foxglove after rain*
BELOW: *A limestone pavement near Colt Park Farm in Upper Ribblesdale*

dale bottoms as terminal moraines, blocking the valleys and forming lakes. At one time the Dales must have been a true 'lake district' but, because of the nature of the stone and terrain, the lakes have largely drained away. Now there are only two real lakes in the Dales: Semer Water and Malham Tarn.

On this basic underlying limestone and gritstone sandwich of the Dales the action of ice, of faulting and weathering has created, over millions of years, a very special landscape. A characteristic hill such as Pen-y-ghent or Ingleborough, for example, has a gritstone cap surmounting beds of limestone, shale and sandstone of the Yoredale series, below which lies the older carboniferous limestones which in turn rest on a bed of older Silurian stone – Coniston Grit. Limestone is soluble in the weak acids of rainwater and over the ages the water has carved out and dissolved away the stone until great caverns, sink pots and potholes, and the clints and grykes of limestone pavements have been formed.

The grykes are the troughs and hollows worn away by the water and the clints are the blocks of limestone left standing. In the grykes, plants such as herb robert and hart's tongue fern flourish, hidden from the tongues of grazing sheep by the great depths of the limestone gashes. There are parts of the limestone pavements that look less like natural forms than sculptures by Henry Moore and, because of the honeycomb nature of the landscape, streams disappear on the fells, sinking into potholes and running through underground caverns until, hitting a bed of hard sandstone, they are driven out as springs upon the hillside. After heavy rains you can see them like snail tracks falling down the fellside.

With the coming of man the landscape began its final stage of change. If we were able to telescope time and look at the thousands of years that have gone before us like a stage show, a 'Night of a Thousand Stars' courtesy of Mankind Promotions Inc., then the first act on stage in the Dales show would be the cave dwellers and food gatherers, men of the Old Stone Age. Act number two, the men of the Mesolithic or Middle Stone Age who came over from Europe, were hunters and fishers, and bone harpoons from that period have been found in Victoria Cave above Settle. The land at the time was still boggy and much of the low-lying ends of the Dales were covered by lakes and tarns. A canoe dating from this period was found when Giggleswick Tarn, near Settle, was drained. The canoe was taken to Leeds Museum where it was later blown to bits by one of Adolf's bombs.

The next performers to arrive on stage were the people of the Neolithic, or New Stone Age, the first farmers and the first true settlers on the land. They grew the crops on the freshly cleared land, ground corn in querns, baked bread, and domesticated cattle and dogs. The metal workers who followed brought with them their organisation and their axes, clearing and settling even more of the land and leaving behind them the earliest enduring monuments to man in the Dales: their house walls, their burial chambers, their forts, and their stone circles.

Later, powerful confederacies of these Celtic peoples, who came to be known collectively as the Brigantes, struggled against the colonising might of Rome and were eventually defeated, though they held out against the invaders until the last on Ingleborough Hill and at Stanwick, near Brough. The Romans in their turn found their glory brought to nothing by the barbarians who marched on Rome, leaving outposts of their Empire like Britain without the sustaining power of the Roman military might, so that, only generations after the fall of Rome, the men who came to people the Dales after them looked upon the Roman remains as 'the weird work of giants'.

There is now an interval known as the Dark Ages during which ice-cream will be served followed by a relatively quick invasion of Norsemen and Anglo-Saxons. The Norsemen, coming to Britain from Scandinavia via settlements in Ireland and the Isle of Man, settled the western ends of the Dales. As shepherds the Norsemen preferred the uplands and so many of the place names of the upper Dales are pure Norse, while the Angles, from the lowlands of Europe, cleared the forests from the dale bottoms and built their settlements there.

After the Norsemen and Saxons the Normans came galloping on to the stage. They parcelled the land and bound it with the chains of law to the great Norman families who turned

Billy Mason of Hill Top Farm, Deepdale, winding wool. He is an expert on sheepdogs and judges at trials all over the North

'Lal' Billy Lambert of Selside, Ribblesdale, dosing sheep below Park Fell

vast areas of the Dales into deer parks for hunting. In the Middle
Ages the monks, in their turn, established the second Empire of
Rome in their great abbeys of Jervaulx, Rievaulx, Fountains,
Sawley and Furness. They walled the land and cleared forests
and began to establish the pattern of the landscape that we see
today.

But now it's time in the pantomime for the appearance of
wicked Uncle Abenazer in the shape of Henry VIII who, needful
of coin, jumped on Luther's bandwagon, pronounced himself
Pope in England and shouted, 'Off with her head and while
you're at it dissolve the monasteries!!' After the dissolution of
the monasteries, the Dales became the property of the new
Tudor and Elizabethan capitalists who invested their money in
the land and, like all good capitalists, expected returns from it.
So the enclosures which began with the monasteries intensified
during the Tudor expansion of sheep farming and the later
agricultural revolutions of the eighteenth and nineteenth
centuries, finally culminating in the enclosures of the moorland
commons in the nineteenth century for grouse moors for the
noblemen's pursuit of sport.

The curtains close on our little drama now as the last star
actors stumble on to the stage: the Lancashire cotton
millionaires, the Yorkshire wool kings and the Tyneside iron
masters, who, apeing royalty, bought thousands of acres of land
and built shooting lodges so that they could travel up on the
Glorious Twelfth and shoot the feathers off birds and the ears
off beaters on moors ringed with notices saying 'Private' where
once all had been free to roam.

Since the enclosures of the nineteenth century, little has
happened to change the underlying appearance of the Dales. The
railways came and in some cases went, the motor car puttered its
way into the Dales and farming turned over from the horse to
the tractor. Two world wars took their toll on the Dales villages
and there isn't a settlement over the size of a hamlet that doesn't
have its memorial to the Dalesmen who died far from their
homes.

*The old Celtic cross on Middleton Fell. It was probably an ancient
phallic stone column, christianised later. It is also known locally as
St Coumb's Cross, after St Columba who brought Christianity to
these parts*

The years between the wars and those after brought the hikers and the bikers as the working class of the cities of industrial Lancashire and Yorkshire, Teesside and Tyneside, discovered a love for the countryside and a taste of the freedom that the hills can give. They came to the Dales for pleasure while to the farmer the hills often meant nothing but work, so that he often saw, and in some cases still sees, the 'hardwicks', as the ramblers are often called, as nothing but a nuisance. Yet the farmer must remember that but for the towns eating and wearing his produce, making and supplying his tractors and cars, his animal feed and medicine, his life would be different indeed. Perhaps he should think on that when he finds a couple of ramblers lost in his bottom meadows.

All of which brings me to the last part of this preamble, my neighbours the Dalesfolk. The true Dalesman are friendly people, and though as an outsider you'll always be an 'off-comed-un', they'll make you welcome, providing you behave yourself. I've met a few I haven't liked, but not many.

They work hard and they play hard. They like a good time and almost every village has its fête or gala or show. Then there are races for children and parents, side stalls, fancy dress, walling competitions, cake and winemaking competitions, brass bands and, of course, Yorkshire teas with plenty of strong tea, scones and jam and buttered spice loaf. Tourism is providing a growing number of people with employment now and is putting some sort of life back into the Dales in the form of tea shops, gift shops and bed and breakfast places, and very good some of them are too; and it has been pointed out that if it wasn't for the tourists many of the things that are taken for granted like the village pubs and Post Offices would have to close.

But farming is still the main occupation of the area. Upland farming is a hard life and Dales farmers are a breed unto themselves. Generations have fought the land for a living and the struggle has bred a toughness and hardness in the people as vital and lasting as the rocks beneath them. The victims on so many occasions of Ministry of Agriculture or EEC decisions, they often look at the future with disquiet. Land is expensive, the prices that stock fetches fluctuate, the costs of high-input, high-

Tombstone at Clapham church. Clapham is one of the prettiest Dales villages and is an important caving and walking centre

A typical porched Dales farmhouse – this one is in the Three Peaks area at Wharfe, near Austwick

*Poor old 'mowdies' hanging from the wire in Ribblesdale. They
serve not as a warning to other moles but to show the farmer that
the molecatcher's work has been well done*

yield farming have been butter and beef mountains, and the use
of expensive machinery and chemical fertilisers has turned the
upland farmer into a cross between an industrial chemist and a
mechanic. Now the small farmer looks around and sees cuts in
subsidies and hears himself being encouraged to grow 'crops of
caravans' in the new tourist boom. That's fine if you want to do
that, but what if you don't? It's a terrible dilemma.

> The farmer is the man, the farmer is the man,
> Lives on credit 'til the Fall,
> Then they take him by the hand
> And they lead him from the land
> But the farmer is the man who feeds us all.
> (Ry Cooder)

The Yorkshire Dales were confirmed as a National Park in 1954
and the boundaries were drawn up largely along county lines.
Thus the northern part of the Howgills was excluded, together
with Wild Boar Fell and Nine Standards Rigg in the north and
Nidderdale in the east. The stupidity and greed for power of
local politicians can be mind-boggling and if you are at all
interested in the history (or perhaps you should call it tragedy)
of our National Parks you should read Ann and Malcolm

MacEwen's book, *National Parks: Conservation or Cosmetics?*

To dispel one myth: the National Parks, unlike those in
America, are not owned by the nation, they are largely in private
hands and are simply areas designated as being of special scenic
and recreational value, managed from a planning point of view
by the National Parks Committees. Under the 1949 National
Parks Act, National Park Authorities were set up to oversee
conservation and recreation in the designated areas. The YDNP
has wardens and information centres, it waymarks certain paths
and builds stiles and repairs footpaths, working closely with
landowners and organisations like the Ramblers' Association to
try and ensure that there is as little conflict as possible. It is not
always an easy task. I happen to have very strong feelings about
the powers, or non-powers, of the National Parks, particularly
with regard to quarrying, afforestation and military use, but this
is not the time or place to voice them. For this is a walking book,
about the pleasure and wonders of rambling in high country,
and though I may curse at the quarries and fume at the forests
from time to time, I want this to be a book that is really about
joy, because as my old grandad used to say, 'You're a long time
dead so enjoy it while you can.'

It would be a sad man who couldn't enjoy rambling in the
Yorkshire Dales, because they contain some of the finest walking
country in Western Europe. There is something for everybody
here, from the nature trails of Bolton Abbey Woods and the
riverside walks around Wharfedale and Aysgarth Falls, to the
hard walking of the Three Peaks and the Howgill Fells. All the
while as you walk there lies beneath your feet the geological
history of our planet, while in wall and tomb, village school and
farm doorway, is the mark of man in the Dales. It's wonderful
country, fragile and delicate in some ways, rugged and tough in
others. Come, enjoy it, walk in its open spaces and wonder at the
grandeur of the hills, the crags and the waterfalls; sit amongst
the ruins of past glories with your flask and sandwiches and
walk old Roman roads and packhorse ways from dale to dale,
enjoy it all, but leave it as it was when you came – please!

1. the three peaks

'INGLEBOROUGH, Whernside and Pen-y-ghent, the highest hills 'twixt Tweed and Trent.' How many millions of schoolchildren have memorised that little chant and never seen the three hills or even perhaps known where they are situated? In a way, this chapter should be headed Ribblesdale, since it is this dale which the hills dominate, but that great triangle bounded by the Three Peaks covers Chapel le Dale, Silverdale and even to some extent Kingsdale, so Ribblesdale would be too narrow a description of what is some of the best and most popular walking country in the Dales.

It was in this area that I did most of my early walking and it was this area that I grew to know the best of all the Dales country. Ribblesdale itself threads the Three Peaks area from Settle to the broad dalehead at Ribblehead. At its lower end lie Settle and Giggleswick, one a busy and bonny little market town where every Tuesday one of the best markets in the Dales is held, the other a hamlet of pretty cottages, a backwater away from the bustling metropolis of Settle and site of the famous boys' public school.

Settle has a number of buildings well worth a look at: the Shambles in the Market Square, with its cellared shops and balconeyed houses; the Folly on the road out to Upper Settle; and the Pig Yard Club Museum, a movable feast that never seems to stay in one place for any length of time. The museum was begun by a local man called Tot Lord, one of the famous characters of old Settle, and it houses some of the best

FACING PAGE: *Whernside from Raven Scar on the flanks of Ingleborough. Like a giant fin dividing Kingsdale from Chapel le Dale, Whernside is the highest of the Three Peaks*

prehistoric remains to be found outside the museums of London and Manchester. Many of the exhibits come from Victoria Cave and Attermire Cave in the scars above Settle and Langcliffe. Here, the first evidence of the earliest known habitation of Western man was discovered in May 1838 when a local man called Michael Horner lost his dog down a foxhole on the scar. Looking down the hole for his dog, he discovered the foxhole to be the mouth of a massive cave. The cave was then excavated and remains of man from the earliest times through to the Roman era were found. There is a local rumour that a lady of easy virtue once lived in the cave not so very many years ago and became known to all the inhabitants around as Mrs Flintstone,

The Folly, Settle, is a beautiful building, once a private residence but now an antique shop

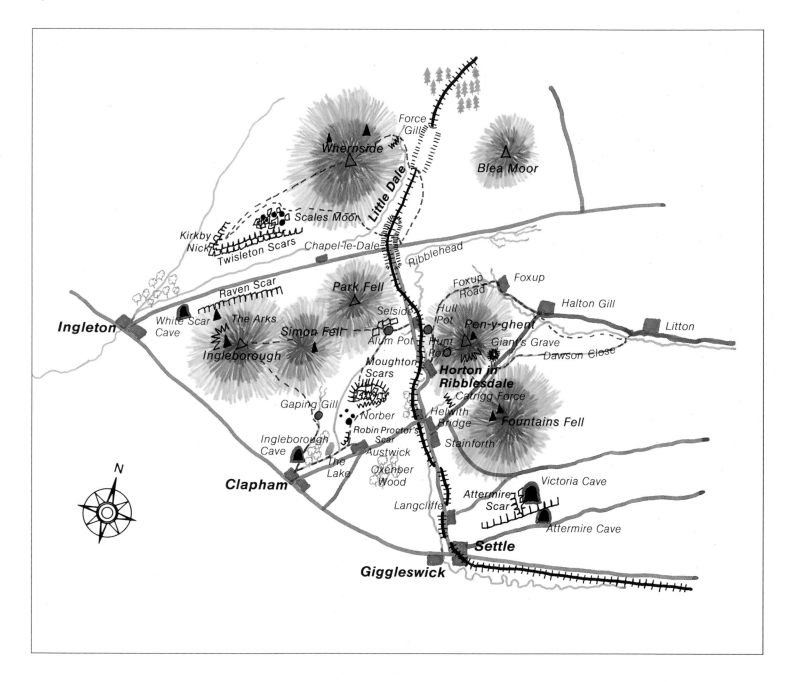

Whernside

Blea Moor

Force Gill

Little Dale

Scales Moor

Kirkby Nick

Twisleton Scars

Chapel-le-Dale

Ribblehead

Foxup Road

Foxup

Halton Gill

Litton

Raven Scar

Park Fell

Selside

Hull Pot

Pen-y-ghent

White Scar Cave

The Arks

Simon Fell

Alum Pot

Hunt Pot

Giant's Grave

Dawson Close

Ingleton

Ingleborough

Moughton Scars

Horton in Ribblesdale

Gaping Gill

Norber

Catrigg Force

Helwith Bridge

Fountains Fell

Ingleborough Cave

Robin Proctor's Scar

Austwick

Stainforth

The Lake

Oxenber Wood

Victoria Cave

Clapham

Langcliffe

Attermire Scar

Attermire Cave

Settle

N

Giggleswick

Ingleborough and Crina Bottom

Pen-y-ghent from near Selside

in honour of a famous children's cartoon series that was being broadcast on television at the time.

Another famous Settle character, now long dead, was a regular drinker in the Talbot public house. He was famous for having 'no clacker'. In other words, he could pour beer down his throat without having to use the usual mechanism of swallowing. His most famous trick, and one on which his reputation was founded, was drinking against the clock – literally. He would, as midnight struck on the town-hall clock, down a pint for every hour struck and always beat the clock to twelve.

Settle has a café, once an inn, called the Naked Man, which has above its doorway a carving of a naked man and the date, while further up the dale is Langcliffe, with another disused inn, the Naked Woman. There is obviously some reason for keeping them apart. Langcliffe is a peaceful little village which has a broad village green and a cobbled area in front of the Post Office with a war memorial and a beautiful old tree. It's quiet now, but at one time it had a candle factory, a cotton mill, a butcher's, a cobbler's and an inn. Now it has only a Post Office, although unlike many other villages in the Dales, it has at least managed to maintain its village school and its church.

Weddings at Langcliffe (and at other places in the Dales) are a hazardous affair. While the ceremony is taking place the local children tie the lychgate fast with baling twine, elastic and skipping ropes and refuse to open it again to let the married couple and guests out of the churchyard until the guests have thrown money over the gate. So far, none of these cases of kidnapping have resulted in prosecution.

From Langcliffe the road winds on to Stainforth, a quiet little village made even quieter recently by the creation of a by-pass. Nearby are two interesting waterfalls, Stainforth Force and Catrigg Force, while above Little Stainforth is the old Iron Age burial chamber known locally as the Celtic Wall.

Beyond Stainforth, Ribblesdale is disfigured with the relics of old quarries and the vivid scars of new ones. It seems ludicrous to me that quarrying is allowed to continue in the heart of one of our major National Parks. When the Parks were first formed, their function was that of the lungs and resting places of a nation. They were to be places where the less

BELOW: *After heavy rain, the becks appear like snail tracks on the hillside*   RIGHT: *Pen-y-ghent from Horton churchyard*

A traffic jam on the Three Peaks Cyclo-cross Race, 1984

Three Peaks Fell Race runners leaving the first stile to ascend Pen-y-ghent, 1985

fortunate of us, forced to work in the dirt, noise and hustle of cities, could retreat for clean air, for exercise and for the recharging of those inner batteries that make us better people.

Cynically, authorities both within and without the National Park have either ignored the original concept of the Parks or have justified their actions in terms of employment or the non-availability of minerals elsewhere. Both are basic untruths. Other forms of employment could be created and other sources of roadstone and chemical lime exist outside the Parks. The plain and simple reason for the destruction of our National Parks is greed. Quarrying and lime-burning have always been part of the way of life in the Dales, but until the middle of this century, always on a smaller scale to meet local needs. Small limekilns dot the landscape and disused quarries lie like natural scars under the scarps of many of our hills. But quarrying on such a vast scale, resulting in massive tears and gashes in the landscape and great wagons thundering along roads that have been rebuilt and which are more like fast

highways than meandering Dales lanes, has destroyed much of the character of Upper Ribblesdale. End of sermon.

Horton-in-Ribblesdale is the heart of the Three Peaks area and the centre for both the Three Peaks Fell Race and the Three Peaks Cyclo-cross Race, when the Three Peaks are covered (a distance of twenty-four miles) in just over two and a half hours. It's a busy, no-nonsense village and is seldom without its legions of walkers, either trudging off on the Three Peaks walk or trundling along the Pennine Way. The station at Horton, now disused except for Dalesrail Days, for years won the Best-kept Station in England Award and under its stationmaster, Mr Taylor, had a beautiful display of alpine flowers.

From Horton, the dale widens, becoming broad and expansive, with views over to Ling Gill and Cam Fell to the east, and Park Fell and Simon Fell to the west. Selside huddles in a kink in the road, a cluster of houses with a sign 'Selside' nailed to the wall of 'the Shant'. The Shant, or 'Selside town hall' as it was called, is a tiny little building once used by locals for whist

Horton-in-Ribblesdale: St Oswald's church caught in a sudden summer storm

drives. Earlier on, as its name suggests, it was probably a railway shanty. This and Stone House further up the dale are all that is left of the old navvy dwellings, while next to the Shant, Hill Foot was once the Red Lion Inn, scene of riots and rants in navvy days.

From Selside, past Top Farm and Alum Pot Lane, the road goes northwards, the flanks of Whernside ahead, Colt Park to the west and a massive drumlin field to the east. At Ribblehead, with its famous viaduct, the road meets the old turnpike road rolling west to Ingleton and east by desolate Gayle Moor to Newby Head where it meets the road to Dentdale before swooping down to Widdale and on to Hawes.

whernside via kirkby gate

WHERNSIDE is in some ways a highly under-rated hill, rarely receiving the praise given to Ingleborough, Pen-y-ghent, Wild Boar Fell or many of the other Dales peaks. This lack of recognition has probably got a lot to do with the shape of Whernside because, seen from almost any direction, the hill does look fairly boring. From Ribblehead it looks like a lump, from Deepdale Head it just looks like a gentle rise continuing the valley slope, even from Knoutberry Haw it doesn't have the shape that Ingleborough and Pen-y-ghent have, that distinct upward curve ending in an outcrop of gritstone and limestone cliffs which makes both these hills look like sleeping animals.

Yet Whernside, though an uninspiring hill to look at, has plenty of places of interest about its flanks. From Scales Moor it does in fact have an interesting shape, with its long

Sunset over Ribblehead Viaduct

flowing slopes sweeping down to Chapel le Dale. On the Deepdale side it has tarns which are lonely and wild, and on the Ribblesdale side it has Greensett Tarn, the haunt of black-headed gulls. The views from its summit across to Ingleborough and down Ribblesdale are superb, while the views down Deepdale and Dentdale from below the tarns are possibly the best in the Dales.

At the foot of Whernside is Ribblehead Viaduct, Bleamoor Tunnel and Force Gill with its two waterfalls, while the old Craven Way, an ancient packhorse lane, curves round its northern flanks making a fine route over from Ribblesdale into Dentdale. Chapel le Dale has a handsome little church in it and at the westerly tip of Wensleydale, Ingleton and Beezley Falls are amongst the seven wonders, if not of the world or of England, then definitely of Yorkshire.

I generally walk Whernside in one of three ways: from Ribblehead by Blea Moor and Force Gill coming back by Chapel le Dale and Winterscales; from Ribblehead through Gunner Fleet and Winterscales to Kirkby Gate and up along the ridge; or from Dent by the Occupation Road and back by the tarns, the old Craven Way and the riverside walk to Dent.

The old Kirkby road is one of the most pleasant ways to walk Whernside. I first walked it alone, five or six years ago now, on a hot August day, leaving Ribblehead about eleven o'clock in the morning and striding under the railway viaduct with the sun hanging in the sky like a big hot brass gong. The Settle/Carlisle line that crosses Batty Moss here by the viaduct was the last line to be built entirely by hand. The Steam Navvy was already in use in America for driving the lines across the new continent, but here the greatest and most scenic stretch of railway line in England was built by what an old navvy from Cork I once worked with on the roads described as 'handraulics'.

As many as three thousand people were living on Batty Moss at any one time in a vast navvy camp of shanties, rough shelters and tents. Life was tough and hard. A hundred and eight men died building the viaduct alone and a tablet on the wall of Chapel le Dale church was erected in their memory at the expense of their fellow workers. Cattle were driven here on the hoof from Hawes and slaughtered and roasted on the spot to feed the navvies. According to Terry Coleman in his excellent book, *Railway Navvies*, four pounds of beef and fourteen pints of ale a day was the navvies' ration. There were camp followers too, women who followed the work-gangs from job to job. Marriages were usually performed without the benefit of clergy by the couple simply jumping over a lighted candle or a broomstick, which is probably where the expression 'Living over the brush', used about unmarried people living together, comes from.

Many more men died than were accounted for and were buried rough on the moor. Those that were identified often had no names other than their 'navvy names', Banjo-Jack, Wheelbarrow-Charlie and One-eyed-Dick being just some of the colourful names that they sported. It was probably the worst job any of these navvies had ever worked on. What should have taken three or four years took seven. The boulder clay that much of north Ribblesdale and beyond is composed of was turned by the rains of winter into a glutinous mass that stuck in the tip-up trucks and caused them, when they were tipped on end, to be

FACING PAGE: *Ingleborough from Whernside. In the foreground are the limestone scars of Ingleborough's flanks*
BELOW: *Ribblehead Viaduct from Batty Moss*

dragged down the embankment. In winter, or after hard frosts, that same boulder clay would become rock hard and had to be blown apart with dynamite. Even when it wasn't frozen, the boulders in the clay deflected blows from picks and shovels, often causing men to throw their tools down and 'jack' in disgust.

I know from personal experience how hard frozen boulder clay can be. One Christmas, after I'd been away from home for a couple of days, I came home to find that a landslide had partially blocked the path to the house and had frozen hard in the winter frosts. I broke a pickaxe and a sledgehammer clearing a few feet of clay away – not to mention the cuts on my face from the razor-keen shards of clay that flew off at every blow.

There were other incredible difficulties for the navvies too. Viaducts had to be built to span Batty Moss, Dent Head, Arten Gill, Dandry Mire and Aisgill. At Blea Moor a beck had to be diverted and culverted over the railway, and at Blea Moor and Rise Hill, massive tunnels were driven through boulder clay and solid rock.

At Dandry Mire, where the railway crosses Garsdale Head, the contractors came across a particularly treacherous bog. Special bog-carts were built with wheels like barrels that could ride across the moss, yet still horses and waggons left out overnight would vanish into the bog. The moss swallowed up thousands of tons of stone that were poured into it to make a footing for the piers, and legend has it that the viaduct was eventually built on bales of wool. 'Rabbitty Dick', a one-time poacher and ganger on the Settle–Carlisle tells how, less than forty years ago, the funnel of a train that had been derailed at Dandry Mire and had gone down into the moss could still be seen sticking up out of the bog, but I can't help feeling that it was the same funnel that he pulled his rabbits out of.

The Settle to Carlisle line runs through some of the most spectacular scenery in England, pulling up the 'long drag' from Settle to Ribblehead below Pen-y-ghent then continuing under Whernside through Bleamoor Tunnel over Dentdale, with

Kirkby Nick at the end of Kirkby Gate

wonderful views looking north to Dent town. From Garsdale Head the line runs along the Upper Eden Valley by Ais Gill, Hell Gill and Wild Boar Fell to Kirkby Stephen, then along the beautiful Vale of Eden to Appleby and Carlisle. Now British Rail want to close it down. The Settle to Carlisle line is one of the finest, if not *the* finest, monuments to the skill of Victorian engineering and the labour of nameless navvies still standing in the country, and British Rail want to shut it 'for financial reasons'. It would cost less to repair the entire line than to build two military jets. A plague on all accountants.

Kirkby Gate, the old way that leads under Ribblehead Viaduct and on from Winterscales by Bruntscar, Ellerbeck and Ewes Top Moss, is an old packhorse route leading ultimately to Kirkby Lonsdale. It is a fine walk on a hot summer's day with good views over to Ingleborough and back to Batty Moss

Viaduct, and on this particular day the path made wonderful walking.

A long dry summer had turned muddy lanes into dusty lanes and boggy patches into springy patches. Beyond Ellerbeck the open moss began and I cut off from the track slightly to my left to look at the limestone pavements above Twisleton Scars. Across the dale stood the great hulk of Ingleborough, seeming closer in the heat, while immediately before me was the boulder field of Scales Moor, a good spot to have a break. Walking here on one cool spring day with my brother John, we found a sheep trapped down one of the grykes in the limestone. It looked about done in, obviously having been trapped for some time. We reached in and, grabbing a horn apiece, hauled it out. Shaky, but still able to move, it staggered across the moor depositing some droppings on my brother's sandwiches as it went, thus proving

Winterscales Farm at the foot of Whernside

the age-old saying, 'It's as much use as a sheep's thank-you.'

I sat down for a breather in the sunshine near the scene of the sheep-rescue operation, looking out at Ingleborough and back at Whernside. This is definitely the best view of Whernside – looking back to West Fell End, High Pike and the shoulder of Cable Rake. Above my head a flock of black-headed gulls made their way updale towards Greensett Tarn, part of a community of such gulls who came over, so it is said, from the coast one year when there was a plague of fat green caterpillars on Whernside. After eating all the caterpillars, they had either forgotten the way home or didn't want to go back, so they stayed and nested in their hundreds by the tarn. Still, who would want to go back to Morecambe after seeing the Dales?

Kirkby Gate ends at Kirkby Nick on Twisleton Scar End. It's thought that Kirkby Nick, like Sulber Nick on the path from Ingleborough to Horton, is partly manmade. The nicks line up like gun-sights and clearly indicate paths which it would otherwise be quite easy to lose, particularly in foul weather. From Twisleton Scar End I followed a rough track leading to the boundary wall up Rigg End, from which it was an easy potter, still following the wall by West Fell, to the summit.

The trig point is on the Kingsdale side of the boundary wall so most people sit and have their lunch on the Ribblesdale side where there is also a grand view down to Pen-y-ghent and Ingleborough, while below you to the left is the viaduct and Ribblehead. I was lucky once, and only once, to see from this viewpoint a steam train cross the viaduct downline to Settle, and as luck would have it I didn't have my camera with me.

From Whernside summit I cut down by Greensett Tarn to Force Gill, a double waterfall above Little Dale where the dark blue limestone for the piers of Ribblehead Viaduct was quarried to be dressed by Welsh masons on Batty Moss. Below the falls I joined the old Craven Way to cross Little Dale Beck by the aqueduct, a further example of Victorian ingenuity.

It must have been almost as bad for the navvies up here as it was for the Romans. Blea Moor is a wet and dreary place at

ABOVE: *Shepherd's shelter on the approach to Cable Rake*
LEFT: *The strange stones of Scales Moor. Laid here by the melting ice, they look like bowls left behind by giants*
RIGHT: *Force Gill at the head of Little Dale. The stone from Little Dale was quarried to make the piers for Ribblehead Viaduct*

times and it is easy to picture the place swarming with navvies with picks and shovels and barrow runs, cursing the rain as it turned the clay to glue and then sitting after work huddled by the stove in their shacks, steam coming off them in a fog, their clay pipes firmly held in their jaws and pints of mulled ale in their hands. The names of the navvy camps are fascinating in themselves: Batty Moss, Jericho, Sebastopol (named by the navvies who had built the railway in the Crimea for the British army) and Salt Lake, so called after the Mormons led by Brigham Young who had founded a town of that name in Utah in America – it was obviously very much in the news at that time. Today Salt Lake cottages are a row of ex-Midland Railway houses on the track up to Colt Park standing on the site of the old navvy camp.

There are a few songs left behind by the 'bold navigators' ('navvy' comes from the word 'navigator', that is, the men who first dug the canals, or 'navigation', and then went on to work the railway diggings). The words to one of the navvies' songs I found in an old broadsheet in the Manchester Central Library called 'Navvy on the Line'. I later found a clog hornpipe with the same name, the music of which fitted the words perfectly:

> Oh I am a navvy bold
> And I tramp the country round, sir,
> Seeking for a job of work
> Where any can be found, sir.
> I left my native home
> My friends and habitation
> And went to seek a job of work
> Upon the navigation.
>
> *Chorus*
> I am a navvy don't you see
> I love beer in my prime
> Because I am a navvy
> That is working on the line.

This bold navvy followed the old Craven Way over Batty Moss to Ribblehead and the Station Hotel unable to have a beer, a cup of tea or even an orange juice because, thanks to the English licensing laws, it was closing time.

pen-y-ghent from horton by foxup and litton

PEN-Y-GHENT has for long been my favourite of all the Dales hills. It was the first hill I ever climbed when I was a lad and I have walked it so many times now that I have completely lost count. The shortest and probably easiest way up Pen-y-ghent is by Horton Scar Lane and the Pennine Way, passing close by Hull Pot and Hunt Pot on the way to the summit. The classic way up the hill is by Brackenbottom and the well-worn and now badly eroded Three Peaks route, coming over the summit and back to Horton by the Pennine Way.

Several summers ago I left the car park at Horton with an old walking pal, Tony, and walked up the lane by the vicarage and the studio of Norman Adams, the painter, and his wife

Anna, who is both painter and poet. It was clear and fresh with the promise of a good day ahead of us, one of those mornings when your legs feel as though they could go on for ever. At the lane-end, instead of turning right by the old shooting box, we carried straight on to Hull Pot, a deep cleft in the fellside, 300 feet long, sixty feet deep and sixty feet across. Hull Pot Beck runs into it and George Perfect, the Horton game keeper, and one of the funniest men I've ever met, tells stories of it filling to the brim after particularly heavy rains, and though I've never seen it myself, I don't doubt his words for a minute.

From the Pot our way to Foxup (the Valley of the Foxes) lay slightly upfell along an old track half hidden in the grass and

FACING PAGE: *Pen-y-ghent from the Silverdale road. From Stainforth to Halton Gill the road runs below Pen-y-ghent and Fountains Fell* RIGHT: *The nab of Pen-y-ghent where the gritstone outcrops and the path leads through a crazy field of slabs and boulders to the summit* BELOW: *The tiny hamlet of Foxup where the chickens are often the only sign of life*

Halton Gill from the Silverdale road. The path leading over Horse Head Pass snakes up behind the hamlet

heather called Foxup Road, which curves round the northern flank of Plover Hill. The turf was springy underfoot and by Swarth Gill Gate we passed through the pastures along the steep valley that led to Foxup, opening up below us to the left. By Far Bergh and Low Bergh, where there are the remnants of Iron Age huts on the hillside, we walked in the late morning sun to the little hamlet where chickens ran scolding before us in the dusty lane. We stopped a while at Foxup for a drink from the beck before pushing on along the metalled road to Halton Gill at the head of Littondale, tucked away below Horse Head Pass. A tiny hamlet now, it's hard to believe that Halton Gill once had enough children in the village and outlying farms to warrant its own school. Today it seems a sleepy little place, well out of the mainstream of life.

It was getting towards lunchtime now, so we crossed the bridge over the Skirfare and walked through the river meadows by Heber Side and the cluster of houses at Hesleden, to Litton and the Queen's Arms, where we sat outside with our ploughman's lunches in the hot sun. Litton was peaceful that afternoon, the occasional cyclist trundling past seemed to be the only life beyond the bees busy in the flowers in the hedgerow. Outside the Post Office as we passed, an old dog was catnapping with his head on his paws and there was a yellowing poster stuck in a window advertising Kilnsey Show.

It was a magical afternoon and it seemed a pity to have to leave Litton for the open fell but, like old Daddy Fox, we'd many

Sheep on Upper Heselden – a storm coming on

The Giant's Grave tumulus looking down on Silverdale

miles before us still to go, so we left our bench and shouldering our packs set off again. We followed the footpath to New Bridge, crossing the river there to climb up the steep sides of Litton Fell by Dawsons Lane, a bridleway that would bring us above Pen-y-ghent Gill and close by the Giant's Grave. The Giant's Grave is now little but a gravel mound with a few upright stones to suggest walls, but before the larger stones were carried away for gateposts and doorheads, it was the extensive site of a Neolithic passage grave, a communal long barrow where many of the important members of the Celtic tribe would have been buried.

Leaving the Giant's Grave, we carried on by road (the only boring part of the walk) to Dale Head Farm and the Pennine Way route over Pen-y-ghent. Dale Head was once an old packhorse inn at the junction of routes from Ribblesdale, Littondale, Malham and Stainforth. It's now a holiday cottage and on the day we passed nothing stirred but the cow parsley and nettles in the yard where at one time there would have been literally scores of horses laden with packs meeting there, some stopping to break their journey, others pushing on the last few miles to Horton. Dr Arthur Raistrick's excellent book *Green Roads in the Mid-Pennines* gives a fascinating insight into the packhorse routes and the lives of the men and the horses that travelled them.

The ponies were short, sturdy animals that came originally from Germany, called Jaeger ponies, later corrupted to Jagger. (People called Jagger will, in all probability, be descendants of these old packmen.) Each pack train was composed of twenty or thirty horses with panniers slung either side. The lead horse had a harness of bells that rang out as it walked, leading the rest through mist and bad light and warning other pack trains along the narrow lanes that they were coming. The packhorses carried, amongst other things, salt, coal, spun wool, finished goods, lead, charcoal and hides. Salt was important for the salting of meat to last through the winter and Salter's Gate or Salter's Lane is a commonly found name for tracks in the upland Dales.

As well as being packhorse routes, many of the green lanes were also drove roads where cattle, sheep and even, in some cases, geese that had been shod for the journey by being walked through hot tar and stone chippings, were driven to markets and fairs. Many of the cattle were Scots brought down from Galloway, and there are many old green lanes crossing these hills called Scotsman's Lane. In Dentdale the Coal Road, a wild old road going over Rise Hill into Garsdale, is still known as the Galloway Gate.

The pull up to Pen-y-ghent from where the Pennine Way leaves the packhorse route at Churn Milk Hole is a bit of a slog, for it's here that the alternate scarps of limestone and millstone grit outcrop most steeply. I once got a pal of mine, Big Phil, who, as his nickname implies, was not small, to climb Pen-y-ghent this way by telling him that there was a pub open at the top, a small bothy hut run by the Mountain Rescue Association to raise

The purple saxifrage that grows on Pen-y-ghent's limestone cliffs in early spring. The plant is rare and only flowers here and in a few other places in the Dales. If you're lucky enough to see it, then please leave it alone. If you pick it, it will die

funds. Tetleys Best Bitter, I told him, cooled by the mountain winds. I have never forgiven myself for the look on his face as he staggered on to the summit to find nothing but a pile of stones. The language he used followed me down the hill in a torrent and even shocked a team of soldiers who were climbing the hill as part of an exercise.

Tony and I paused on the summit in the afternoon light. Fountains Fell was glowing in the sun, and to the south Pendle Hill, well over twenty miles away, stood out clearly in the summer haze, while closer at hand Ingleborough and Whernside bounded Ribblesdale to the north and west.

The old miners' footpath down Pen-y-ghent is so severely eroded now that ash palings have been laid in strips down the side of the hill. However, the palings themselves are sinking while the cord that binds them together is coming away. People don't like walking on them anyway and have tended to walk either side of the palings, broadening the erosion. As I see it, there are two alternatives: one is to divert the footpath temporarily, giving the damaged path time to recover; the other, and I feel more realistic, way is to accept the fact that a track has been eroded and to pave with narrow stones at regular intervals

Hull Pot on the flanks of Pen-y-ghent. The walkers give some sense of scale

The stone sentinel on the limestone cliffs of Pen-y-ghent

as was done by some of the builders of the packhorse routes in the south Pennines above Hebden Bridge. If flags of millstone grit are used they will soon weather and blend into the landscape and the bare, peaty soil on either side can be re-seeded and encouraged to grow. The first priority, though, is to call for an end to all mass challenge walks over the Three Peaks. The fell race and the cyclo-cross race are enough; let the rest of us walk for pleasure, not for fund-raising or endurance.

We left the path a few hundred yards before the shooting box and went to look down that evil-looking slit in the fell Hunt Pot, all of 290 feet deep in one sheer drop. As somebody once said, 'If you fall down there, you go on falling for the rest of your life.' We followed the path by the shooting box and began our descent into Horton.

As we walked down the lane by Squirrel Cottage a blackbird was singing in the trees and the legs that felt as though they could have gone on for ever in the morning didn't any more. They just about carried me the last hundred yards to the Pen-y-ghent Café, halfway house for millions of Pennine Way walkers and the only place for miles around where you can get pint mugs of tea and bacon butties – which we did.

INGLEBOROUGH VIA ALUM POT, BACK BY GAPING GILL

THE Alum Pot/Gaping Gill area of Ribblesdale is classic limestone country. Sink pots, potholes, collapsed caves, limestone pavements, streams vanishing and resurging, are all features of the flanks of Pen-y-ghent and Ingleborough, and Ingleborough has on its eastern slopes the great pots of Gaping Gill and Alum Pot.

One of my favourite walks takes in both of these pots and some limestone pavement and a collapsed cave system for good measure too. The walk begins at Selside, follows Alum Pot Lane via Alum Pot across the clints and grykes above Long Churn and Diccan Pot, and goes on by Borrins Moor to Simon Fell and Ingleborough. From Ingleborough the route descends by Gaping Gill down Trow Gill to Clapham for lunch. After lunch an easy stroll back up Long Lane past Norber and the erratics on to Crummack and Moughton brings me back to Selside via Clapham Lane.

One morning I left the house early, before the sun had cleared the night dew from the grass. It was an August day with high light broken cloud and a gentle breeze stirring air that was already promising to become fat and heavy with sun. In the lane leading to Alum Pot some cavers had debouched from a van and were stripping off to their underclothes and pulling on their wetsuits as I passed. They were a university party getting ready to drop the 200 feet to the bottom of Alum Pot via Upper Long Churn Cave, a trip that would take anything up to five and a half or six hours, depending upon how many other teams were attempting the pot. On busy days you have to wait your turn on some of the ladder pitches as lamps vanish before you into the distance.

I made the trip a couple of years ago and enjoyed every minute of it. I don't suffer from claustrophobia so it's hard for me to understand how it affects people. I do, however, have a bad head for heights and find that on exposed scrambles my knees develop a life of their own and knock like woodpeckers on a tree full of bugs. In Alum Pot I had no trouble at all since, though I was eighty feet above the next bit of solid ground, dangling in space on a flexible alloy ladder, I could see nothing but my lamp-beam gyrating in the empty blackness and my safety rope following the curve of the ladder up into nothing.

The first part of Alum Pot brings you down from Lower Long Churn Cave through two very deep pools requiring a careful traverse and a couple of climbs. Then there is a fifty-foot shaft which you need a ladder for that brings you to a ledge halfway down Alum Pot shaft. Ahead of you is the Bridge, a slab of limestone that has fallen across the pothole at this point. Looking up from the Bridge, you can see above you the wide mouth of Alum Pot and the daylight streaming down into the cavern, while below you the final darkness waits. The trip across the Bridge gave me a case of the woodpeckers, but from then on it was easy-peasy down another pitch to the sump, where 200 feet below the entrance of Diccan Pot and Lower Long Churn, Alum Pot Beck disappears to travel under the river Ribble and resurge at Turn Dub, a little over a mile away.

Deaths of potholers in Alum Pot are rare, although one unfortunate girl was killed by a stone that fell or was thrown from the daylight above some years ago. It's been the scene of a couple of suicides, though, in recent years – it seems a gloomy and terrifying way to lose your life. Look down the cavern of Alum Pot on a dreary November day when the light is going and the rain is lashing the fell and you can understand how the Victorians 'sank back from it in horror' and how it earned its name Alum, a corruption of 'Helm' or 'Hell', Pot.

FACING PAGE: *Simon Fell from the limestone pavements above Alum Pot*

There are a few local folk tales about Alum Pot, one of which I heard myself from the late Peggy Wilcox of North Cote Farm, a jolly smiling Daleswoman, an expert at making honey-baked ham studded with cloves, and not at all given to fairy tales. Once, she said, when she was a young married woman living at North Cote, she had walked to Alum Pot. It was 'back-end' and had rained almost every day for a month and a half. When she got to Alum Pot she saw that it had filled to the top with water, something neither she nor anybody living had seen before. The water swirled like a whirlpool, and bobbing like a cork in the peaty waters was the body of an old shepherd from further up the dale who had been missing for months.

From Alum Pot, although no formal right of way exists, I climbed the wall by a stile and crossed the limestone pavement where the entrance to Upper Long Churn Cave lies and headed across Borrins Moor to Simon Fell. It's an easy way up Ingleborough though there are two stiff slogs ahead of you: one up the shoulders of Simon Fell, the other being the last pull up Swine Tail on to the summit. As I neared the summit, climbing up the gritstone jumble of Swine Tail in the sunshine, I began to congratulate myself on finally getting the view from the top promised by the direction finder on the wind shelter. No such luck. There was no cloud, true, but there was a thick heat haze that turned anything further than ten miles away into a green-blue sunlit soup.

So, sulkily ignoring the view, I toddled round the summit looking at the hut circles and the few old walls that are all that's left of the Brigante fort which once stood there. The Brigantes, who ranged the hills long before the Romans came, must have had an extensive kingdom, for remains of their dwellings and

Alum Pot

evidence of their way of life is to be found throughout the Dales.

Close by the trig point is a cairn, not the work of the mysterious cairn-builders of Gragareth or Great Coum, but the jumbled monuments of walkers who have carried a stone up the last hundred yards of Ingleborough's western slopes to dump it on the growing pile. A further jumble of stones is all that remains of a tower that was built in 1838 to celebrate the coronation of Queen Victoria. Apparently there was so much rejoicing on the day and the builders got so intoxicated that they immediately tore the tower down that they had just built with their own hands. It must have been some party.

The other feature of the summit is a wind shelter erected to commemorate the jubilee of King Edward VII. The hill needs a wind shelter too, for its summit is one of the most bare and exposed in the Dales and is rarely seen without a cap of cloud. It can be a tricky place in mist and one story illustrates only too well the stupidity of venturing on the hills unprepared.

One September day I set off from Selside by Alum Pot Lane with my brother-in-law Ian and my daughters' dog Sam, who sadly now has gone to the great kennel in the sky. Sam was an Old English Sheepdog, Ian was a young English fell-runner and the fitter of the two. The day was grey but not threatening. What cloud there was was high and, since we were planning to stroll across Ingleborough from Borrins Moor down by Crina Bottom into Ingleton where we were going to be picked up by car, we set off in short sleeves, *sans* map, *sans* compass, *sans* common sense.

Sam, like many Old English Sheepdogs, had poor eyesight and though she was a friendly dog who loved people, children in particular, she was not terribly confident. In the reversal of the natural order of things, sheep worried her. Below Long Churn are some boulders commonly found in limestone regions and called by the French *roches moutonnées* i.e. sheep stones. They are water-worn limestone blocks that from a distance do look a bit like sheep. To Sam they looked like sheep from six feet away. Twenty canine personality crises later, we got to the stile leading over to the limestone pavement.

Stiles were another thing that worried Sam. To her they were the greatest problems in lateral thinking known to dog-kind. She would stand looking puzzled, then confused, then she would back off and sit down looking at the stile again. Finally she would walk up to it and put her paws on the bottom rung. Then her memory bank would fail her and she would stand there blankly waiting to be lifted over. On rainy days a wet dog like Sam weighs as much as two sacks of potatoes and is about as easy to manage. Her favourite trick when you grasped her round the middle and lifted her over the stile was to place two peaty paws on your shoulders and as you struggled up the stile with her she would complete your morning's ablutions

by washing you all over with her very long, very pink tongue.

We lifted her over the stile, crossed Borrins Moor and began the climb of Simon Fell. Halfway up the fell the cloud dropped and we were in a world of whirling mists with visibility down to ten yards. Without map or compass, by the time we reached the top of Simon Fell we were faced with two possibilities: to go back down the way we had come, or to try and find our way hoping the cloud would clear. Stupidly, we chose the latter, believing that the wall we followed led on to Swine Tail. For an hour and a half we wandered round that hill totally lost, the cloud now bringing with it a cold driving rain that had us soon wet to the pink bits.

At one point the cloud broke briefly and we saw below and before us to our left through a gap in the clouds Chapel le Dale and Ribblehead Viaduct, both of which should have been well behind us and on our right. We were on Park Fell. We had wandered totally in the wrong direction. We turned and walked back, keeping as best as we could to what we felt was the right direction, eventually coming to Swine Tail which I recognised and which we followed to the summit. Getting off Ingleborough was even trickier, at one point resulting in us heading down a gully that ended in some hairy-looking crags from which we then had to retreat.

Eventually we found our way off the hill and, walking down below the cloud, saw Crina Bottom below us. By the time we got to Ingleton it was nearly closing time and a walk that would normally take some two hours had taken us four and a half and left us drenched and the dog emotionally exhausted. She lay under the pub settle like a giant dishmop dripping on the linoleum.

It seems funny now, as is the way of such things when time takes the misery away, but it was a very stupid thing to do. A few years later on Ingleborough, in similar conditions, a fell-runner running in the Three Peaks Race died of exposure in May only yards from the footpath.

I walked now, carrying compass and map and a rucksack full of waterproofs, across the summit to the wind shelter. It was

The Arks of Ingleborough from Raven Scar

getting warm and it was really pleasant to sit and watch other walkers arriving sweating and gasping over the summit edge. It's funny how soon after your own heart has returned to normal and your own lungs have stopped wheezing like burst lilos that you become the hard man of the hills smiling benignly at the wet wretches scrambling the last yards to the summit. I allowed myself a bit of smugness, then stood up and fell over my rucksack. Serves me right.

With bruised knees and dignity and followed by the breathless laughter of dying walkers, I set off for Clapham and lunch. At Gaping Gill a clutch of tents spread out above Fell Beck meant that the Bradford Caving Club were getting ready for a winch meet. Two caving clubs, Bradford and Craven, erect winches, one at Spring Bank Holiday, the other on August Bank Holiday. Free of charge they will drop you in a bo'sun's chair to the bottom of Gaping Gill. They do charge, however, for bringing you back up again, the money they make going to club

funds and the local publicans' distress fund.

Gaping Gill is well worth a visit. It's probably the best-known pothole in Britain, if only because most 'O' level geography students have had to memorise its name in connection with the physical features of limestone country. It's 365 feet deep and its main chamber is 460 feet long and 100 feet high and wide. The descent by bo'sun's chair is not to be missed.

From Gaping Gill the path to Clapham continues down Trow Gill, a collapsed cavern and almost a Gordale Scar in miniature, and carries on past Ingleborough Cave, a show cave that was first explored in 1837 when the local landowner ordered a stalagmite barrier to be removed to let out floodwaters that were massed behind it forming a lake. The workmen who drained the lake's waters away walked into a long cave system that when explored was shown to reach a quarter of the way to Gaping Gill. It was known that the waters of Fell Beck vanished into Gaping Gill to reappear again in Ingleborough Cave, but it was 146 years before a brave and skilful team of cavers and cave divers led the first two-way crossing between Gaping Gill and Ingleborough Cave in 1983.

Following the path from Ingleborough Cave brings you on to the Reginald Farrer Nature Trail. The Farrers owned (and one of their descendants still owns) the Ingleborough Estate. Reginald Farrer (1880–1920) was a world-famous botanist who introduced over a hundred new plants into Europe. He was a keen conservationist who wrote, concerning a professor who had offered money for any specimens of rare ladies' slipper orchids sent to him from the Dales, 'Accursed for ever more, into the lowest of Eight Hot Hells, be all-wreckless uprooters of rarities from professors downwards.' Many of the plants he introduced were gathered on trips to Japan, China, Tibet, the Alps, the Dolomites, and the Himalayas, where Farrer eventually embraced the Buddhist religion. After the First World War he went on a final plant-collecting expedition to upper Burma, where the climate proved too much for him and he died and was buried in a simple grave.

Harry Rée's marvellous book on the Three Peaks has some interesting stories about Reginald Farrer. Apparently he used to cover the cold frames in his garden with ice to fool the Himalayan plants into believing that they were at home. Then when the warmer weather came he removed the ice and the plants 'happily sprouted and sent out shoots'. When he wanted to establish plants on an unscalable cliff face overlooking Clapham Tarn, he rowed across the lake with a shot-gun in the boat. He replaced the shot in the cartridges with seeds and fired them into the cliffs where many of them took root in the crevices and ledges and flourished.

On the way down the trail you will hear at times a strange knocking sound made by a ram-pump that drives water up to Clapdale Farm where the witch of Clapham is reputed to have lived. Below the ram-pump the waters of Clapham Tarn were used to drive an early form of turbo generator installed by Reginald Farrer's father James to power a saw-mill and to generate electricity for Clapham village, which made Clapham one of the first villages in England to have streets lit by electric light.

But not everything that the Farrers did seems equally sensible or ingenious. The family fortunes were founded by a man called 'Penny Bun' Farrer, who was so called because of his frugal habits as a law student in London. He bought shooting rights on Ingleborough and a farm here and there until eventually the Farrers owned land as far as Ribblehead. About 1833, his two nephews, Oliver Farrer and James William Farrer, brought about a transformation of the entire top end of the village. They demolished the vicarage, the tithe barn and several other buildings, re-routed roads and made two dank, gloomy and dark tunnels that lead out from Clapham to Long Lane. Through them goes the old drove road that leads eventually to Clapham Lane and to Austwick Lane. Apparently, James and Oliver when they extended the estate did not like to see the Scotch drovers crossing their land on the old right of way driving their cattle across into Ribblesdale, so they re-routed the right of way through the tunnels so that their eyes would not be offended by the sight.

Clapham is a pleasant little village and one that I have often used as a watering hole when I have been walking or cycling round the area, and each New Year's Day for the last few years I

Clapham parish church

Robin Proctor's Scar

A Norber erratic. The boulders lie scattered all over the fellside, many of them suspended like this one on limestone pedestals

have walked over to Clapham and back to start the New Year off in a proper and civilised manner. There is a good pub there, a couple of shops, a fine packhorse bridge across a leafy beck with stippled trout lingering in pools. There is an information centre and a tea shop, the Bridge Café, which sells good pots of tea, Yorkshire ham and eggs and crisp salad sandwiches. What more could you want? Down a back lane in Clapham are the offices of *The Dalesman* publishing company, where Bill Mitchell and David Joy produce books on the Dales and a magazine, *The Dalesman*, that is read all over the world by expatriate 'tykes' and other lovers of the Dales.

From Clapham I walked through the two dark, wet tunnels, slipping over rough stones in the gloom to re-emerge in the warm sunshine of Point Lane. Just beyond the tunnel Point Lane joins Long Lane and you can follow Long Lane back to Selside

where it becomes Clapham Lane if you want, though I prefer to carry on down Thwaite Lane past Robin Proctor's Scar to Norber, Crummack Dale and Moughton. Robin Proctor's Scar is said to get its name from a young farmer, thwarted in love in years gone by, who rode his horse over the scar top in a last desperate act, and much good it did him – although he did get his name on the Ordnance Survey Map, which is more than can be said for most of us. From Point Lane I turned up by Dear Bought (i.e. expensive) Plantation on to Norber. There I stopped for a while to wander amongst some more 'O' level geography, the Norber erratics.

At school I had a wonderful geography teached named Bill Whalley. 'Wild Bill Whalley', we called him, though a gentler man never put chalk to blackboard. He knew and I knew that I would never get my 'O' level geography in a month of wet

The limestone pavements of Moughton. This is one of my favourite places in the Dales

Mondays. My brain refused to memorise lists of exports and imports and the position of the Lanarkshire coalfields and the Snowy Mountains of Australia. Apart from Boy Scout camp in Devon and Kent and my cycling holiday in the Yorkshire Dales, I had never left Manchester for more than a day in my life.

Physical geography, however, was another thing. When he mentioned Pen-y-ghent I knew it because I had climbed it and when he mentioned Norber I knew it because I had nettled myself scrambling over it. I did fail 'O' level geography and poor Bill is dead now, but if it's any consolation, I never lost my love for physical geography and since leaving school I have been fortunate enough to visit most of the places I had only read about in text books, from Aberdeen to Australia, Canada to Crete.

The Norber boulders are freaks of nature. By rights they should be lying on the floor of the valley, but the rivers of ice that scoured the area during the glaciation of the Ice Age picked them up and dropped them down again on top of the very limestone that they should have lain beneath. Over many thousands of years the limestone has worn away around them leaving many of the boulders of Silurian stone suspended on thin limestone pedestals, Silurian gritstone being much harder and more resistant to weathering than the limestone.

From Norber I followed Crummack Lane on to Moughton Scars, Beggar's Stile and Thieves Moss. Moughton Scars is a magical place, a place I love dearly, an enormous natural amphitheatre where a limestone pavement is cupped by a semi-circle of limestone cliffs. I have often wandered here alone just to sit and soak in the quiet and tranquillity, particularly of an evening when the sun is sinking in the west and the clints and grykes of the limestone pavements stand out in the falling light. Hut circles of Bronze Age man have been found here and from below the scar, Moughton whetstones were taken by packhorse to Sheffield in the eighteenth and nineteenth centuries where they were used to sharpen the best Sheffield blades. I found some unfinished lengths of stone in the stream below the scar once, together with what I think is a stone scraper used by men who came here before the bronze workers.

There is a wonderful echo on Thieves Moss – shouts roll around the walls and come back at you. It is said that Thieves Moss was where thieves were tried and executed, but why they should be so treated here is a mystery to me. From the Moss, Sulber Gate leads to Clapham Lane and back to Selside. I returned home, crossing the path of bands of weary Three Peakers making for Sulber Nick on their way back to Pen-y-ghent Café to clock off.

The sun dropped behind Simon Fell and a curlew startled by my footsteps rose swiftly into the air. First it gave out a bubbling distress call, then as it wheeled across South House Moor it gave that soulful cry by which it is known so well, and went before me, circling above the roof of my cottage in the evening light.

2. Swaledale

Beautiful Swaledale the land of rest,
Beautiful Swaledale I love thee the best,
The land it is set in a cultivate style,
The extension of Swaledale is twenty long mile.
(Old Yorkshire Ballad)

SWALEDALE has been called by many the most beautiful of all the dales and though I would argue with that definition, it is certainly one of the finest.

At the western head of Swaledale, Birk Dale, West Stones Dale and the beautifully named Whitsun Dale are tributary to the main dale, their becks joining below Wain Wath Force to become the river Swale, supposedly the fastest flowing river in England.

It is near this point that the Pennine Way crosses Swaledale from Tan Hill over the bleak mass of Stonesdale Moor, falling down into Keld and on by Thwaite to Shunner Fell. If you've never seen the Tan Hill on a bleary winter's day when winds are driving wet sleet over the hellhole of Sleightholme Moor and the sky and the land are welded together in one sullen, sodden grey, then you've missed a treat.

The Tan Hill Inn is the highest public house in England and for my money just about the loneliest. I remember staggering in there one afternoon after crossing Sleightholme Moor. It had been raining all day and by the time I got to the inn I looked like a pink sponge in a cagoule. In the pub were twenty or so other walkers, similarly soaked, all crowding round a massive wood stove. By closing time the place was like an alcoholic Turkish bath, and leaving it for the trip over Stonesdale Moor in the lashing rain was a sore wrench indeed.

ABOVE: *Looking down into Swaledale from the Butter Tubs Pass* FACING PAGE: *Thwaite and Swaledale from the Pennine Way on Kisdon Hill*

Possibly one of the finest views of upper Swaledale is the view from the Butter Tubs Pass above Cliff Side, where the narrow upper dale begins to widen out towards Thwaite. The valley, homely and tree clad, is spread below you and as you drop down from the pass, just above Thwaite, you can see Muker down the dale looking like a toy village. From Muker by Ivelet and on to Gunnerside the dale is steep sided but pleasantly

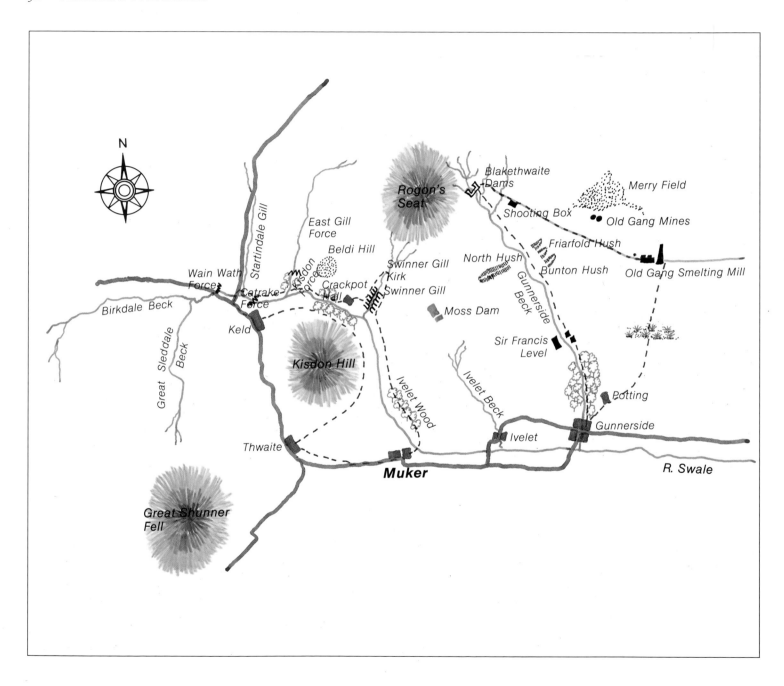

N

Startindale Gill

Blakethwaite Dams

Merry Field

Rogon's Seat

Shooting Box

Old Gang Mines

East Gill Force

Friarfold Hush

Beldi Hill

North Hush

Bunton Hush

Old Gang Smelting Mill

Swinner Gill Kirk

Gunnerside Beck

Wain Wath Force

Kisdon Force

Crackpot Hall

Swinner Gill

Catrake Force

Moss Dam

Birkdale Beck

Keld

Sir Francis Level

Great Sleddale Beck

Kisdon Hill

Potting

Ivelet Wood

Ivelet Beck

Gunnerside

Thwaite

Ivelet

Muker

R. Swale

Great Shunner Fell

ABOVE: *Muker*   TOP RIGHT: *Swaledale from Gunnerside*
BELOW: *Ivelet Bridge*

wooded while Gunnerside itself is on the site of an Old Norse settlement. Its name comes from 'Gunner's sett', the word 'sett' meaning upland summer sheiling, so Gunnerside was the summer pastures of a man called Gunner.

The area from here to Reeth is rich in the history of lead-mining and the moors about are riddled with shafts and workings. Reeth is a fine Dales town more typical of an old East Riding town than a town of the Craven dales. It has a broad village green, a Post Office stores and a good selection of pubs and cafés. Reeth has always been a good walking centre, particularly for walkers from Tyneside and Teesside, and on many occasions I've heard the hills round about echoing to a sound I love so well, the lilt of Geordie accents.

Swaledale is most famous, I suppose, for its sheep, a hardy black-faced breed that survive the winters well and cross well with other breeds such as Suffolks. According to Billy Mason of Deepdale, they are also good sheep to keep because they 'heugh' easy. That is, they keep to their own area of fell and don't wander. Swaledale is one of my favourite little dales, secret and full of character.

thwaite to keld, back by crackpot hall to muker

THWAITE hides itself away at the upper end of Swaledale as though it were trying to shelter from the rush and madness of twentieth-century life, and I can't say that I blame it. Little cottages line lanes that jut off from each other as though they too were trying to hide away. It has a telephone box, a bed and breakfast place or two, and a shop-cum-guest-house called the Kearton Guest House.

The Keartons were two brothers who were pioneers in the study of nature and wildlife photography. Richard was born in 1862 in Thwaite and when he was twenty years old or so he left Swaledale to work for a London publishing firm. He retired in 1898 and devoted the rest of his life to nature study and wildlife photography. His brother, Cherry, joined him in his work and together they became the first men to illustrate books on natural history throughout with photographs. Richard died in 1928. Cherry went on to become a popular radio broadcaster and was sadly killed when leaving Broadcasting House during an air raid in 1940.

Thwaite is also on the Pennine Way and it was the Pennine Way route I took one August cloudy day up and out from the village towards Keld. It would be hard to miss the path out of Thwaite, because it is well signposted by a farmer who has painted 'Pennine Way, single file' on every stone or stump available, and why not? A crowd walking eight abreast can trample a good-size swathe through a hay meadow and single file just makes common sense, although I must admit the signs did seem to be something of an overkill.

I followed the path through the grass and flowers, and Bill the dog, who has no aesthetic sense at all, occasionally attacked a clump of cranesbill by rolling on it. At a wall corner I stopped to look back at Thwaite's collection of stone houses shimmering in the dale. Behind them hulked the great mass of Shunner Fell below the flanks of which the Butter Tubs Pass wormed its way over into Wensleydale. The fields between my viewpoint and the village were typical of Swaledale. Each field had its own small barn for wintering stock, a custom said to be typical of the early Norse settlers that came to this dale, leaving on the landscape the marks of their hands and on the speech the sound of their tongue. At this end of Swaledale many of the place names are of pure Norse origin. 'Thwaite' means 'clearing', 'keld' means 'spring', and 'muker', where this walk would end, means 'small cultivated field'.

FACING PAGE: *The Literary Institute, Muker*   BELOW: *Thwaite and Kisdon Hill in February*

A barn near Keld

Above Thwaite the Pennine Way branches off towards the right, behind the intake wall, while a signpost to the left reads 'Bridleway to Keld'. This is part of the old corpse road that leads from Keld over the flanks of Kisdon Hill and turns above Thwaite to follow a line above the river, passing by Muker and on to Grinton.

Before ground was consecrated at Muker in 1580, the nearest ground to Keld consecrated for the burial of corpses was at Grinton. The dead were carried in wicker coffins from Keld along the corpse road, stops being made along the way for food and drink, and every so often there were great 'coffin stones' at the side of the way where the pallbearers could rest the body (one such stone still stands at the side of Ivelet Bridge). Much of the old corpse road is still there and can be traced on the map.

The route stretches some twelve to fifteen miles and parties often took two days and a night to make the journey, leaving the corpse in the 'deadhouse' at Blades (now in ruins) overnight. The corpse road avoided the villages along the route for fear that

the spirit of the dead should be enticed to return, a fear that in fact stemmed from Norse mythology, in which the corpse way was thought to mirror the last journey of the soul from the earth into the underworld.

The spirit was dissuaded from returning to haunt the living by the relatives placing soil on the corpse to fasten it to the ground, putting burning embers outside the door to bar its path and whispering in its ear the plea that it would not return. The myth of the returned loved one is rooted deep in both Celtic and Norse mythology and has carried over into more recent times. 'The Unquiet Grave', 'The Grey Cock' and 'She Moved Through the Fair' are just three examples of folk songs that deal with the subject. In a version of 'The Unquiet Grave' collected from an old singer in 1906 the ghost of the dead lover returns after a year and a day and asks:

> What do you want of me, sweetheart,
> Or what is it you crave?
> I want one kiss of your lily-white lips
> And that is all I crave.
>
> My lips they are as cold as clay,
> My breath be heavy and strong,
> If you have one kiss of my lily-white lips
> Your life will not be long.

When the corpse arrived at Grinton churchyard it was buried without a coffin in a linen shroud. In the seventeenth century a law was brought in which forbade the burial of the dead in any but woollen shrouds, because it was hoped by this decree to support the failing woollen trade of the Dales. Further to the west the Ingleton Parish Register for the period records after many burials that the dead were 'buried in wool according to the act' and in Swaledale itself, when Ann Baker was buried in 1692 at Grinton Church, her father, Adam, a lead-miner from Oldgang, was fined five pounds for not burying his daughter in wool.

Swinner Gill from the Pennine Way

Corpse roads exist throughout the Dales. There is one on Cross Fell and another that runs from Cotterdale by the ruins of High Dyke Farm to Lunds Chapel. The most famous of all is the one that runs from Osmotherley to Raven Scar known as the Lyke Wake Walk, along which corpses were carried forty miles.

Today I was following not the valley path of the corpse way but the pathway to Keld that runs above Northgang Scar from which the views across to Black Hill and up to Swinner Gill are wonderful. In fact one of the great things about this walk is that it keeps for most of the time to the shoulder of the fells so that they fall away steep sided below you giving you clear views out and down. Approaching Keld I dropped down into the dale where Great Sleddale Beck falls over a succession of stairs, hard bands of limestone that have resisted the action of the water to form an impressive series of falls all of which are within a mile or so of Keld village. Downstream from the village are Ease Gill Force and Kisdon Force while upstream are Catrake Force and Wain Wath Force. At Kisdon Force, Bill the dog fell in the river and, because I had laughed at him, shook himself all over me.

Keld, like Thwaite, is a sleepy little place and will be forever remembered by me as the milkless village. I had made a flask of tea and some sandwiches but had run out of milk at home, so I brought a stoppered bottle along planning to buy some milk in Keld. The youth hostel was closed, the only shop was disguised as a garage and had no window, a local Quaker family had helped to close the only pub in the village in the 1950s, and a farmer I asked said he had none. As the Ancient Mariner might have said,

> Cows, cows everywhere
> Yet ne'er a drop to drink.

Keld is more famous, however, in Dales folklore for being the birthplace of Neddy Dick. Neddy was an old Dales character who played the harmonium and who found an old bell one day which he placed on top of his harmonium because he liked the sound of it. Eventually he built up a collection of bells which he played in time to the tunes he would play on his harmonium. His most famous invention, however, was a stone xylophone, invented when Neddy noticed that a stone he had found in a beck gave out a clear note when struck. He built up a complete instrument and travelled round the Dales on a horse and cart playing it. After his death his 'rock band' disappeared and was last seen, rumour says, broken and tumbled together in an old wash-house.

From Keld to Wain Wath Force was a quarter-mile of road-walking and, leaving the road below the force, I sat by the bridge

The ruins of Crackpot Hall

on the track to West Stonesdale Farm with my milkless tea and sandwiches. The beck falls away under the bridge here in a short cascade and it was a pleasant spot to sit watching clouds crossing the sky and the breeze shaking the delicate water avens on the bank.

Lunch over, I walked on to where the Coast to Coast Path and Pennine Way cross above Ease Gill Force. It was two years since I had stood on this spot on the way from Tan Hill to Hawes; then the force had been a sluggish trickle after a dry spring, now, two years later almost to the day, it was a respectable torrent. From the force the path left the Pennine Way and climbed towards my next port of call, Crackpot Hall.

Crackpot Hall is in ruins now, with its roof gone and floors crumbled in, leaving bedroom fireplaces suspended crazily high above the ground. Behind the hall and further to the west at Beldi Hill are the great humps of spoil heaps left behind by the lead-mines. 'Crackpot' comes from the Old Norse meaning 'pothole of the crows', and there is a fine view from its ruins downdale to Muker.

It's hard to imagine now the armies of men working here

ABOVE: *A hay meadow, detail*   LEFT: *Ease Gill Force*

and at Beldi Hill, but at one time the area must have been loud with the noise of men and their picks, crowbars, shovels, barrows, crushing hammers and water-wheels. Although not as devastated as Gunnerside by the effects of mining, this end of the dale none the less has its scars and wounds. Beldi Hill was the scene of pitched battles between rival gangs of lead-miners in the 1770s when workings were flooded, and Spoutgill Smelt Mill became the scene of violent fighting when a man called David Brunskill was thrown bodily into the hush, a deep gully scoured out of the fellside during the search for lead-bearing veins.

From Beldi Hill and Crackpot Hall I walked below Buzzard Scar into the deep gash of Swinner Gill where more lead mine workings, spoil heaps and ruined huts lent an air of sad majesty to the valley. A fine stone bridge spans the beck below Swinner Gill Kirk and I crossed it to follow the gill back below Moss Dam Hags and out along the top of Arn Gill Scar. The sun had moved towards the west now and the cloud had broken, sweeping sunlight along the Dales, silvering the river and cutting hard shadows by walls and hedges.

I dropped down following a lovely track through the woods below Ivelet Boards and followed the pathway down to Ramps Holme, disturbing a weasel on the way. Across the bridge the track followed the old corpse road back to Muker through meadows fuller with flowers than I had ever seen before. Purple patches of cranesbill lay amongst lakes of buttercups, clover and sweet cecily, the whole hay meadow looking like a painting by Monet. Bill, no lover of the scenic, ran ahead to Muker where the Farmer's Arms had just opened. Bill and I sat outside, in the sun, and wetted our respected throttles, he with water, I with a pint of Theakstons Bitter – well, it's wasted on a dog.

GUNNERSIDE AND THE LEAD-MINES

THE area of fell and moor that strikes north from Swaledale towards Tan Hill, Stainmore Gap, Keld and Reeth is a scene of some of the worst devastation visited by man on the landscape of the Dales. Derelict buildings, old workings, dams and hushes scar the land and everywhere there are the cones of spoil heaps that stretch acre upon acre in some places, so that you feel at times that you could be standing on the surface of the moon. This is the area where, like Grassington in Wharfedale, lead was mined from pre-Roman times until early this century. We know that lead was mined by the Brigantes because after the battle of Stanwick and the defeat of Venutius in AD 74 by the Ninth Spanish Legion under Petilius Cerialis, many of the defeated warriors were taken as slaves to work the lead-mines at Hurst in Swaledale and Greenhow Hill in Wharfedale,

where lead pigs bearing Roman markings, probably stolen by native workers, have been unearthed from their hiding places.

During Anglo-Saxon and monastic times, lead continued to be mined throughout Swaledale, although on a small scale and a

RIGHT: *Richard Chambers looking at the winding gear in the engine room of the Sir Francis Level*   BELOW: *Looking out of one of the Bunton levels*

fairly unorganised basis. The rise of the Elizabethan merchant class, however, meant that capital and management were available for the exploitation of both land and people. Under their stewardship and that of their descendants, development of the lead-bearing fields expanded until by the eighteenth and nineteenth centuries the pattern of lead-mining in the Dales had become established.

Landowners such as the Earl of Cumberland and the Duke of Devonshire employed agents to develop the mining fields, bringing skilled men from Derbyshire and Cornwall with their knowledge of mining and mine drainage. Since so many of the walks in this area are dominated by the old lead-mine workings it's probably worthwhile looking for a little here at the history and techniques of lead-mining.

At the time of mountain building in the development of the earth, molten granite was injected into the earth's crust from a great depth. These intrusions caused the limestone and sandstone rocks above to buckle, crack and fault over the subterranean peaks of granite. As the granite cooled it squeezed out hot fluids containing mineral ores in solution. These filled the cracks and crystallised to form veins of quartz and lead-bearing ores, mainly sulphites. They lay within the cracked rocks like the jam in a crazy sponge cake.

The heart of the Swaledale mining field is a vein called the Friarfold Vein running from the neighbourhood of Keld across to Arkengarthdale. From the Friarfold Vein complicated branch veins run off in all directions in what is called a ribbon deposit. The standard way of exploring for lead was by searching for veinstone pebbles in the becks of gills, and when enough of the veinstones were found to indicate a good deposit of lead-bearing ores a dam was built up above on the fell at the head of the beck. When the dam had collected enough water behind it, it was smashed apart letting tons of water race down the gillside to scour out the bed of the stream, exposing the lead-bearing rocks. These manmade gullies, some massive scars on the landscape thirty feet deep or more, are called hushes.

The miners would then search the hush for the vein and would cut trenches in the hillside, herring-boning outwards from the hush to discover the direction in which the vein led into the hillside. From then on there were three ways of winning the ore. Open cast, the earliest form of working, usually led to the second method when shafts were sunk into the hill. When the ore got too deep to be raised by surface workings, the third method was tried and levels were driven into the valley side.

Once won, the 'bouse', a mixture of rock spar and ore, had to be separated ready for smelting. This was done on dressing floors. Firstly, the ore was hand picked over to take out 'deads' (that is, any rock that bore no ore whatsoever); then it was crushed by hand or by machines to a workable size; then last of all it was washed on racks that shook heavy ore to the bottom while the lighter spar came to the top and was washed or scraped away. It was now ready for smelting. Lead in the Pennine area exists largely in the form of lead sulphide, or galena. The sulphur was burned off, thus producing a lead oxide which then had to be reduced leaving behind the pure lead.

The smelt mills had long flues that in some cases snaked up the hillside and across the fell. The flues induced fierce draughts and also, because of their length, allowed vaporised lead to condense within them. When the vaporised lead cooled, it was collected by small boys with brushes and shovels. Fortunes were made by some mine owners and millions of pounds'-worth of lead was taken. From one mine alone in this area, Blakethwaite Mine, lead worth more than £120,000 (£48 million in today's money) was taken in the early nineteenth century.

For the miners, however, life was hard and short. A walk of often three or four miles across wild and featureless moorland to some of the furthest workings would be followed by hours of bone-twisting work in the most miserable conditions. Then, at the end of the day, wet and tired, they would have to make the same walk back again. In winter that walk back home must have been hell: sleet, rain, snow and ice blowing across the moss, wet clothes clinging to chilled skin and ahead and behind a long line of miners' lanterns 'bobbing like glowworms in the dark'.

Lung complaints from working in foul, damp mines or from inhaling the sulphurous fumes from the smelting mills were widespread. In the 1940s Ewan McColl, the folksinger, and Joan Littlewood, the playwright and theatre director, recorded an old Dales lead-miner singing a song called 'Fourpence a Day' which tells more truthfully than the industrial archaeologists' sometimes ebullient picture of the grandeur of Victorian enterprise, the real benefits of lead-mining for the many – simply hardship and poverty.

The ore is waiting in the tubs, the snow's upon the Fell,
Canny folk are sleeping yet but lead is reet to sell.
Come me little washer lad, come let's away,
We're bound down to slavery for fourpence a day.

CHORUS
Fourpence a day me lads, and very hard to work,
And never a pleasant word from a gruffy-looking Turk.
But his conscience it may fail him and his heart it may give
*   way,*
Then he'll raise our wages to ninepence a day.

It's early in the morning we rise at five o'clock,
The little slaves are at the door to knock, knock, knock,
Come me little washer lad, come let's away,
It's very hard to work lad for fourpence a day.

Me father was a miner he worked down in the Town,
Hard work and poverty, they always kept him down.
He aimed for me to go to school but brass he couldn't pay,
So I'd to go to the washing racks for fourpence a day.

Me mother gets up at five o'clock with tears upon her
    cheeks,
She packs me bag upon me back which has to last a week.
It often breaks her great big heart when she to me doth say,
'I never thought you'd work lad for fourpence a day.'

Because of rising costs and the import of cheap foreign lead in the late 1800s, the market collapsed and by the early years of this century the mines had all closed. Thousands left Swaledale to work in the pits of Durham and the mills of Lancashire. Some even went to America across 't'Girt Dub' (the Big Pond), while others went to work in lead-mines in Spain. It's a sad story but not one without some humour, for I can't help but wonder if in some tiny village in Spain there is a child with the name Jesus Francisco Brunskill or José Fothergill.

There are so many paths and old miners' tracks around this area of Swaledale that you could spend years walking them and exploring the old workings and still not cover them all. One classic route follows Gunnerside Gill to the dams at Blakethwaite and returns back to Gunnerside by Hard Level,

Looking up Gunnerside Gill through the mists of early autumn

Gunnerside Pasture from Potting

The track across Long Bank

Old Gang and the track over Brownsey Moor by Long Brae to Potting. I walked this path one July Sunday with Tony, Bill the dog, my wife Pat and Matt (Matt is a lugubrious Yorkshireman with a very droll sense of humour and together with Tony has been a walking companion for many years).

Tony and Matt had brought lamps to look in some of the levels and we left the car in Gunnerside and followed the sign by the bridge that said 'Public Footpath to Gunnerside Gill'. It was a pleasant walk along well-trodden paths through Birbeck Woods beyond which we came upon the first set of workings in Gunnerside Gill: the remains of dressing floors belonging to the Old Gang Mining Company.

Across the gill a rusting compressed air chamber and a few ruined walls were all that remained of the Sir Francis Level, one of the last and most mechanised mines driven in the dale. The miners used rock drills and compressed air to drive through hard rock and the level had a hydraulic engine, worked by water from the dam at Sun Hush, which had such a head of water that it developed up to fifty horsepower and worked both the water pumps to drain the deep levels and the winding gear. The mine was opened in 1864 and closed in 1882, by which time the company had mined almost £40,000 worth of ore, which at today's prices is perhaps the equivalent of £16 million.

Matt muttered something about the Sir Francis Level and said he had been here before. 'If I remember rightly there's a way into the Sir Francis Level and I think that a lot of the old machinery is still down there. There's a big engine room a couple of hundred feet underground or so with all the winding gear and the cages and the hydraulic pumps.' Matt often says things like that and he's usually right. His remarks start, 'If I remember rightly,' and finish, 'Ah yes! There it is.' Tony and I reckon that when Matt goes to heaven he'll have his nose in an

Ordnance Survey Map and he'll be saying, 'If I remember rightly there should be an old bloke around here with long grey hair and a grey beard and a long white nightie on. Ah yes! There he is.'

As we walked further upstream, the gills showed increasing evidence of the works of man and at Friars Hush and Bunton Hush the old levels, the tailings of spoil and the ruined buildings haunt the landscape. Looking across the valley to the scars of North Hush, it seemed hard to believe that these deep gouges in the earth were manmade and were not the result of some massive upheaval in the earth's crust.

We stopped for a while and, leaving Billy well secured outside with Pat, took our headlamps and torches and walked into the level. I hate the sort of book that says, 'Now a word of warning here,' but I've got to say that all these old mine workings are dangerous. Some are in a state of imminent collapse and in others, side passages branch off in all directions and shafts can suddenly appear at your feet dropping down hundreds of feet into the darkness. Tony and Matt are both experienced cavers, they have the right equipment, have had a guide to the mines produced by the Northern Association of Caving Clubs, and, more importantly, Matt at least has done this sort of thing before, or as he said, 'If I remember rightly . . .'

Had I not been with Matt and Tony I wouldn't have considered setting foot inside the level. Knowing I had two members of the local cave rescue team with me, I followed them in. The first hundred yards or so of the level were stone dressed and arched over our heads in a well-made curve. Water some six inches deep or so was running along the old rail bed. After eighty yards we came to the rails and sleepers themselves under a foot of water leading onwards into the blackness. A few yards further in, the lining of the tunnel finished and we were on good ground. Straight, clean-cut stone walls and a steady slabbed roof led on into the hill. A side tunnel branched up slightly into a chamber that must have been worked as an exploration into the vein. On the roof I could see the marks of the picks of long-dead miners cut into the rock as they crouched here in the dark, hacking out

the ore with no light other than the dim wicks of the oil lamps or the candles stuck on their helmets.

We carried on for a few more yards, then retraced our steps down to the main level and back out into the sunshine. It was easy to imagine what relief the miners must have felt at the end of a long day's work in those conditions when they saw the mouth of the tunnel framing the daylight before them.

At the head of Gunnerside Gill beyond the ruins of Blakethwaite Mine are the ruined dams of Blakethwaite, and it was here that we stopped for our lunch. The dams themselves have long been disused. The lower dam has been breached and most of the signs of its previous existence are gone, while the upper dam, though it still has a fine water race below it, is silted over and is now a peaty, muddy reed-bed.

From Blakethwaite Dams we walked on south past the shooting box belonging to Lord Peel's estate through a landscape which was now a desert of lead-mine spoil, called on the map by the strangely incongruous name of Merry Field. A broad Land-rover track led us down to Hard Level where lived poor Adam Baker who was fined for not burying his daughter in a woollen shroud 'according to the law'.

Coming to Old Gang Smelting Mills we stopped to look for a while at the most complete collection of buildings still standing in the mining field, although comparing them now with photographs taken in the 1930s it's obvious that they're slowly falling apart. They're still impressive, with the chimney, flues, dressing floors and the remnants of the smelting hearths clustered together in a valley whose sides are covered with heaps of spoil. Far above on the moor we could see some new machinery which meant that someone was working out the tailings for spar and barytes for the North Sea oil industry where they're used in the drilling processes.

The Old Gang Smelting Mills reminded me of an old deserted coal pit I played around as a child. It had the same air of dereliction and sadness, but something else too. Old colliers used to say that in the mines sometimes you could hear noises that

were not just the noise of settlement or movement but something different, the feeling that someone else that you couldn't see was working near you. It's something that runs through mining folklore and can be traced right back into the lore of medieval German miners. In England they called the noises 'the old man working'.

Now, at Old Gang there's that same air that certain places have, as though what has gone on before has left on the landscape not just scars but a presence. There's a poem by Percy Bysshe Shelley about a traveller in the desert who finds in a vast empty plain the feet of what once was a colossal statue, and engraved on the plaque below the feet are the words,

> My name is Ozymandias, king of kings:
> Look on my work, ye Mighty, and despair!

That same air of confidence that has ultimately come to nothing but dust pervades the area of the Old Gang Smelting Mills and the workings and hushes roundabout.

We cut out from Old Gang across the grouse moor of Lord Peel of Gunnerside Lodge with its shooting butts and its newly cut Land-rover track, a great scar bulldozed across the moor, and followed the path down to Potting. Swaledale opened up below us as we stepped down off the tops. Gunnerside lay dozing in the Sunday sunshine and the new-mown fields patching the valley towards Muker had on their best Sunday golden-green.

As we dropped down towards Gunnerside, rabbits exploded in all directions and Bill had so many to choose from he lay down confused, unable to make his mind up, looking at us pitifully as though we could make up his mind for him.

'If I remember rightly,' said Matt, 'there's a tearoom in Gunnerside that sells strawberry scones about this time of the year.' He was dead right.

ABOVE: *The wasteland of Merry Field* FACING PAGE: *The ruins of the Old Gang Smelting Mills*

Old Surrender Smelt Mill

Later on in the year I went back to Gunnerside with some friends and explored the Sir Francis Level. Richard Chambers, a fine caver who had helped me photograph the Yordas Cave main chamber, Jeff Clegg and Matt Kirby of the Earby Mines Research Group and myself left the road near Gunnerside Lodge and clanked our way up the old miners' path along the west side of Gunnerside Gill one damp late September evening. We were wearing wetsuits, helmets and lamps and carrying ex-army ammunition boxes that were watertight and into which had gone the cameras and flashguns we were going to use to photograph the mine.

A short ladder pitch from one of the ventilation shafts led down into the level. It was flooded with water that in my case came up to my armpits and in Jeff's case the back of his knees. Ploughing through this for almost an hour brought us well into the hillside and at length to where the rail bed rose out of the water and into the old engine room. There, two hundred and more feet below the moor, is a truly amazing relic of the Industrial Revolution. It had taken us an hour to walk but had taken the men who drove it thirteen years of drilling and blasting through 748 fathoms of solid rock to build it.

Some 4620 feet from the side of Gunnerside Gill lies the engine room and hydraulic engine that pumped the mine clear of water and wound up the tubs of lead ore from the levels another 130 feet below the engine room. The passageway here splits into two, one branch leading to the engine sump where a cage lies jammed for ever, the other leading to where a small spiral stairway runs up from a hole in the wall, over the tunnel, to the engine room which, apart from a few acts of vandalism and the ravages of time, is very much as it was on the day it was left. The hydraulic pump and the winding gear, the great pipes which brought the water down from the fell above to drive the engine, were almost intact, although somebody (a famous industrial museum, it is rumoured) has pinched some of the valve rods.

We stayed for an hour and a half taking photographs and looking round before wading back for another hour with our ammo boxes again. Then, emerging to a night full of stars with our helmet lamps lighting our path before us, we walked across the fell back to Gunnerside and closing time.

Old 'If I remember rightly' had been right again.

3. wensleydale

WENSLEYDALE is a big, fat, friendly dale, full of green fields, waterfalls, brass bands and cows. It has two castles, a Roman fort, a giant, the Devil and a sunken town. Rightly called Yoredale in the Middle Ages after the river Ure which flows through it, the dale later came to take its name from the little market town of Wensley, further down the dale.

From the heights of Newby Head the old turnpike road sweeps down through Widdale and over the foot of Ten End to where Hawes marks the head of the dale. At Hawes there are

FACING PAGE: *Evening, Upper Wensleydale*   BELOW: *Askrigg with Addleborough beyond, autumn evening*

shops, cafés, pubs, a rope works, the biggest sheep mart in the Dales and a cheese factory where the traditional Wensleydale cheeses with their distinctive mild flavour and crumbly flesh are made.

Across the river from Hawes is Hardraw with its much-visited waterfall, while further down the dale lie two bonny villages, Askrigg and Bainbridge. Askrigg, the village that was the setting for the television series 'All Creatures Great and Small' based on the books by James Herriot, was also the centre of a great clockmaking tradition that was begun by John Ogden, who came there from Halifax in 1681. His brass-faced clocks had only one hand and a calendar because, in the years before bus and train timetables and television programme times, all the Dalesmen needed to know was the hour and the day. Ogden's craft was carried on by Christopher Caygill, who made brass-faced clocks with minute hands, and one of his apprentices, who married his master's daughter, took over the business and made clocks with painted faces.

Bainbridge has a lovely village green which was the setting for nothing more remarkable than the fact that I arrived there one day to walk over from Bainbridge to Cam Houses with Tony and Eddie, the landlord from my local pub, only to discover that I'd left my walking boots back at home in Dentdale and had to do the entire walk in a pair of fur-lined cowboy boots, which earned me the nickname of Roy Rogers for the rest of the week. A mile and a kick south-west of Bainbridge itself are 'the shining levels' of Semer Water and above them the flat-topped hill of Addlebrough, where the Devil and a giant are said to have thrown stones at one another.

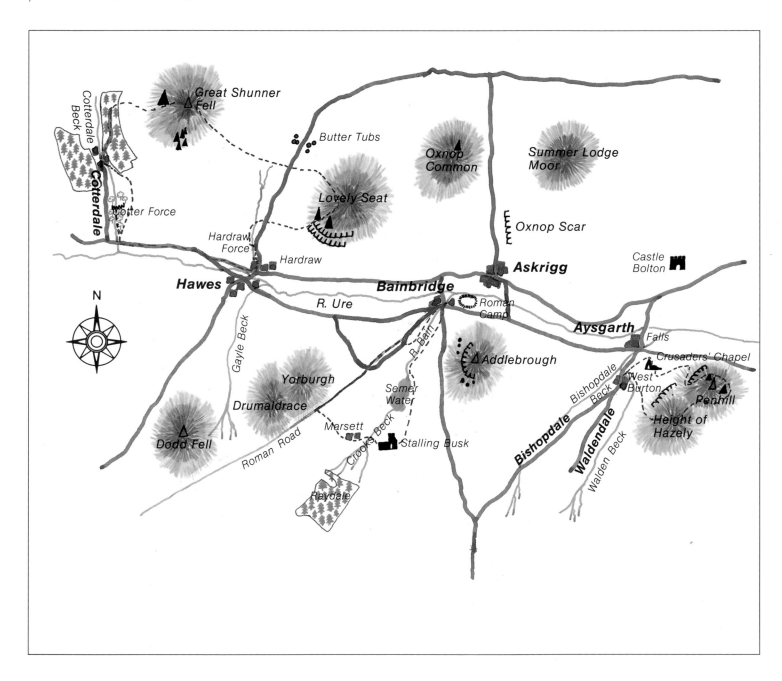

Great Shunner Fell

Cotterdale Beck

Cotterdale

Butter Tubs

Oxnop Common

Summer Lodge Moor

Lovely Seat

Cotter Force

Oxnop Scar

Hardraw Force

Hardraw

Castle Bolton

Hawes

Askrigg

Bainbridge

R. Ure

Roman Camp

Aysgarth

N

Falls

Gayle Beck

Crusaders' Chapel

Yorburgh

R. Bain

Addlebrough

Bishopdale Beck

West Burton

Drumaldrace

Semer Water

Penhill

Dodd Fell

Marsett

Crooks Beck

Stalling Busk

Bishopdale

Waldendale

Height of Hazely

Roman Road

Raydale

Walden Beck

Further down the dale lies Aysgarth, with its National Park centre and spectacular falls. Where what is now a carriage museum was once a woollen mill where the red shirts for Garibaldi's army were made. So the man who unified Italy and gave his name to a biscuit bought his shirts in Aysgarth. Fame indeed for such a little village! Across the dale from Aysgarth, Penhill Beacon and West Burton lie at the northernmost end of that beautiful secluded dale, Waldendale.

LEFT: *Tree roots, Aysgarth upper falls*   BOTTOM LEFT: *Aysgarth parish church*   BELOW: *The middle falls*

Waldendale means the dale of the Welshman, Welsh being a word once used to describe any foreigner, though in this case it probably refers to the last remnants of the Celtic peoples who retreated to this dale in the face of Norse and Anglo-Saxon expansion.

Where the main dale leaves the National Park and opens out into the flatter farmland of the old North Riding is Wensley itself, now a tiny village compared to its bigger neighbour of Leyburn, a busy typical northern Dales town with its wide main street and broad pavements laid out for market stalls.

If I was asked what I felt characterised the walking around Wensleydale, I would say that it has all the expanse and sweep of the bigger dales like Wharfedale but that it also has jewels of villages like West Burton and Askrigg and the fine falls of Hardraw and Aysgarth. It's a friendly rolling dale, green and fertile, yet with limestone scars, gritstone crags and high ridges, giving miles of walking along the high wild peaks or the gentler riverside paths.

Bolton Castle

BAINBRIDGE, SEMER WATER AND THE ROMAN ROAD

BAINBRIDGE is a handsome little village on the Hawes–Leyburn road with a broad village green, complete with village stocks, where miscreants of olden days, instead of being fined or having their licences endorsed, were pelted with rotten garbage and sometimes even worse. The rolling forest of Wensleydale that surrounded Bainbridge has gone now, with its deer and wild boar, but the horn that was blown at dusk every evening between Holyrood and Shrovetide to lead travellers out of the forest to safety still hangs behind the bar of the Rose and Crown, although it is blown now only at village weddings.

Bainbridge stocks and green

Just out of Bainbridge by the road that snakes up by Brough Hill are the remains of a Roman camp built by Agricola in the first century AD to police the area. A fast marching road led from Bainbridge to Cam High Road to meet up with the Roman road running from Chester to Carlisle. Legionaries would be marched up the road on and under Ingleborough to quell the troublesome Brigantes. They were not always successful, however: the fort was rebuilt in AD 158 and was sacked again in AD 197.

There's a grand walk that begins and ends at Bainbridge, travelling along the Roman road, cutting across to the bottom end of Raydale by Marsett and Stalling Busk to Semer Water and back along the river Bain to the village green. It's one I first came across in one of the handy little circular walk leaflets published by the National Parks and, though I generally like to devise my own routes, it's a cracking walk and at ten miles of easy walking a good stroll for hot high summer day or days when low cloud and drizzle make high fell-walking a grey punishment.

I've walked the Roman road on wet windy December days when clouds have sailed across Drumaldrace and the stone walls have been silvered with rain and I've sat by Semer Water on sweltering August days when the shimmering haze has turned the wild summer colours into pastel shades. But the best day of all was in high summer when the sky was a deep blue spattered with shoals of small flat-bottomed clouds and the sun turned the flowers and leaves in hedgerow and field into a giddy mosaic.

I left Bainbridge by the lane leading out of the village from the Post Office. The path took me under trees in full leaf and out across open fields where below me to the left the river Bain, the shortest river in England, flowed on its two-and-a-half-mile journey from Semer Water to the river Ure. Somebody (a clever 'university type', so it is said) in a pub in Bainbridge once loudly informed one of the locals, 'Do you know that the river Bain is the shortest river in England?' 'Aye,' said the old farmer, 'that's 'cos it smoked when it were little.'

After crossing several fields I turned down to the right to follow a metalled road for a while until I reached the first real treat of the day, the Roman road. It is not hard to imagine legionaries marching briskly along this track because, even though it is now walled as a result of the nineteenth-century enclosures, it runs straight as a spear across the fell, totally unlike the whirligig roads of the drovers and packmen.

The breeze which before had been cooling the morning, dropped now and the lane grew loud with bees and heavy with the scent of summer. Ahead of me, to my right, the humps of Yorburgh and Drumaldrace shimmered in the heat as I dropped down following a kink where the road crosses a beck. I climbed a wall to drink at the beck, sitting for a while on its banks in the sun before walking on up the legionaries' highway crossing the Burtersett road under Green Scar Mire and heading up towards Fleet Moss and Kidhow Gate. Some day, I decided, I would walk the entire length of the road in the opposite direction from Gearstones by Cam Fell to Bainbridge. Not today, however, and now my route took me off the road by a stile and up over the hill by an old quarry track.

A dip in the hill, much like those at Sulber Nick and Kirkby Nick, led over the crest by an outcrop and as I walked out from the dip I saw ahead of me Raydale with, to my left, Semer Water and Addlebrough behind it. Below lay my next goal, Marsett. A green lane, on this day made even greener by the sunlight filtering through the leaves, led to a farm drive and the road to the village.

The one part of this walk that I dislike is the short but sodden path that leads from the rough lane out of Marsett towards Stalling Busk. In the driest of summer days the bottom meadows are a ducks' paradise. In winter, unless they're frozen over, they're a lagoon. I picked my way across the bottom meadows like a clockwork ballerina dancing from dry tuft to dry tuft and followed the footpath to Stalling Busk Old Church.

ABOVE: *Looking down towards Semer Water from Stalling Busk*   FACING PAGE: *Looking towards Semer Water with Addleborough above*   BELOW: *Stalling Busk Old Church*

A water-logged tree, Semer Water

The church is a ruin now. Built in 1722 on the site of an older church, it once had a central pulpit with pews arranged round it in a circle. It was abandoned when the new church was built in 1909 and in less than seventy years has fallen into complete ruin – a good indication of how severe the Dales weather can be and how quickly buildings succumb to its assault. I stopped at the church for my lunch, sitting on a hot tombstone looking out across the fields to Semer Water.

Semer Water is one of the few natural sheets of water of any size in the Dales. It would be difficult to build water-gathering reservoirs of the size of those found in other parts of the Pennines in the Dales because of the many caves and potholes that would carry the water away. The water authorities have not ruled out the possibility of flooding large parts of the Dales, however, and, ever greedier in their search for uplands to despoil and destroy, will have to be watched carefully. It was the water authority of Bradford that was largely instrumental in keeping Washburndale out of the National Parks.

Semer Water was formed when the last glacier to carve its way down Wensleydale melted, leaving behind a bank of moraine that formed the nether end of a lake that is now nearly three miles in circumference and, at its deepest part, forty-five feet deep. Like many lakes, Semer Water has its legendary sunken village or town, complete with underwater church bells tolling as storm winds move the surface of the lake. The story of the sunken village under Semer Water has been repeated so many times that it may be pointless me telling the story once again, yet there may be some of you who won't have heard it, so if you're sitting comfortably, I'll begin.

Once upon a time, an angel came down to earth to test the charity of man. Where Semer Water stands now there stood a fine city with towers, domes and spires reaching to the sky, and its streets, houses and shops were full of busy people. The angel, disguised as an old man, went from door to door begging for food and drink. At all of them he was turned away empty-handed and was cursed at as a beggar by the proud townspeople of Semer Water. On his way out of the city he came to a poor crofter's cottage. He knocked on the door and begged for aid. The old couple, poor as they were, took pity on him and gave him food to eat and water to drink. Then, throwing off his tattered rags and appearing in 'bright, shining raiment', the angel raised his staff and cried:

> Semer Water rise, Semer Water sink,
> And swallow all save this lile [little] house
> That gave me meat and drink.

At the far end of Semer Water is a ruined building that is said to be the dwelling place of the charitable old couple. On summer evenings rowers on the lake have claimed that they have heard far below them through the still waters the sound of church bells tolling. There may be a basis of fact in the legend of Semer Water in that the lake is known to be the site of an Iron Age lake village built on piles out from the shore. Its destruction and decay may have lodged in folk memory and been Christianised into the version we have today.

ABOVE: *A windsurfer on Semer Water*   BELOW: *The stones at the lake's edge*

I finished my lunch and walked along the track above the lake at the northern end. There lies a group of stones deposited by the glacier, the largest of which, the Carlow Stone, is said to have been used by the druids for human sacrifice. To be honest, the evidence for druids having ever performed such grisly ceremonies is very dubious and the whole thing is probably nothing other than a piece of Romano-Christian propaganda aimed at destroying the pagan religion of the Celts. The Romans were known to have accused everybody they didn't like of having committed human sacrifice in the same way that nations have always labelled their enemies 'Frogs', or 'Nignogs', or 'Argies'.

I remember that the first time I came to Semer Water was as a boy on my bike. It was a day much like today, hot and sunny, but unlike today there were no tourists about and Dave and I had stripped off to the skin and stepped through the shallows with mud squidging between our toes to the pebbly beach, swimming out into the cool water. You couldn't do that now. Even on a quiet mid-week summer's day the beach is fringed with people picnicking or sleeping in their cars, while the lake itself is often used for windsurfing or water-skiing. I like watching windsurfers with their brightly coloured sails skimming the water. Their sort of sport harms nobody, adds colour to the scene, and doesn't fill the air with noise, tearing the peace and tranquillity apart as water-skiing does. Before you accuse me of being a spoilsport I think there's a place for water-skiing, but it's not in a National Park. More than that I will not say.

From Semer Water I crossed the road and followed the track above the river Bain through summer meadows, by stiles, some of which were gated and had the rubber soles from wellington boots for hinges. Past Bracken Hill beyond Out Brough I looked down at Bainbridge snoozing in the sun before dropping down the last half-mile to the green and the Post Office for something to still the dust.

the giants hill and the crusaders' chapel

IN the Dales, history and legend are welded into the landscape as firmly as the rocks beneath. Iron Age tribes, the legions of Rome, the Norsemen and Danes, the monks, and the lay landowners who followed them: all of them, from the great lords and princes of Christendom to the little men who kept their huts on the commons, along with Quakers, Methodists, travelling packmen, lead-miners, quarrymen and railmen, all have left the print of their passing on the land. When you look at maps of the Dales, particularly the new 1 to 25,000 series, you can read in the patterns on the landscape and the names given to settlements and landforms, the intricate story, incomplete as it must of necessity be, of the pageant of life in the upland valleys.

In Wensleydale, Bolton Castle looks across the broad valley to Penhill, which, legend has it, was once the haunt of a fierce giant, while the castle itself is the place where Mary Queen of Scots was placed under house arrest before she was taken to London to be executed. Almost midway between the two and marked on the map as 'Chapel (remains of)' is the ruined church of a settlement of Knights Templars, a military organisation formed to protect pilgrims travelling to the Holy Land. They were an organisation of 'warrior monks' who became so powerful that they were eventually disbanded by the Crown.

There is a walk that takes in two of these sites of history and legend and gives you grand views across the Dales to the third. The route begins at the bonny little village of West Burton, climbs on to Penhill and then descends by drove road and field path to the ruined Crusaders' chapel, returning at last by leafy lanes to the village.

West Burton has been called by many 'the prettiest village in the Dales', and though I think that Dent village has them all beat hands down for style and atmosphere, West Burton runs a close second. Dent, with its narrow cobbled main street and its white buildings, could almost be taken for a Westmorland village, whereas West Burton, by-passed by the Bishopdale road and standing with its houses clustered round a broad wedge of a village green with cross, stocks and children's swings, is very much a village of the eastern Dales. The local stone here is gritstone, much of it brought down I suspect from the quarries on the flanks of Penhill, and on a summer's evening, when the children are playing on the swings and people are sat talking quietly in the dying sunlight outside the pub while an old dog wanders across the green sniffing his way towards the children, then, when every building is tinted with amber and the gardens are heavy with blooms, it could well be said to be 't'prettiest lal spot i't'Dales'.

One July morning I left the car and, with a heat haze

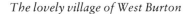

The lovely village of West Burton

West Burton Falls

softening the details on the hills in the further distance, turned down the lane at the village's north-eastern end marked 'To the Waterfalls'. The falls are the upper and lower Cauldron Falls. Here, Walden Beck drops into a deep stone hollow fringed with trees before it flows downdale to join Bishopdale Beck and finally the river Ure by Adam Bottoms. It was cool in the shade and I stayed for a while by the deep pool below the falls before turning back to the path and climbing through the heat of the late morning past Poor's Land towards Knarlton Knot.

As I climbed higher, the dales of Walden and Wensley began

to appear below. Walden away to my left was patterned with meticulously regular fields built during the time of the later enclosures. Across the dale, through the haze, the flanks of Brant Lea above Bishopdale and the edge of Carperby Moor above Aysgarth came slowly into view.

The climb continued by Knarlton Knot to Hudson Quarry, where wild sage was growing thickly amongst the limestone and grass, until I came at last to the rougher pasture below Hazely. There was no footpath from here on, so I followed the boundary wall and fence dividing West Witton and Melmerby parishes until I came, dripping and thirsty, wet on the outside and dry on the inside, to the Height of Hazely.

Bill the dog always seems to walk at least twice as far as I do, running ahead for a while and coming back to check that I'm following before he dives down a hole after rabbits that he never catches. I always keep him under tight control when I'm walking and make sure that he never goes near sheep or lambs, and on the open fell he's usually on his best behaviour. However, ever since an incident with a chicken which resulted in a bald-arsed chicken and a dog with a mouthful of feathers, I've kept him on a lead whenever I've been near a farmyard.

On Hazely Peat Moor Bill waited for me, grinning as I slogged through the heather in the heat. Cloudberries, or knoutberries as they're known in the Dales, studded the moor, set amongst the dark fleshy green leaves like clusters of red beads. The sun, which had been hidden all day, broke through the cloud at the very moment that Bill fell tail first into a peat hole filled with boggy water and couldn't get out. His front paws rested on the heather as his back legs thrashed about in the dog-sized hole. He gave up after a bit and just stayed there looking at me. I've never been one for crediting animals with human feelings, but the expression on that dog's face definitely said 'Stop laughing and get me out of here'.

I pulled him out and, taking a compass bearing, walked across the moor towards Hodge Holes. As we walked, grouse rose from the heather, calling out in alarm. This call has been said to sound like 'go back, go back', but to me it always sounds like a duck laughing (to be honest I've never heard a duck laughing, so I'm probably totally wrong).

At the Hodge Holes it was 'baggin time' (a Northern word for lunch break) and this was very fitting because Bill, who is a pedigree Bitzer (bits'er this, bits'er that), rejoices in the name of Bilbo Baggins, a name given to him by my daughters on the day he was bought from the dogs' home. Much as I love the works of J. R. R. Tolkien, I refuse to call any dog Bilbo Baggins, so Bill he has become; anyway, the only resemblance between Bill and a hobbit is that both have hairy feet and a liking for grubbing around in sandy holes.

From the Hodge Holes, where the views across Coverdale, even through the heat haze, were grand, we climbed up through waist-high bracken, where Bill disappeared completely, to the cairn on Penhill End. From here, the whole of Wensleydale from

Cloudberry

Leyburn to Aysgarth lay spread before us. There's nothing finer than standing on the edge of a Dales hill like this looking down at the landscape strung out below.

We walked on round the summit edge to Penhill Beacon itself, where the beacon mound marks the possible site of the last resting place of an Iron Age chieftain. The similarities between this mound and that on Wild Boar Fell in terms of placement and structure are remarkable. Both are basically shaped like upturned saucers set on rocky promontories above crags, and both look across dale in a basically northerly direction. The Penhill site may be the source of a story that goes back to Celtic mythology, 'The Legend of the Giant of Penhill'. The story, for which I'm indebted to Dr Arthur Raistrick, goes as follows:

There was once in the olden days a giant who lived on Penhill who had all below him in the dale in his thrall. He owned a

The Iron Age chieftain's grave on Penhill

savage wolfhound called Wolfhead and a herd of swine who roamed the forest and fields below Penhill. He was cruel and vicious and cared about nothing but his flock of swine.

One day, as the giant and Wolfhead were hunting in the dale, they came upon a shepherdess called Gunda who was minding her flocks. The giant, for sport, set Wolfhead to worrying the sheep and when Gunda pleaded with him to call the dog off, the giant turned upon her and, struck by her beauty, tried to ravish her there and then. However, Gunda struggled free and ran for her life; but the giant set Wolfhead on her and the dog pulled her down and began mauling her.

Being a true Yorkshire lass, Gunda reached out and with a lump of stone that was to hand beat the dog off. The giant, who by now had reached her, was maddened with what he saw and battered her to death with his club. Afterwards, he washed Wolfhead in the blood, but when the dog growled at him while he was doing this, he took his spear and killed it.

Later that year, when the giant's favourite boar was killed by an arrow fired from an unknown bow, he was so enraged by this that he took the first-born of all his tenants and threatened to kill them unless the guilty one came forward or some other person informed on them. The wise hermit of the dale, the Seer of Carbaby, warned the giant that if he carried out his threat he would never see his castle again alive or dead. The giant ignored this and killed all the children, at which moment there appeared to him the ghosts of Gunda and Wolfhead. Terrified, the giant backed away from them as they came towards him and fell head first over the crag, never to be seen again. Thus perish all giants, slayers of dogs and children and ravishers of Yorkshire lasses.

From Penhill Crags, where the only bones I saw were those of a less than gigantic sheep, we walked by the disused quarry to Stony Gate and the old drove road of Morpeth Gate, now a peaceful broad green lane and very pleasant walking. Through the haze, Bolton Castle was just beginning to show itself across the dale, square and massive. In its former glory it must have

dominated the whole dale below from Richmond to Hawes.

The castle was built by the first Lord Scrope who fought at Crécy and was knighted for his efforts. It took eighteen years to build, every piece of stone used in its construction coming from the quarries in Apedale (the valley of the Norseman Appi). Bolton housed poor Mary Queen of Scots from July 1568 to January 1569. It was besieged by Cromwell's merry men in 1645, and when it surrendered Cromwell ordered it to be dismantled (if that's what you do to castles). It now belongs to Lord Bolton and has a grand little tearoom where I have slaked the dust absorbed on summer cycling trips on many an occasion.

From Morpeth Gate we turned right following the path towards Swinithwaite, striking off at a kink in the lane to the field gate that led to the ruined Chapel of the Knights Templars. I must admit that I was disappointed to find there was so little of the wall of the chapel left standing and that what remained was surrounded by a wooden fence. A little bit of imaginative nettle clearing and further excavation of domestic buildings which, though they are known to exist in the proximity, have never

been uncovered, could make all the difference to the site. The most impressive of the remains are the tiny stone coffins on the ruined floor of the chapel which indicate that either the Knights Templars were very small men or that their bones were broken after death and they were buried with their limbs beneath them. A hole in one of the largest stone coffins was there, so Dr Raistrick told me, 'to let the juices drain away'.

Billy was not at all impressed by the chapel and was trying to out-stare some heifers in the next field. We walked on above Long Bank Wood and Spring Bank where wild deer are said to roam and where Bill was made a fool of by several rabbits. It was late in the afternoon now, later than I thought it would be, and shadows were long on the grass before us, so that by the time we'd travelled the leafy lane to Flanders Hall and had followed the road past the Grange to West Burton village green, it was early evening. Children were playing on the green, a wet labrador that had been swimming in the beck was drying out by the village cross, and there was just room amongst the people sat at the table outside the pub for one man and his dog.

FACING PAGE: *Morpeth Gate as it comes down towards Flanders Hall* LEFT: *Looking down to Morpeth Gate*
BELOW: *A Crusader's coffin*

shunner fell and lovely seat

DYSGARTH Falls, Ingleton Falls and Hardraw Force are probably the most visited waterfalls in Yorkshire, for like Malham Cove, Bolton Abbey and the show caves of White Scar and Ingleborough, they are amongst the 'honeypots' that attract coachloads of trippers to the Dales. But besides the falls I've just mentioned there are many more falls and forces like Cotter Force, Catrigg Force and Scaleber Force which, perhaps because they are a little less accessible, are visited by far fewer people, although they are also arguably less impressive because they don't fall as far or there aren't as many of them.

The writers of the nineteenth century who first created the cult of the picturesque and peopled the Dales with 'awful caverns and frightful ravines' were only impressed by waterfalls that had height or were 'raging spouts' in flood. So strong was this hankering for the Gothic and everything that went with it that many of them refused even to look at nature first-hand, but looked at it through a special lens called a Claude-glass, Claude being a French painter of the Gothic who designed his glass especially for looking at ancient ruins and alpine chasms.

For a confirmation of this, you only have to look at some of Turner's paintings of the Dales and compare them with the reality to see how much poetic licence has been taken for the sake of the 'phantasmagoric'. Turner's painting of Hardraw Scar shows a vast rocky amphitheatre with a torrent gushing over the lip of the furthest wall, while leading us into the scene there is a wide, almost treeless valley, with cows grazing on its slopes and a milkmaid perched on a dry-stone wall in the foreground. Turner is one of my favourite painters, but for a long time I have had a theory that he had 'wide-angle eyes' that filled the camera with distorted shapes. He also had a graduated filter in front of his eyes that turned every sky into a backcloth for 'Maria Martin or the Murder in the Red Barn'. I know that artists aren't expected to paint exactly what they see, and that interpretation and expression are all part of the game. However, I can't help wondering how many people after seeing the engraving based on Turner's painting by Middiman and Pye of Hardraw Force got off their wagonettes and hurried through the door of the Green Dragon Inn – only to be underwhelmed by a narrow, peaceful, tree-clad valley that leads serenely to a rocky bow with a high fall dropping from its lip to the valley floor which, impressive though it certainly is (particularly after heavy rains), is nothing like the falls depicted by Turner.

Hardraw is a friendly little place, particularly on the day of the annual brass-band contest when bands from all over Yorkshire and beyond come to compete against each other and the treeless side of the little valley is carpeted with supporters and spectators picnicking on the grass and the ringing of the sounding brass echoes from the steep gillsides.

One year I walked from Newby Head by Cam High Road to Hawes on a wonderful late spring day and carried on to Hardraw to watch my local band, Settle and Giggleswick Brass Band, take first prize from amongst a great deal of strong opposition. It was a smashing walk on a beautiful day and sitting listening to the bands playing in the sunshine was as near to heaven as I'll probably ever get.

Not many people who come to Hardraw realise that the lip of the waterfall is totally artificial. After the disastrous storms and floods of 1890 in which vast sections of Grisedale and Garsdale were washed away, bridges destroyed and people made homeless, the stone lip of the waterfall was found to have been destroyed completely by the force of the water, so much so that instead of falling from an overhanging shelf a majestic hundred feet on to the rocks below, the waterfall now raced down in a series of cascades. The landowner, Lord Wharncliffe, conscious of the loss of one of Britain's greatest natural assets, immediately

Hardraw Force brass-band competition   INSET: *A Settle and Gigglewick player*

instructed his workmen to reconstruct the lip exactly as it was before, and it is to him that we now owe the sight of Hardraw Force in all its almost-original splendour.

Hardraw is a good starting point for Shunner Fell and Lovely Seat, the two hills that flank the famous Butter Tubs Pass, and is known to many who have walked the Pennine Way as either the end or the beginning of the day that takes you from Tan Hill to Hawes or vice versa, depending on which direction you are walking.

I used Hardraw as a starting and finishing point of a walk that goes first to Cotter Force, then passes along Cotterdale up on to Shunner Fell, crosses the Butter Tubs to Lovely Seat and returns by the upper falls above Hardraw Falls to the village itself. It was a warm but cloudy day in June with high shifting cloud leaving only the occasional gap of blue to send fleeting shafts of sunlight across the fells. I left the road halfway between the Cotterdale Road end and Hardraw and walked with Bill the dog and Eddie the landlord from the Sun in Dent along to the signpost that pointed the way to Cotter Force. The fields were spread thick with buttercups and the may blossom which had been particularly plentiful this year was beginning to turn and fall. Bill the dog, happy as ever to be out and about, was sniffing everything in sight, his tail whirling round in a completely circular motion like a helicopter rotor; Eddie, however, having no tail to wag, was simply smiling, something he's very good at.

Ahead of us I could hear the noise of the waterfall – there had been plenty of rain and when we arrived at the foss, the beck that eventually joins the Ure to travel down Wensleydale was hammering over the lip of the force. We sat for a while just watching and listening to the water and turned back to follow the path out of the steep-sided gill towards Cotterdale. At a bridge above the fall a friendly sign said 'Keep out, private property', while another sign told me that a bull was loose with cattle in the field I had to cross. I crossed the field, keeping extremely close to the top wall ready to jump over it if two tons of Fray Bentos came visiting, but there was no sign of either bull or cattle.

Above the collection of stone-built houses that comprise Cotterdale, the fields were giddy with colour. Buttercups, daisies, cranesbill, the red purple of clover, all were pushing through the new grass of the meadows. Below the wood, a curlew started from the grass and winged beneath us, its mate calling from across the dale. They circled in the wind, their cries filling the morning air as we crossed the bottom meadows into the hamlet. The half-dozen or so houses were neat and well cared for, yet there was no sign of life at all, not even the yapping of a dog or the cluck of a hen, just the wind stirring the flowers at the road end.

ABOVE: *Cotter Force*   BELOW: *Looking down Cotterdale from Cotter Force*

Beyond the houses the lane became a rough track crossing a bridge towards the forestry development, climbing up through the young trees of the forestry and out on to open country towards the summit of Shunner Fell, where, after much bog-trotting and splashing about, we hit the line of ash palings that had been laid down here to stop further erosion of the Pennine Way but which had very largely sunk into the bog. At the summit cairn on Shunner Fell, we paused only for a few seconds to look towards Swaledale and back towards Mallerstang before moving on. The wind was chilling and we wanted to find somewhere sheltered to have our sandwiches. It was just enough time, however, for Bill perform in a way that he usually (being then only a puppy) performed on the kitchen floor.

'That's a good dog,' I said, patting his head in a friendly way. 'Now that's where you should do it, not on the kitchen floor.'

'It's a long way for him to come every time he wants a crap,' said Eddie, running off before I could hit him.

The last time I had been on Shunner Fell two years previously I had been walking the Pennine Way and had left Tan Hill on a rainy June day, with heavy clouds following me south as I travelled. Leaving the pretty village of Thwaite I climbed the green lane to Shunner and below the summit had overtaken 'the Dog Man'. I had heard about the Dog Man before on my week-long journey from Kirk Yetholm towards Edale – travellers going north had told me as I journeyed south at first that the Dog Man was only three days ahead of me, then two days ahead of me, and then the final group of walkers had told me that it wouldn't be long before I caught him up. I asked them who this mythical creature was, but each time they just said, 'You'll see when you meet him.'

The Dog Man was a walker like myself doing the Pennine Way. He had been out of work for a year and some mates had clubbed up to give him enough money to take a three-week walking holiday on the Pennine Way. He hadn't done much walking before, and had made what I think was a mistake in deciding to carry all his food with him from day one. He started off carrying something like a seventy- to eighty-pound pack of tinned foods and dried foods, his only companion a lurcher dog walking beside him on a length of clothesline.

The idea was that he would eat the food in the pack while the lurcher dog would provide itself with rabbits and hares along the journey. The only problem was that every time he let the dog off the lead it tried to provide itself with a sheep supper, so consequently he had to keep it on the lead and feed it on tins of beans, sausages, bacon and egg, which had so exhausted his stock of food that now he was living on porridge and giving the dog the rest of his sausages.

He had also walked the whole way in a pair of ex-NATO boots, high-laced stiff things that could reduce an SAS regular into a hobbling wreck in five minutes. His blisters had blisters on them. He was limping dejectedly towards the summit of Shunner when I overtook him and garnered his story. We sat down and talked for a while before setting off towards Hawes, as the sun broke through the clouds and the dog pulled him downhill towards the cairns.

'The only fun I get,' he muttered in the voice of a man with nothing left to live for, 'is at the end of every day when I have fed the dog and I climb in the tent and change the bandages on my blisters.'

As we made our way down towards Butter Tubs Pass following the boundary fence, Bill found the head of a freshly killed grouse, possibly the work of a fox, and refused to put it down again but walked along with it head first in his mouth, the neck feathers sticking out like a shuttlecock. When we sat down for our sandwiches, I made him go away with the grisly thing, but we could still hear him crunching away behind a rock – first a crunch then a cough as he swallowed a feather, then another crunch then more coughs until he realised there was no future in it and came round for a sandwich. They were cheese and onion. Bill hates cheese and onion sandwiches. It wasn't his day.

The light changed for a few minutes and a watery sun hit the flanks of Lovely Seat. Lovely Seat (from the Norse words meaning Lorn's summer pasture) is a broad expansive hill with wonderful views down Wensleydale from its southernmost and Swaledale from its northernmost flanks. We crossed the Butter Tubs Pass, keeping to the contour at the head of the pass so as not to lose height, and began to ascend the flanks of Lovely Seat.

The Butter Tubs Pass links Swaledale and Wensleydale, snaking airily up from Hardraw, crossing the saddle between Lovely Seat and Shunner Fell at 1100 feet before dropping down to Thwaite. The pass gets its name from two groups of deep limestone potholes set either side of the road. They are fenced now and those on one side have steps leading down to them. There are signs too, telling you that these are the Butter Tubs, in case you didn't know. The name is supposed to come from their usage as cool stores for butter that farmers travelling the pass had failed to sell at market. The butter was lowered down on ropes into the cool depths to keep until next market day.

It was a gentle pull up Lovely Seat to the cairn, but again the June winds of our English summer were too cold for anything but a brief look over to Shunner and south to Dodd Fell and the distinct hump of Ingleborough before taking a compass bearing and walking off towards Hardraw. The clouds broke a little and the sun that had previously looked like a tarnished shilling in a bowl of porridge came out and lit the sweep of Wensleydale below the cairn.

We cut off down through a sloping jumble of gritstone boulders, rabbits everywhere starting for cover, all thankfully too fast for Bill or Eddy. Below the crags a well-built tunnelmouth and a lined tunnel leading into the hill marked the site of one of the old stone-mines on Stags Fell.

The Stags Fell stone-mines are typical of a phenomenon found only in this area. Good-quality gritstone that could be

FACING PAGE: *Looking across Wensleydale from the stone-mines*   RIGHT: *The Butter Tubs*

ABOVE: *Hardraw Force, detail, summer*   FACING PAGE: *Hardraw Force, winter*

dressed for architectural purposes was found deep beneath the fell. The alternatives were either to make a massive quarry or to mine into the fell. It was easier to mine in for two reasons: firstly, if you mined the stone, massive amounts of earth did not have to be shifted before the stone could be got at, and secondly, the men of Swaledale and Wensleydale, many of them experienced lead-miners, had all the knowledge and expertise necessary to dig stone from the mine, and furthermore labour was plentiful because of the decline of the lead industry. Most of the stone for Victoria Station, Manchester, for example, came from these stone-mines above Hawes.

Heaps of spoil lay between Stags Fell and the road, so we picked our way through them and down by a wall to the road, following a pleasant series of falls through Shaw Gill Wood above Hardraw Force for a while before hitting the road again where a footpath took us down through flower-spattered meadows to Hardraw. There we walked through the Green Dragon to the force, at a hundred feet the longest unbroken waterfall in England, and known to freeze into a massive ice tube in winter – Wordsworth and his sister Dorothy visited the spot and were impressed by its grandeur, so much so that William, ever the florid poet, wrote ebulliently to Coleridge, describing the visit:

We soon reached an Inn at a place called Hardraw, and descending from our vehicles, after warming ourselves by the cottage fire we walked up the brook side to take a view of a *third* waterfall . . . We walked up to the fall and what would I not give if I could convey to you the images and feelings which were then communicated to me. After cautiously sounding our way over stones of all colours and sizes encased in the clearest ice formed by the spray of the waterfall, we found the rock . . . from the summit of which the water shot directly over our heads into a bason and among fragments of rock wrinkled over with masses of ice, white as snow, or rather as D. says like congealed froth . . . I cannot express to you the enchanted effect produced by this Arabian scene of colour as the wind blew aside the great waterfall behind which we stood and hid.

We less poetic mortals sat for a while in the afternoon sunlight and shadow, then we turned down the path again for a pot of tea and a scone for myself and Eddy and a biscuit for Bill before we began the road walk back to the car. While we were drinking our tea, the lady at the shop told us that the water that flows over Hardraw Force is in York within an hour. When I told Tom Stephenson this, he said nonsense, so I'll leave them to fight it out.

4. dentdale

IN my opinion the loveliest of all the dales, Dentdale is also the most secluded, cut off both by the hills which hem its eastern and western ends and by the narrowness of the roads that lead in and out of it. At Dentdale's eastern end, Dent Head and the viaduct lead into the dale, the road winding on to Lea Yeat and Cowgill where the narrow winding Coal Road climbs by Monkeybeck Grains and below Shaking Moss over into Garsdale, its highest points often being blocked by snow in the winter months. The Dentdale road carries on from Cowgill by the chapel past Scotchergill and on by Church Bridge to Dent 'Town', as the village is called. West of Dent the road passes by Helmside and climbs the foot of Frostrow by Millthrop into the 'big city' of Sedbergh behind which loom the great Howgill Fells.

It may be the fact that this end of the dale is shielded by the Howgills and the other by Wold Fell and Blea Moor, which, combined with its narrowness, makes Dentdale so lush and green – I don't know. But it does seem (and locals swear) that the climate is milder in Dentdale than the rest of the Dales. It gets less rain, they say, and the snow if it does fall never lies long. It's a woody dale with more trees than many of the other dales, and hedges replace the stone walls of limestone country. Be that as it may Dentdale certainly is, as I have said, the bonniest of all the Dales and Dent village, with its cobbled streets and whitewashed houses, the bonniest of all the Dale villages.

Dent has been called a 'chocolate-box village' by some writers who have assumed that the preservation of the village is due to the action of the green welly and Barbour jacket brigade (2.4 children called Timon and Amarintha, Range Rover with macramé or tie die seatcovers and this year's Booker Prize winner on the back seat), but the fight to prevent the cobbles being ripped up and the narrow bridges widened was led, not by middle-class 'off-comed-uns', but by the Dalesfolk, the farmers, joiners and builders, the ordinary people who cared about their dale.

Dentdale is superb walking country: the high ridge walks along Rise Hill and Barbon Fell are amongst the best in the

FACING PAGE: *Great Coum from near Cowgill*   BELOW: *Helmside, late autumn*

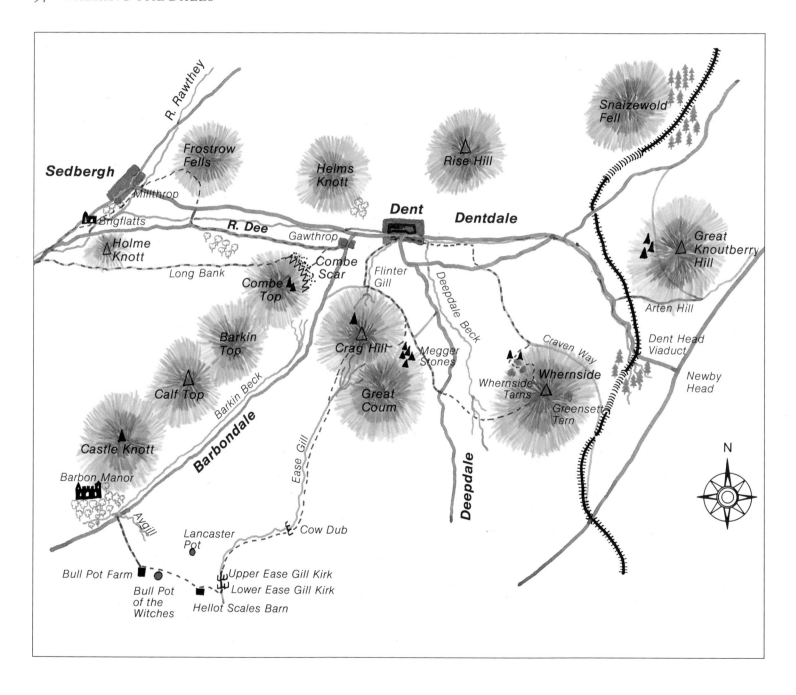

Rook settling across sun, Gawthrop

Dentdale, winter

Dales, while lower down, the Dales Way long-distance path follows the river for much of its length into Sedbergh, and some of the wooded gills like Flinter Gill, which are a typical feature of Dentdale, have footpaths along them leading on to the fells or on to the old packhorse routes. The dale is dominated at its lower end by two scars, Great Coum and Combe Scar, both carved out by the passing glaciers, while the sweeping fells of Barbondale mark the point at which the Dent fault has thrust the older Silurian gritstones thousands of feet above their original bed.

Dent is a popular walking centre with a Post Office, stores, a knitting shop, an outdoor clothing shop, a craft centre, two good pubs, plenty of bed and breakfast and camping accommodation; it also has Stone Close Café, the best little tearoom in the Dales.

The village itself is rich in local history and lore. Dent had its 'coiners', men who clipped the edges of gold coins and melted the clippings down. It had some connection with the Brontë sisters, and two of the houses in the dale, High Hall and Whernside Manor, may have been the models for Wuthering Heights and Thrushcross Grange. But Dent is famous for many other things: its 'Terrible Knitters'; Dent marble; Adam Sedgwick; and, of course, its vampire.

Until the end of the last century, knitting was not a pastime in Dent but a livelihood. Everybody knitted, children on their way to school, shepherds minding their flocks, men on their way to market, all would knit, and women would gather and sit by the fires at night knitting and singing and reading aloud. The stockings they knitted went on to the feet of the British Army, and so great was the demand and so determinedly was it met that

Mr Williams taking out the sheep, Dentdale

Children drinking at the Sedgwick Memorial Fountain, Dent

the Romantic writer Southey called them the 'Terrible Knitters of Dent', terrible meaning not bad but fierce, terribly good.

Dent marble is not a true marble but a fossil limestone containing a variety of crinoids. It comes in two forms, black and grey. The black 'marble' was considered the finest and was quarried at Arten Gill and at Binks Quarry below Great Coum. Until the introduction of cheap Italian marble killed the industry in the late nineteenth century, Dent marble was cut and polished at Stonehouse. Fireplaces of Dent marble can be found all over the Dales, while the columns of Ingleborough Hall and the staircases of the Inns of Court, London, Owens College, Manchester, and the Cartwright Memorial Hall, Bradford, were all made of the crinoid limestone of Dentdale.

Adam Sedgwick, whose life is commemorated in a fine book by Colin Speakman and in a memorial fountain of Shap

granite that stands in the main street, is Dent's most famous son. He was the son of the Vicar of Dent, went to Sedbergh School and later on to Cambridge, where he became one of the most important founders of the present science of geology. He never forgot Dentdale and credits much of his earlier love of learning and his interest in rocks and their formation to the days he spent as a boy rambling the fells around Dent.

The legend of the Dent vampire is in all probability nothing more than an elaborate leg-pull, but it's worth relating in case you haven't heard it before. George Hodgson was an old man of ninety-four when he died in 1715. For years before his death rumours had spread all over the Dales that put his rude good health and longevity to dealings with the Devil and pointed to his long canine teeth as evidence of vampirism.

After his death and burial in a far corner of the churchyard, several Dalespeople swore that they had seen George Hodgson walking by moonlight and after the mysterious deaths of a number of them, his body was exhumed and buried by the church porch with a stake through its heart. When the coffin was opened, so it is said, the hair and nails had grown and the flesh was glowing pink as though the corpse were alive.

Well, the gravestone certainly stands by the porch and it does have a hole drilled through it, said to have been where the iron stake was hammered through the stone into the coffin, but I'm afraid that I agree with the general consensus voiced around the bar of the Sun Inn and the George and Dragon that George Hodgson was guilty of nothing but old age, that the only thing he sucked were his gums, and that the hole in the stone was made for a railing or gatepost.

It's certainly difficult to imagine anything dark or dastardly happening in Dentdale – it seems such a friendly, cheerful, always happy place, with its rounded fells, its lush fields and the river appearing and disappearing below its limestone bed. See Dentdale in summer when the hay meadows are on fire with wild flowers and the roadsides are crowded with the pale lilac of the bell flowers and you will find it hard to disagree with one early writer's description of Dentdale as 'an earthly paradise', even if it does have a vampire buried in its churchyard.

LEFT: *The grave of the 'Dent vampire', Dent churchyard*   BELOW: *Bridge Cottage Café, Gawthrop, and Oliver Bridge where Oliver Cromwell is said to have marched his troops on his way to lay siege on Middleton Hall*

the occupation road to whernside tarns

FROM Barbondale, a walled track leads along the flanks of Great Coum above Dentdale and Deepdale over the watershed to Kingsdale. It is one of the many old drove and packhorse roads that, before the coming of the railway and the motorcar, were the main links in the chain of communication that ran throughout the Dales. When the rough land above

Dentdale was enclosed or 'occupied', the road was walled for most of its length (which shows how important it was in the life of the Dales) and became known as the Occupation Road.

The track from Dent Town up Flinter Gill on to the 'Ocky', as locals call it, is an old green lane, with rough boulders and stones paving the steep way out of the dale used in former days

FACING PAGE: *Deepdale and Dentdale from Whernside*   BELOW: *The Howgills from Flinter Gill, Helms Knott in the left-hand foreground*

ABOVE: *Bull calf on the path to Flinter Gill* LEFT: *The head of Flinter Gill* BOTTOM: *Flinter Gill in winter*

by packhorse trains and coal-carts coming over from Ingleton and Barbondale. A series of falls hidden from immediate view follows the gill on the left-hand side and one May morning as I walked up the gill the falls were roaring after the heavy rains of the week before. It had been a wet May with a few scarce hours of sunshine at the beginning of the month and little since, but today the grey skies that had hung over the land like a shroud had broken, and high white clumps of cloud were bowling swiftly across the blue sky betokening a day of good weather.

From the top of Flinter Gill I looked out to the Howgills and across to where cloud shadows were moving across Dentdale and over Rise Hill. The fields shone a new green in the sun, and the air which for days had been hazy had been cleaned by the rain so that I could make out the shapes of sheep

Lockin Garth Force

grazing near the old Coal Road above Cowgill as I walked down the lane.

I cut off from the lane up towards Great Coum and the Megger Stones. The Megger Stones, like Nine Standards Rigg and the Three Men of Gragareth, are a group of cairns standing sentinel below Crag Hill. I have heard it said that they were built by Iron Age men in honour of Megan, a Celtic goddess. Another suggestion is that they were put there by shepherds so that they could find their way off the fell in bad weather, the idea being that by the number of cairns the shepherds would be able to tell where they were and by the pattern they would know which direction to follow. Both are possibilities but some of the smaller cairns look as though they were thrown together by walkers while they were having their tea break.

I climbed through the Megger Stones and on to Great Coum looking down Dentdale and Deepdale. Below the coum near the County Stone are the strewn remains of a Second World War plane that crashed killing all the poor lads that were in her. Miley Taylor of Deepdale, who was in the Home Guard at the time, went out with a horse-drawn sledge to bring the bodies of

the crew, all French-Canadians, down into Dent. It's just one more indication of the madness of war that four lads from Montreal or Quebec should lose their lives on a Dales hill. It proves to me once again that war is not just immoral, it's stupid. As somebody once said, 'Military intelligence is a contradiction in terms.'

It's easy to see how important the Occupation Road used to be, because every so often the little becks that run down from the fell to cross the track are culverted underneath the lane through well-made stone-lined tunnels. Some of the culverts have been smashed by the passage of heavy-wheeled vehicles such as tractors and Land-rovers over the years, so that in places beyond Nun House Outrake after heavy rains the Ocky is a lagoon of peaty mud and you need the agility of a ballerina and the balance of a goat to skirt round it.

I had neither, so I plodded stoically through the mire turning a corner eventually to see the summit of Ingleborough framed by the walls of the lane. At Kingsdale I stopped by the road and had a bite to eat before striking off up the fell to Whernside, following the wall that leads upwards towards the summit. The view down Deepdale as I climbed was beautiful. Farms and outbuildings stood out grey-white against the green of the fields and the darker green of the hedges that parcelled and patched the land. I could see the line of Gastack Beck above Lockin Garth Force and traced the curve of the Ocky below Great Coum.

Another pull for ten minutes or so brought me up on to the summit, where I sat down to have my lunch. Below me were Ribblehead and the viaduct, while to my right was Ingleborough which for the first time in days looked fresh and green instead of glowering and grey.

A number of people close by on the summit were busy like me holding the wall up with their backs and their morale up with cheese and onion doorsteps. I remember when I was working on the building sites in Manchester, the Irish lads called onions 'navvies' apples' and some of them would peel them and eat them whole like fruit. As one of them said, 'Your onion is your better class of vegetable. It clears the blood and be God it'll drive the colds out of you faster than any medicine you could care to name.' Doctors have recently come to the opinion that garlic and onions do in fact lessen the risk of heart disease, but as somebody pointed out, they also lose you friends.

I packed my rucksack again and walked off the summit towards the tarns. After the heavy rains of the past days I expected them to be full, and they were, a lot fuller than when I had seen them the year before. Then, after a long hot summer, they had dried up until they were small circles of stagnant water surrounded by mud and silt. Now they were once more full and shining under a blue sky and a breeze that shook the surface into tiny waves.

From the tarn, I followed my nose down to a cairn that stands on the shoulder above Deepdale Side where the view down Deepdale into Dentdale was so good that I sat and looked at it for a good half-hour until the thought that I needed to be home by late afternoon pushed me on down to the green lane of the old Craven Way. The old Craven Way is a wonderful way of coming into Dentdale from Ribblesdale. Like the Occupation Road, it's an old packhorse lane rising out of Ribblesdale by Blea Moor and Force Gill. Follow the old Craven Way on a frosty October morning when skies are clear and the whole of Dentdale opens below you tinged with autumn and you can keep your Grand Canyon and your Taj Mahal.

From the old way I took the track down to Whernside Manor and Deepdale Methodist Chapel, crossing the road there and taking the path through the woods where a millstone propped against a tree is all that remains of the old mill that once stood here. By the riverbank in the warm afternoon sunlight I meandered back to Church Bridge and Dent. The fields were full

Whernside Tarns

of early summer flowers, and on the banks butterbur spread its thick green leaves. At Church Bridge people were paddling in the still pools beside the running water and throwing sticks out into the mainstream which reluctant dogs stared at and barked as though to say, 'I may be daft but I'm not daft enough to go splashing through that lot.' I walked slowly back into Dent for a pot of tea and a slice of buttered spiced loaf at Stone Close Café. As my grandad used to say at the end of a grand day like that, 'That's another one they can't take away from you.'

Dent to Brigflatts and Back by the Dales Way

THE hamlet of Gawthrop (the village of the crows in Old Norse) clusters round the road that makes up from Dentdale to course down Barbondale below the impressive sweep of Barkin Fell. At Bridge Cottage Café, where the road crosses the beck, there is a bridge called locally Oliver Bridge. Legend has it that Oliver Cromwell on his way to lay siege to Middleton Hall during the Civil War found the old packhorse bridge too narrow for his cannons and wagons and so had the bridge widened.

A footpath leads from Dent across the fields to Gawthrop and from Bower Bank a little way down the back road to Sedbergh, a footpath leads up to Combe Scar via Tofts. I often go this way to walk to Brigflatts, a very special building that lies a field back from the river Rawthey near the Sedbergh to Kendal road. Brigflatts is the very first Quaker meeting house established in England. It is a peaceful house in a peaceful place, an air of stillness and quiet lies all around it, and everybody I have taken to see the house has said that it has a very special atmosphere.

Though I am not superstitious or religious in any formal sense, I do feel that certain places that have had working within them strong forces for either good or evil absorb something and retain some of that force. In the early seventies I worked in Bergen in Germany, which had been the site of the Belsen concentration camp, and the whole place was heavy with an air of misery, fear and evil. It was said that birds had not been seen nesting or singing in the area of Belsen since the war. You can feel the same oppressive sense of place at Culloden, where great numbers of Scots were massacred, and I felt a similar sense of sadness and grief as I walked through Glencoe where the Macdonalds were treacherously murdered by the Campbells.

I also think you can feel such sensations in places where great acts of religious worship have taken place. Stonehenge still has a very special air in spite of the official attempts to destroy the place; York Minster has it, and Chartres has it to an incredible extent. I remember when I was cycling through Normandy and along the Loire valley a couple of years back, I stopped at Chartres and went into the cathedral. Great pillars of stone swept up to a roof that seemed an infinity away, sunlight was pouring through the stained glass and falling through space to the floor below, and in one of the side chapels a group of French nuns were singing the Angelus by candlelight, their voices weaving round the stone pillars and the shafts of dark and light. It was a very emotional experience.

If we accept calmly and scientifically that stone in the form of silicone chips can accept messages and retain them, then it doesn't seem too impossible to me that the stones of buildings can absorb strong emotions such as fear and terror or the positive feelings of worship and devotion. If Chartres has an atmosphere of almost hysterical ecstacy, then Brigflatts has an air of honest calm and loving peace.

Somebody once said, 'I have never met a bad Quaker yet.' There may well be some truth in that – certainly the Quakers I've met have given me the impression of being caring and loving people. They are peaceful people, too, and many of them have been persecuted for that love of peace: Arthur Raistrick, Yorkshire Dalesman and the greatest living Dales historian, was imprisoned as a pacifist during the First World War, while in earlier times, the Quakers led by William Penn fled to America where they founded Pennsylvania, the capital city of which is Philadelphia, the city of brotherly love.

Quakerism must be one of the most sensible religions of all, since it has no ministers and no hierarchy but involves all its members in its organisation and its acts of worship. The movement was founded by George Fox, who was walking one day on Pendle Hill when, as he said, the sky opened and the Lord showed him a great multitude of people waiting to be saved. He travelled the country round, like Wesley after him, preaching

ABOVE: *Storm clouds over Helms Knott* FACING PAGE: *Brigflatts meeting house* BELOW: *Campanula* (top left) *A very rare butterfly orchid* (bottom left) *A common spotted orchid* (right)

and converting, often being persecuted and physically assaulted for his beliefs. At Firbank, where the chapel proved too small, he went out on to the fell to preach to the people, saying that God's church was not made of stone but of the air and the countryside around. That afternoon he preached to three thousand people, so it is claimed, and the place where he preached that sermon is known as Fox's Pulpit. If you walk up the hill above the Pulpit, you will be rewarded with one of the finest views of the beautiful Howgills Fells.

Brigflatts can be walked to from Sedbergh following the Rawthey Way, coming back via Birks and the wonderfully named Elysian Fields, but my favourite walk to Brigflatts begins from Gawthrop and follows the edge of Middleton Fell to Holme Knott and Brigflatts Moss. It continues on to Jordon Lane, crossing the Rawthey at Middleton Bridge and following the road and the Rawthey Way to Brigflatts meeting house. The return route follows the Dales Way and involves a bit of road walking, but since the road is a backroad and sees at the most two or three cars a day, it is a pleasant way of returning.

I did this walk once on a bright June day with Pat and Bill the dog. There were a few light clouds about and a cooling breeze, and everywhere the hawthorns were heavy with may and the hedgerows thick with wild garlic, campion, bluebells and the little star-flowers of chickweed. I know next to nothing about wild flowers, and what little I do know I learnt largely when I was a pink-kneed 'Boy Sprout' in Manchester and in order to pass some badge or other I had to be able to burn some dough on a stick over an open fire, make smoky porridge and recognise six kinds of trees and flowers from their leaves and blossoms. I can show you hawthorn, beech, oak, ash, elderberry and sycamore; after that I have to take a leaf home and look it up in a book. The flowers I know at sight are bluebell, foxglove, dandelion, buttercup, campion and wild garlic. (Well, you don't get many soldier orchids growing between the paving stones in Manchester. The only flower that did grow in abundance was fireweed (rosebay willowherb), which grew rapidly in the years

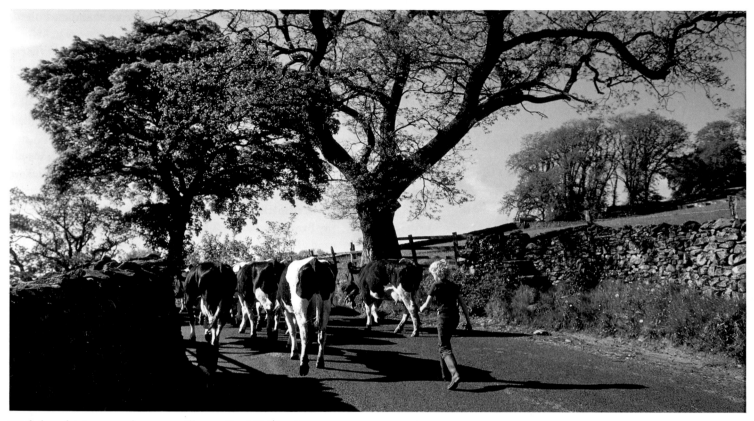

Little boy driving cows home to milk near Rash Bridge

Wood where there are some magnificent waterfalls hidden amongst the trees. After wet weather their thunder can be heard from across the dale and once, and only once, in winter when many of the trees had lost their leaves, I caught a glimpse of them from Frostrow: shimmering skeins of white foam through the wooded gill.

At Ellers we stood on the bridge watching swallows skimming and bumping the water after a hatch of flies that the late afternoon warmth had brought out. As we walked the river path towards Dent a pair of curlews rose in alarm close by a pool where one autumn morning I had watched a heron fishing. Seeing me, it had taken to the air, clumsily at first, then with increasing speed as its great wings beat it downriver to Rash.

We crossed the fields below Underwood and made our way back home as cows were brought in to milk and children were brought in from play for their tea. A beautiful day.

ease gill, great coum and the megger stones

ON the edge of limestone country, Ease Gill is classic limestone: at its lower end it is a dry valley with an impressive cavernous 'kirk', and further upstream it has the waterfall at Cow Dub where the beck leaves a pure white flowstone bed to drop twenty feet through a collapsed cavern into a deep pool where it is again cupped in limestone. The gill is easy walking and leads up on to Crag Hill, which is near my home in the Dales, so one day, throwing work to one side, I cadged a lift down Barbondale to Blind Beck Bridge and set off in bright sunshine up the track to Bullpot Farm and Bull Pot of the Witches.

It was midwinter but one of those strange warm days that seemed to come from nowhere to tell you that spring isn't really far away. The bracken on Barkin Fell was the colour of new rust and the sky over Barbon Manor a deep blue. The manor always looks out of place to me, a Victorian shooting lodge built in the style of a German castle for the wealthy Kay Shuttleworth family. Sir James Kay Shuttleworth was a successful physician in Manchester during the great cholera epidemic of 1832. He was shocked at the condition of the working class employed in the cotton manufacturing industry in Manchester and became a leading reformer and campaigner for better working and living

Looking down Barbondale towards Dent

Storm above Barkin Fell, evening

Barbon Manor hidden amongst the trees

conditions. He built Barbon Manor, which now lords it over the pines perched halfway up Barkin Fell like a Bavarian schloss. It must be a nice spot to live, though I wouldn't like to have to pay the window-cleaner's bill.

Bullpot Farm is a caving club now, owned by the Northern Association of Caving Clubs. A lot of people say that cavers are mad, that they cause a lot of trouble getting themselves stuck, and that they wouldn't do it themselves for a gold onion. Most of the cavers I have met, and I have met hundreds, have been careful and courageous people who cave for the adventure, challenge and hard physical exercise, and most of whom have a deep appreciation of the beauties of underground limestone. Like climbers and fell-walkers, they frequently attract animosity, oftentimes from locals in the areas they use for their sport. I think this is unjustified – some people don't like anybody coming into their area. They resent the 'off-comed-un', the 'bloody potoiler', the 'bloody hiker', forgetting that no matter how far back their own roots go, they or their ancestors were at one time 'foreigners' too. It's unfair for another reason: most of

the walkers, climbers and cavers that come to the Dales, the Lakes and the mountains come because they love them, because they respect them and care for them and want to keep them the way they are so that the people of the future can enjoy the wildness and the greatness of the earth.

There are cowboys, admittedly, idiots who leave smashed bottles in grass, throw lit cigarettes away carelessly, leave gates open or even vandalise them. You get that in any society, but I would say that these loonies are in the minority and certainly would get the 'clog pie' from any walking or caving club.

At the other end of the argument, there are farmers who block footpaths, set dogs on walkers, block cave entrances with rubbish, run dangerous bulls in fields with rights of way through them, rip footpath signs down and who have, in some cases, threatened people or actually hit them. Quarrying companies blast away the sides of beautiful valleys, destroy footpaths, old woodlands, Iron Age settlements and other antiquities and leave areas of the Dales looking like the surface of the moon. Water boards flood valleys, culvert streams, run concrete open drains across hillsides and fence off millions of acres of wild and open land. The MOD have again taken millions of acres of beautiful wild land and made it, if not unwalkable, at least dangerous to walkers. 'Do not stray from the path', said a notice I saw in the Cheviots when I was walking the Pennine Way. 'Do not pick anything up. It may maim or kill you.' Strange sort of welcome?

If you are looking for vandals then I think some people should look closer to home.

Walking past Bull Pot of the Witches was a sad occasion for me, as a couple of years ago a very fine caver friend of mine died while diving Bull Pot. 'In memory of Ian David Plant', a plaque reads above the pothole, 'a fine caver who died while diving Bull Pot of the Witches, 14 October 1981'. Ian was the youngest editor ever of the *Craven Herald*, one of the most important papers in the Dales. I first met him when he came to interview me as a young reporter. He was intelligent, cared about people, loved the Dales and was a good newspaper man. He was a caver too, probably one of the top ten cavers in Britain, and known well in potholing circles far and wide for his work with Oliver Monks in diving the Kingsdale master system. His death was accidental, a million to one mishap. His tragic loss was shared with his wife Sally and daughter Katie by everyone who knew him.

Beyond the tree-fringed mouth of Bull Pot of the Witches, the path to Ease Gill cuts left on to the fell's edge and passes close by a trap door covering a shaft that leads into Lancaster Hole, the first route into the main cave system of Leck Fell. Lancaster Hole was found in 1949 when a caver sitting having his lunch on a still sunny day noticed the grass nearby waving and stirring as though a wind were moving it. Being a bright lad, he worked out that it was an updraught from underground and a few removed boulders later the entrance to Lancaster Hole was revealed.

Bull Pot of the Witches, by the way, may mean just that, that it was named after a witch or witches that lived in the area. Over the fell, near where Deepdale meets Dentdale, is a farm called Coventree, which, Miley Taylor told me one night in the Sun Inn, is named after a tree beneath which the hairy crones of Dentdale would hold their covens and throw eye of newt and armpit of toad into the stew while waiting for the Dales equivalent of Macbeth and Banquo to come riding out of the night.

The ruins of Hellot Scales Barn mark the beginning of Ease Gill and the rise of Leck Beck, where all the waters that drain beneath

ABOVE: *Bullpot Farm*   BELOW: *Lower Ease Gill Kirk*

Leck Fell resurge. The first hundred yards' walking up the gill leads you into the rocky vault of Lower Ease Gill Kirk. Sheer walls thirty feet high enclose you, the way upstream being a clamber up the smooth lip of a nine-foot dry waterfall that takes you into Upper Ease Gill Kirk. Although it was dry when I visited it, Kirk Pot in the Upper Kirk is a deep pool in flood conditions. There is no way out of the Upper Kirk other than scrambling to the left or right on to the higher ground.

As I started to make my way up through some bushes on the left of the kirk, something caught my eye and I stopped. Staring at me through the branches of a twisted thorn was a tawny owl perched on a rock ledge. He blinked; I held my

BELOW: *The Megger Stones looking to the Howgills*   FACING PAGE: *Where Cow Dub drops through the beck bed*

breath. He had obviously been sleeping out the daylight in the gloom of the kirk, never expecting that some idiot with a camera, rucksack and heavy boots would come crashing into his bedroom. With what I swear was a scathing look that said something like 'Wally', he launched himself gracefully on to the air and noiselessly flew down the gill out of sight. I scrambled noisily and gracelessly out and up into the sunlight.

Another half-hour's walking brought me to Cow Dub where a stream thunders down from a lip of flowstone, crashing through a narrow tubular cavern to scour out a perfectly formed round pool below. Climbing up to the right and beyond Cow Dub, I followed the beck, dry where it had drained away through the limestone but flowing where the bands of sandstone outcropped, until on the open fell the limestone gave way to glacial moraine and the beck gurgled noisily back down towards Cow Dub.

As I struck northwards, climbing heavily towards Barbondale, I looked back and saw the river Lune cut like a golden scratch on the face of the earth leading towards Morecambe Bay, the far fells of the Lake District just visible through the afternoon light. On Crag Hill I stopped at the cairn to look down on Dentdale spread below me, Helms Knott, the Howgills and the distant forms of Cross Fell, Dun Fell and, facing me, the long ridge of Barbondale.

Cutting round to the right and following the track north-eastwards, I came down a path that led towards the Occupation Road via the Megger Stones. At the Megger Stones, the views across Dentdale and over the fells to the Howgills were superb. I sat down to watch the late afternoon shadows climb Rise Hill before striking out for the Occupation Road. This took me in a gentle curve round the flanks of Great Coum towards the Barbondale road, Combe House, the track past Tofts, and back to my home for tea and crumpets. When I eventually got home the crumpet packet was lying empty on the kitchen floor while Bilbo Baggins, the new puppy my daughters had brought home from the dogs' home, was lying full beside it. I didn't fancy his biscuits, so I made do with some toast.

5. malhamdale

MALHAMDALE stretches in a vaguely northwards direction from the gentle swelling lush lands of Craven to the wilderness of Fountains Fell and Malham Moor. At its southernmost end is the village of Gargrave where the river Aire, the Skipton – Kendal road, the Settle–Carlisle Railway and the Leeds–Liverpool canal all meet to travel among the low-lying valleys of the Aire and the Ribble.

Gargrave is the home of Johnson & Johnson of babies' bottoms fame and is also a good stopping point for a traveller on

FACING PAGE: *Malham Cove*   BELOW: *Malhamdale from the Settle–Kirkby Malham road, winter*

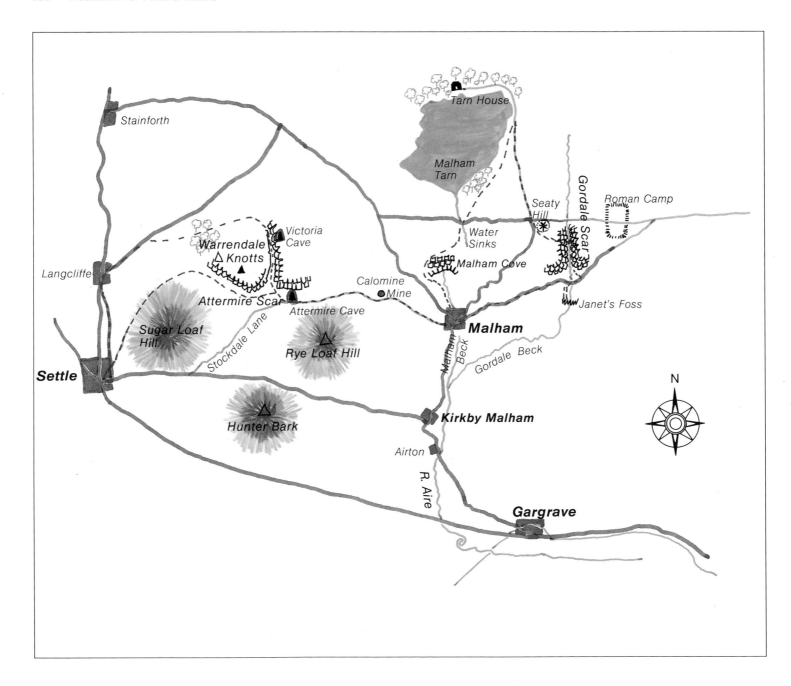

ABOVE: *The old monastic road of Mastiles Lane*   BELOW: *Medieval field system above Malham*

the Pennine Way, for there is a wonderful café here known to generations of walkers and cyclists at the very spot where the Way crosses the busy turnpike.

Walking north from Gargrave the Pennine Wayfarer follows a meandering path over a series of drumlins to Airton, where an old cotton mill was once used for the manufacture of Dettol. On the last Saturday in August the Malhamdale Agricultural Show takes place here, one of the most important shows in the dale.

From Airton the Way follows a peaceful riverside path to pass below Kirkby Malham and come close by Aire Head to Malham itself, dominated by the great scar of the Cove, which for generations of Yorkshire folk has been a place of pilgrimage and picnic. Northward of Malham is the Tarn, while to the east lies the gorge of Gordale Scar.

Fountains Fell dominates the northern end of the dale and from its flanks looking southward you can see the Tarn and the head of the dale spread before you. If you come into the dale from Stainforth, then the road into Malham winds down by Ewe Moor giving you a good view of the Cove and the lychetts under Shorkley Hill. Lychetts are strips of land one oxen-width wide that were ploughed into the hillside by Anglo-Saxon farmers. A little like the paddy fields of China, they were a sensible way for unmechanised farmers to grow crops on steep land without causing erosion.

Within its narrow boundaries, Malhamdale contains probably more of interest to the historian, geologist, naturalist and the casual tripper than any of the other dales. It has the natural beauties of the Cove Scar and Tarn, prehistoric circles and burial mounds, monastic highways and dwelling houses and, at Kirkby Malham, one of the most beautiful churches of the Dales. It's fine walking country in any weather, though it's probably best avoided on Bank Holidays and summer Sundays.

LEFT: *Malham village* (top) *Pennine Way walkers near Beck Hall* (bottom) RIGHT: *Abbot Moon's Bridge otherwise known as the Clapper Bridge* (top) *The stepping stones at Gargrave* (bottom) CENTRE: *A little owl on a post by the road to Airton*

malham, the cove, gordale scar and back by the tarn

MALHAM village is one of the 'honeypots' of the Dales and, to some extent because of this, it has suffered badly from the effects of visitor pressure. I'm thinking particularly of the footpaths leading to and climbing up the side of Malham Cove, where artificial ways have had to be created to cope with erosion caused by millions of feet. The area is popular because it contains, within a short walking distance of the village centre, the great crag of the Cove, the chasm of Gordale Scar and the glacial lake of the Tarn. Visit Malham at mid-day on a sunny Bank Holiday and it will be 'fair thranged wi' folk', yet wait until evening when the charabancs have gone and the cars have motored their way back downdale, and Malham becomes again a quiet little place, the only noise coming from the Hikers' Bar of the Buck Inn where legions of Pennine Way pilgrims have slaked their thirst; or from the bar of the Listers Arms where Dalesfolk have been coming for years to taste the best steaks in the Dales.

I like Malham because, in spite of the hammering it takes from visitors, it has still managed to keep its character. The Post

A curious cow at Seaty Hill

Office sells a few souvenirs and the café sells sandwiches 'to go', and there is a converted barn selling walking gear and souvenirs with a smashing little tea shop. There is also, of course, Beck Hall across the Clapper Bridge, which does afternoon teas and is a grand spot to sit with your scones and jam and good strong tea in the sun watching the ducks do ducky things in the water. But beyond all this, Malham goes about its business of being a living Dales village, with its farms and farmers, its village hall and little shops, very much in the way it has always done.

Malham has been a favourite stopping-off point of mine for years now. While walking the Pennine Way I cooled my feet in the beck before continuing south to Airton and Gargrave. Another time when I was walking with Tony we paused for an hour at Malham to break a long day's walk from Langcliffe to Arncliffe by Malham and Yew Cogar Scar by the old monks' road.

I remember two summers ago crossing the Dales with a backpack and camping at Malham after a glorious hot day's walking from Horton over Pen-y-ghent and Fountains Fell. The evening was cloudless and warm and after pitching the tent and cooking something called 'Hunter's Goulash' (a freeze-dried meal that I'd brought home from a trip along the Appalachian Trail – it tasted like fried sofa stuffing doused with monosodium glutamate), I walked up the narrow lane above the youth hostel to watch the sun going down behind Pikedaw Hill tingeing the sky a dusky orange – a wonderful sight.

The next day I walked through a hazy, warm day up Gordale Scar to Seaty Hill and then followed the old monastic road of Mastiles Lane to Kilnsey in Wharfedale. The few days I spent on that trip will stay in my mind as some of the most pleasant times I have ever spent. I love camping and don't feel that anything can compare with waking up in the morning with the day just a few hours on from dawn, dew still on the grass, so that when you open the tent flap the smell of a new day comes to

you with the early morning sun. Nothing in the world tastes
better than bacon and eggs cooked on a wood fire as the sun
dries the tent ready for packing away again. Having said that,
there have been times, one particular occasion in the west of
Ireland I remember only too well, when after four days of heavy
rain, I would have swapped tent, pack, pots and all for a warm
bed and a hot bath.

Malham, though, has also been a favourite spot of mine for
little walks, the sort of walks that only take an afternoon. Or, if
it's a terrifically hot day and you don't feel like burning out a
gasket on the tops, Malham is just the place for an easy stroll,
going 'just steady on', as they say in the Dales. I suppose the
most regular walk I do around Malham begins and ends at the
village itself, going first by Janet's Foss to Gordale Scar then on
to the Tarn and back by the Cove. It means that you don't get
the good views of the Cove until you've reached Malham Beck,
but I think that it's better doing the walk this way round than
going at it clockwise and having to clamber down the scar. This
walk, by the way, although it's only short, does involve a bit of
scrambling which, though hardly dangerous, does need a fair
amount of agility – fit grannies and grandads would make it,
overweight VAT inspectors with beer bellies wouldn't.

I did the walk last summer on a fine sunny afternoon,
leaving Malham by the beck that runs from the village to the
pretty little waterfall at Janet's Foss. Janet's Foss
(foss = force = waterfall) is said to have been the haunt of a
witch or water sprite called Jennet. Her cave lies just to the right
of the waterfall. But when I reached the foss I encountered not a
fairy, but my first school party of the day.

Like Alum Pot and Gaping Gill, Malham is known to
generations of 'O' level, 'A' level and CSE geography students as
a superb example of limestone scenery. During the spring and
summer, thousands of minibuses bearing such legends as 'St
Mungo's School, Larking in the Marsh' crawl down
Malhamdale, eager noses pressed to the windows and hands
clutching clipboards full of papers scrawled with questions,

ABOVE: *Courting couple above Malham Cove*　FACING PAGE: *Janet's Foss*

measurements and such amatory statements as 'Ruth loves
Simon Carr – true'.

So there at Janet's Foss was my first school trip of the
season. It was a party of sixth-formers with an instructor
teaching them about the effects of weathering, the differing levels
of hardness of limestone and how the two combine to produce
waterfalls. One of the boys, wearing shorts and a T-shirt and
little else, climbed round the pool and up below the fairy cave.
He was showing off, as is the way with adolescent boys in the
first flush of manhood (let he who has not sinned throw the first
stone), and, as is the way with adolescent boys in the first flush
of manhood, he slipped and fell in the pool – collapse of stout
party etc.

From Janet's Foss my way led across the
road and through a gate where the Dales Park
have placed a plaque telling me that this is
Gordale Scar and to keep to the path. I did as I
was told, although I did go off it once, I confess,
to watch a lad from Leeds ferreting for rabbits.
Back on the path I came to the 'chasm' said by
many geologists to be a collapsed cave system
and suggested by others more recently to have
been carved out of a weakness in the limestone
by the raging melting ice waters of a glacier.

This morning the school party, including
the wet member, having gone on well ahead, I
crossed the beck and sat in the warm sun
outside the gorge, simply looking. It has always
inspired awe and wonderment. Even
Wordsworth, who had never been there, took
it on himself to describe it as 'terrific as the lair
where the young lions couch', then went on to
say that if the 'pensive votary' enters Gordale
at 'shadowy eve when the air glimmers with
fading light', he or she will meet 'a local deity
with oozey hair and mineral crown'. Local
writer Thomas Hurtley (who also, by the way,
thought the Dales peaks at least as high as those
in the Alps) called Gordale a 'Stupendous
Pavilion of Sable Rock apparently rent asunder
by some dreadful although inscrutable
elementary convulsion'.

The scar itself is part of the Mid-Craven
Fault, one of the same set of faults which
produced Giggleswick and Attermire Scars.
The gorge which cuts through Gordale Scar,
whether a collapsed cave or simply a water-
eroded cleft, is impressive in its grandeur.
Although the literary effusions of Hurtley and

Wordsworth and the exaggerated landscapes of James Ward and J. M. W. Turner seem a little over the top to us dwellers in the twentieth century (who, since the advent of the camera and the picture postcard, like our landscape more real and our prose less flowery), the scar nevertheless overhangs and dominates the scene as an example of the incredible forces at work when the landscape we now see was formed. The Mid-Craven Fault is so deep that if you were to look south of Malham for the limestone that you see on Gordale Scar you would have to drill many thousands of feet below the earth's surface before you came to it.

I walked out of the sunlight into the cool dark shadow of the gorge, meeting no deity with oozy hair but a couple eating sandwiches and two crag rats. The crag rat, or *Rattus lithographus*, is a strange specimen rarely seen in limestone hitherto because of the friable nature of the rocks, until now usually preferring Lakeland granite or Pennine gritstone. The creature is often seen on the Idwal Slabs in North Wales and

FACING PAGE: *Gordale Scar*   BELOW: *Crag rat on Gordale Scar*

Stanage and Laddow Rocks in the South Pennines but has of recent years migrated on to the Craven limestone.

When they first made their appearance in this country, crag rats sported nailed boots and tweed plus-fours. Now they wear little except shorts and light rubber-soled pumps and hold on to vertical cliff walls like flies with a combination of sticky powder on their fingers, the faith of an Indian fakir, and tons of hardware in the shape of bolts, runners and slings hammered into the rocks. For all that, as somebody who gets jelly knees on anything as simple as Jack's Rake in the Langdales, I admire their bottle.

Passing the crag rats who were climbing Cave Route Right Hand, I climbed my own bit of grade E6 over the tufa and out past the block of stone with a hole eroded through that is said by some to have been the lip of a water chute when the chasm was a cave. Then I climbed up into the warm sunshine and the dry valley of Gordale Beck. Access to the dry valley is forbidden, which is a shame since it is in fact one of the best examples of a dry valley in the area. Steep cliffs of limestone line its sides, while higher up in the bed of the beck which flows through it you can find, according to Dr Raistrick, 'Cave Pearls', small, rounded calcite pebbles formed by the deposition of layer upon layer of calcium in solution.

Visitor pressure and the often mindless or downright destructive behaviour of some of the people who come to this area have annoyed some farmers so much that they look on walkers as just another kind of vermin – and there are many times when I can sympathise with this attitude completely. The unfortunate result is that farmers, angered by the attitude of the careless few, block footpaths or refuse access to such places as the dry valley of Gordale Beck to the many considerate walkers who respect not only the countryside but also the problems of the working community who for centuries have fought to make a living from the land.

It's long been a custom to knock farmers and the high subsidies that many of them receive. I might agree in terms of

ABOVE: *Malham Tarn, evening*   FACING PAGE: *The duck that pinched my sandwich* (inset)

lowland farming where farms are more often controlled by investment groups than by single families, but hill farming has always been, and still is, a hard and often heart-breaking as well as back-breaking job.

To work all year and then watch your entire flock of sheep be killed by a long savage winter, as happened in Malham in 1940 when drifts ten and twenty feet deep covered the moor of Spiggot Hill and Tarn Moss, must be cruelty itself. The sheep had huddled together to keep warm and as the drifts covered them the weaker animals were trampled and crushed beneath the stronger sheep that were struggling for air. Then they too died as, too exhausted to fight any further, they were covered by a crust of snow which froze on in the bitter winds. In 1947 again the winter closed in after Christmas, as often happens in the Dales, only this time haytime had been ruined by a terrible summer and, in spite of the RAF airlift of fodder, many thousands of animals died of starvation.

From the forbidden dry valley I followed the path to Seaty Hill, a Bronze Age tumulus standing close to the point at which Mastiles Lane joins the main tarmac road and an indication of the deep roots of man's existence in the Dales. The day was moving on faster than I was now and a heat haze shimmered over the Tarn as I came to its banks to sit and eat my lunch.

Malham Tarn was first formed when glacial meltwaters gathered on a thick bed of boulder clay at the end of the last Ice Age. In a landscape renowned for its water sinks and disappearing streams, it's unusual to find lakes of the size of Semer Water and Malham Tarn. 'Tarn', by the way, is an interesting word coming from the Old Norse word for tear. I suppose for the early settlers the smaller tarns such as those on Widdale, Baugh Fell and Whernside looked like tears on the face of the fell. Malham Tarn is a fascinating place. The monks of Fountains Abbey fished here for trout in the Middle Ages after William de Percy granted the Tarn to the Abbey 'for the good of the souls of his father and mother and all his ancestors'.

The Tarn is still famous for its trout, and boats can be hired from Tarn House. On the day I fished the Tarn, however, a long summer heatwave and a freak wind had brought algae up from the lake bottom so that they hung in suspension, turning the lake the colour of pea soup. I caught precisely nothing, not even a pea.

The Tarn House, now a centre for nature study, was largely rebuilt on the site of the hunting lodge of the Lords Ribblesdale by Walter Morrison around 1852. Morrison was host to such Victorian worthies as Ruskin, the great art critic, and Charles Kingsley, who is said to have been inspired to write his book *The Water Babies* by his visits to the Dales (Vendale being based on Littondale) and who once told somebody that the black marks on the face of Malham Cove were made by 'the fingers of little chimney boys'.

The Tarn is home to many varieties of water fowl including the curlew, the greater crested grebe and the lesser spotted sandwich-pinching duck, one specimen of which had my last tuna-fish butty while I wasn't looking.

I could see the beginning of cloud formations in the far west that looked as though they might thicken up and, since I wanted to get some shots of the Cove while the light was still good, I set off by Water Sinks, where the water from the Tarn sinks and doesn't reappear again until some miles down the valley at Aire Head, and followed the footpath that would take me west of Watlowes dry valley and bring me down to the Cove by the pasture land above the Pennine Way. It was as fine an afternoon as you could wish for as I slowly descended to Malham Beck, the Cove coming into view on my left as I walked down. Children were splashing in the beck, their cries echoing from the cove face, a courting couple were doing what courting couples have done since time immemorial, oblivious to the world and its wife passing by, and old ladies on a coach trip from Bradford were walking gently through the sunny afternoon, all grey hair, handbags and giggles. I stayed at the Cove watching cloud shadows racing across the great limestone cliffs until the sun moved round to the west when it was time to race the old ladies back to the village for the tea and scones of Beck Hall. I beat them, but only just – those handbags are lethal.

malham to settle, back by victoria cave

'VE always been fascinated by prehistory, particularly the time of man's first settlement in the northern Dales. The area between Langcliffe and Malham is probably the most interesting area in the North for anybody interested in prehistoric man, for in the limestone cliffs of Attermire and Langcliffe lie some of the earliest traces of man's habitation in Western Europe.

A couple of years ago I was staying in Malham for a few days and decided to set out one morning for Attermire by the old pack lane from Settle to Malham. It was a sunny morning in late autumn and the frost was melting on the stiff blades of grass as I climbed the lane out of Malham and crossed the meadows climbing steeply upwards to Pikedaw Hill.

On Pikedaw Hill is the now covered shaft of a calamine mine where men descended deep into the earth to dig out zinc bearings, a memorial to the fact that Malhamdale was once a very industrialised valley. Cotton mills were built and worked at Airton and Kirkby Malham: by the side of the path up Pikedaw Hill is the entrance to a disused lead-mine, while further up the dale is the old smelt mill chimney on Malham Moor.

Beyond Pikedaw Hill I followed the track over the saddle of Kirkby Fell and below Rye Loaf Hill to Stockdale Farm. It's smashing walking along this track because it's firm underfoot and the views back to Malham and over to Great Scar and Attermire are worth nine out of ten in anybody's book.

FACING PAGE: *The smelt mill chimney on Malham Moor*   RIGHT: *Looking westwards towards Stockdale Farm*   BELOW: *The calamine mine on Pikedaw Hill*

ABOVE: *Attermire Scar* RIGHT: *Langcliffe and the war memorial* (top) *Scaleber Force just off the road to Stockdale* (bottom) FACING PAGE: *Looking across the main street to the Naked Man Café* (top left) *The Naked Man, Settle* (top right) *Victoria Cave* (bottom)

From Stockdale Lane End, I climbed a stile and followed the footpath under Attermire Scar. High above me was the narrow gash of Attermire Cave and the craggy outcrop of the scar hanging over the valley like a wave of stone about to break.

Some more crag rats were further proving the delights of Yorkshire limestone, holding on to ledges with their eyelashes and hanging on to spars of rock by their nostrils, swarming in a team of a dozen or so all over the face of the scar like a plague of dayglo flies.

I turned away from the scars near Warrendale Knots and dropped down by Middle High Hill to Settle and lunch at the Naked Man where the nicest ladies you could ever wish to meet serve real Yorkshire food, and plenty of it. They do, however, insist that you keep your clothes on.

After lunch, full of roast beef, Yorkshire pudding, apple pie and custard, I took the back lane from Settle to Langcliffe and began the long climb out of the village by road. I had to sit down twice because of the roast beef and everything, which had gone straight to my legs. It isn't a good idea to climb hills after eating at the Naked Man – ideally you should find a quiet corner and sleep it off like a boa constrictor does after it has swallowed a goat or two too many.

Eventually, having decided that calling out the Cave Rescue for a simple case of overeating wouldn't look good in the newspapers, I recovered and got to the lane by Clay Pits Plantation that leads to Victoria Cave.

Clouds were moving across the far north-west of the landscape as I got to the cave, and I'd just reached the mouth when the first drops of rain spattered on the stones at my feet. In minutes the sky had darkened and a heavy rainstorm was lacing the fields before me.

As I sat in the mouth of the cave looking out at the change in the weather, I wondered how a man in the Old Stone Age must have felt, staring out at the rain, knowing that if it didn't let up soon he'd have to go out in it and knock a mammoth on the head for tea. Amusing myself with such trivial thoughts, I waited for the rain to give up.

It didn't, I did and clad in my cagoule, glasses steamed up, and mouthing curses at the weather, I walked through the grey rain to Attermire and back to Malham. I'd like to say that I remember something about the rest of that walk but I don't, only that it rained, then it rained some more, and when it got fed up with that, it rained again. I reached the Buck Inn just at opening time and stood by the fire steaming so much that two Swedish students got lost in the fog going to the gents.

6. GARSDALE

FROM Sedbergh to the lonely Moorcock Inn runs Garsdale, a deep and secretive valley, and one of the northernmost dales, flanked by the long ridge of Rise Hill to the south and the mass of Baugh Fell to the north. The road into Garsdale from the west leaves Sedbergh and rises below Frostrow Fell and Tom Croft Hill. Just before the road drops down into Garsdale there is a parking place which is well worth pulling into if you're in a car, for there is a fine view of the Howgills from this spot. You can also begin a short walk from here called the Adam Sedgwick Trail, which will take you along by the river Clough to the Danny Bridge where the rocks of the Dent Fault lie exposed above the river. A plaque in the car park shows the route.

From the car park the road runs into Garsdale hugging the banks of the river Clough as it goes by New Bridge and Slack Farm and by Dandra Garth to Garsdale Head and Dandry Mire.

Garsdale's one settlement of any size, The Street, is made up of a collection of cottages, a Post Office, a petrol station and a church. Some of the cottages have their windows painted red and this 'Garsdale Red' is said to stem from a custom established in Garsdale when a goods train belonging to the Midland Railway Company tipped over at Garsdale Head, tumbling thousands of tons of Midland Red livery paint into the fields. For years after, all the farmhouses and cottages in Garsdale were painted the maroon and cream of the railway company. I don't know if that's true or not but it makes a good tale.

FACING PAGE: *Looking towards Swarth Fell from Grisedale, at the western end of Garsdale* RIGHT: *River Clough, Garsdale*

There seem to be more chapels and churches in Garsdale than anywhere else I've been. This may be because Garsdale used to be one of the most powerful centres of Methodism in the Dales. Revivalist meetings were common, some of them going on until one or two o'clock in the morning, and the famous

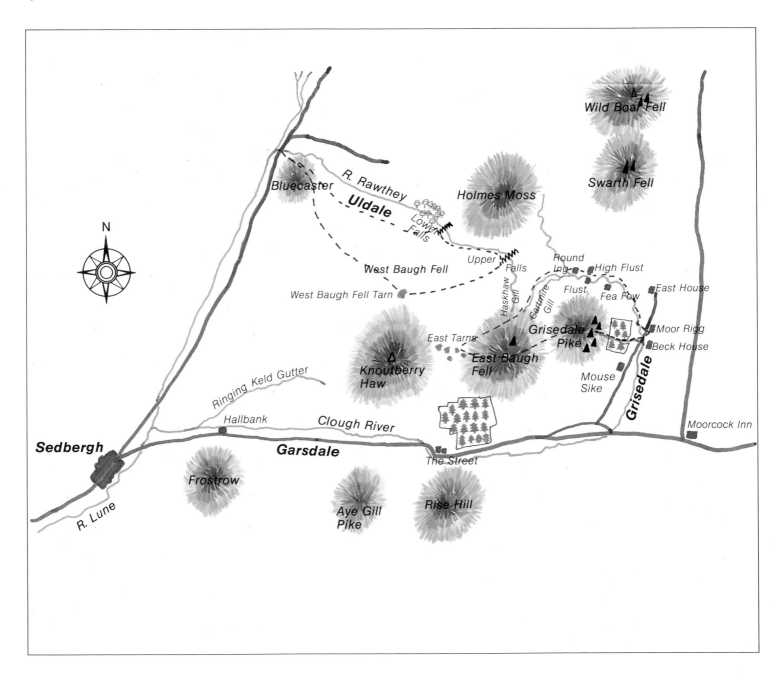

Richard 'Dick' Atkinson of Grisedale was so well known in Methodist preaching circles that he was invited down to London to preach, but refused to go, saying that his place was in the Dales with the people he knew.

Richard Atkinson was by all accounts a hell-fire preacher of tremendous power who converted thousands to Methodism. He prayed alone on the fell under a solitary hawthorn where it is said you can see the hollows made by his knees to this day. On one occasion he is supposed to have climbed up on to the ledge of the pulpit in full view of the congregation and challenged the Devil to fight. Apparently on this occasion the Devil did not show up, although Dick claimed to have met him many times on the fell.

ABOVE: *Dandrymire Viaduct, Garsdale* BELOW: *Garsdale Head Methodist chapel* (left) *The Street, Garsdale* (right)

ABOVE LEFT: *Slack Cottage, Garsdale*   ABOVE RIGHT: *Early lambs, Grisedale*

Garsdale finds little mention in literature, although it was the birthplace of John Dawson, a shepherd who was born in the late eighteenth century. While watching his flocks on the fells, he taught himself algebra and geometry. He later went on to become a surgeon and one of the most brilliant and renowned mathematicians of his time.

Garsdale also features in a remarkable work by Richard Braithwaite called *Drunken Barnaby's Journal*, a wandering inebriated trip through these dales which brings Barnaby to 'Gastile', as Garsdale was pronounced in the dialect then:

Thence to Gastile I was drawne in
To an alehouse neare adjoining
To a Chappell; I drunk stingo
With a Butcher, and Domingo
The Curate, who my discerning
Was not guilty of much learning.

Garsdale is a little-known dale, hidden and winding, but well worth a visit for, although it can be wild at times, it is generally peaceful, still and cut off from the bustle of some of the more popular dales. In all the times I've walked in the Garsdale area I haven't seen a soul on the tops. Not even Old Nick.

BAUGH FELL BY RINGING KELD GUTTER

'I'D rather be here than in Philadelphia' – W. C. Fields, when asked what he would like carved on his tombstone.

Writers and walkers alike have often discounted Garsdale and Baugh Fell, calling them dull and dowdy, uninteresting, sad, uninspiring and, perhaps most damning of all, miserable. They've been neglected in most walking books and in all but the most regional topographical books, and I have to admit that I too used to be guilty of thinking of them in that way. My ideas changed one hot late summer's day a few years ago when Pat and I were walking along the ridge of Rise Hill that lies above Dentdale running from

Arten Gill to Helms Knott. It had been a wonderful day and as we walked the late afternoon gave way to early evening.

To the south, Great Coum was tipped by the lowering sun and the walled fields of Deepdale and Dentdale were thrown into relief by the falling light as they stood, a stark network of dry-stone walls and hedges piecing and parcelling up the valleys. To the west, Combe Scar, a cup-shaped slash in the fell with sheer gullies and twisted thorns clinging to its face, was darkening now as the sun moved towards Barbondale, and as I turned to look back I saw Garsdale spread out below me and the slow rise of Baugh Fell travelling east–west, ending in the desolate but hauntingly lovely Grisedale.

Baugh Fell edge looked as though it would make an interesting walk, and that night by the fireside I took out my maps and traced what looked like a fair route from Hallbank along Ringing Keld Gutter and on to Knoutberry Haw, the highest point on Baugh Fell. Once on the top I saw that I could either strike back to West Baugh Fell Tarn and follow one of the many gills that drain westward off Baugh Fell back to my starting point, or I could travel eastwards to Grisedale Pike, cut north to Scale Farm and follow the track round to Rawthey Gill Foot and follow Uldale down to the falls. There seemed to be any number of interesting possible walks, ranging from pleasant strolls to serious circular tours of the whole fell, all centering on Baugh Fell and Garsdale.

In the event it was winter before I was able to get out for a few days' walking and, leaving the car at Hallbank, I walked across the footbridge and headed out across the fields towards Ringing Keld Gutter. It was ten days before Christmas and a mild autumn and mild though wet early winter had given way to

LEFT: *Frost on the fence, Baugh Fell*

ABOVE: *Cloud inversion, Baugh Fell*   FACING PAGE: *Baugh Fell from Garsdale*

the first serious frosts. Branches and walls were coated with floury ice while grass stems and wire fences had gathered frost on frost, in some places almost a centimetre thick with rime.

The fell tops were under low cloud as I set off but there was a good chance it might clear, and with a map and compass, plenty to eat and drink, warm clothing and enough hours of daylight to see me clearly through it, it seemed hardly likely that I would get into any serious trouble. The path to Ringing Keld

Gutter crosses the Clough, Garsdale's own river that rises close to the source of the Rawthey on East Baugh Fell: the Rawthey turns north and east while the Clough turns south and west to circle the fell.

It has always struck me as fascinating how on these high uplands water can appear, disappear and resurge in what sometimes seem very mysterious ways. Rain falling on one side of the dry-stone wall on Pen-y-ghent's summit, for example,

ABOVE: *Sheep in winter* FACING PAGE: *Looking across Ringing Keld Gutter towards the Howgills*

me and obliterating anything more than a few yards away. I climbed on until I came to a narrow gully that cut through a wall; I checked the map. I was below the pike. I climbed expecting a cairn to appear through the mist. Instead I was met by a jumble of stones that looked more than a little like the hut circles on Ingleborough.

As I stood amongst the stones, the clouds dropped suddenly and I found myself looking down in pale but bright sunlight across Garsdale to Rise Hill. Below me, inverted clouds rolled unreally in waves and a lagoon of mist lapped the shores of Rise Hill and Baugh Fell. I stood held by the scene for some time, then moved over to the wall, sitting behind it in the lee of the wind to drink my brew and eat my sandwiches.

Within minutes the mist had rolled in again and I set off one step ahead of the cold, following the wall and coming at last to Knoutberry Haw and the trig point. By now it was obvious that the weather had set in and that the mist was going to be about for the rest of the day. There is no fun and no future in wobbling

about in chilling mist, so I took a reckoning and walked south-east towards Swarth Gill Wood. As I dropped below the crest of the hill the mist thinned until at about 2,000 feet it cleared completely and I walked out below it into clear day to see Garsdale stretching before me.

The valley was tinted by the misty wintry light of the sun so that dry-stone walls, barns, trees and farmhouses took on the tones of burnished brass. At my feet a beck whose banks were hung with ice-rimed whiskers gabbled and muttered on its way downfell while to my left a lone tree stood stark and golden against an icy blue sky.

And so, through broken light and below skies that were alternately thick cloud and clear blue, I walked down the fell to the road. After a mile of road I cut across country again by the old track from Bellow Hill to Hallbank and back to my car. It was a shame that I'd been forced off the fell early by the mist but at least I had been able to prove to myself if nobody else that Garsdale is not the walker's wilderness it is claimed to be.

uldale and the falls

At the northern fringes of Baugh Fell and at the northern boundary of the National Park, the river Rawthey flows down the narrow valley of Uldale, a little-visited gill that contains some of the loveliest scenery in the Dales.

I have collected books ever since I was a boy and in recent years have collected anything I could lay my hands on that dealt with the Yorkshire Dales. A bibliophile friend of mine had managed to get for me a copy of a book long out of print, *Three Picturesque Yorkshire Dales – Sedbergh, Garsdale and Dent*, by the Reverend W. Thompson, M A, formerly scholar of Queen's College, Oxford. Published in 1910, the book is a labour of love written by an old boy of Sedbergh School. It's quirky in parts, verbose in others and is illustrated by some fine old photographs. About Uldale the book says: 'On its way through the sequestered glen of Uldale, the Rawthey meets the Uldale Gill, and the streams separately and unitedly descend by a succession of cascades, of which two at least are of more than ordinary interest and beauty.' Though I had walked the Howgills and the fells around for years I had never walked in Uldale, nor, with the exception of the Reverend Thompson, had I read much about it.

It was a clear winter's morning when I left the Kirkby Stephen–Sedbergh road at Rawthey Bridge and began walking through the snow-covered fields below Bluecaster. Bluecaster, a mound by the roadside, was probably the site of a Roman camp or signal station on the Roman road from Sedbergh to Brough. Certainly the track called The Street which runs beyond Bluecaster going northwards is still what remains of an old Roman road. The day was cold and crisp, and though the snow slowed me down a little, it was good walking with all the signs of a settled day ahead.

I was well prepared for the weather in thick winter walking boots, woollen over-jacket and mitts and all the stuff that a modern walker wears on a winter's day on the fells, but I couldn't help but wonder how the poor old Romans managed in weather like this. Imagine some raw recruit legionary from a village in southern Italy with its hot sun, its olive groves and vineyards, being stationed up here in the biting northern winds and snows, watching through the northern gloom for the rebel Brigantes on the rampage. I know that the Romans, where they could, recruited men from local tribes into their armies, but there must still have been a fair smattering of Mediterranean

FACING PAGE: *Looking across Uldale*   BELOW: *Uldale lower falls*

types shivering in their cloaks, staring out over the Howgills with icicles hanging from their togas, cursing the natives and banging their chilblains together to keep warm.

The route I had chosen took me slightly away from the river and on to what, in spite of the snow, was still visible as a Land-rover track running below Bluecaster and slightly above a sheep fold. As I followed it I could make out in the near distance the ruins of a barn, its rough edges smoothed now by time and the snows.

Further down the Dales, particularly in Swaledale, Littondale and Ribblesdale, the traditional pattern of Dales farming is plain to see from the fell tops, as the farms line the valley between the river and where the good land ends, obviously built where good fresh springwater is to be had. Above them are the 'laithes', outlying barns where cattle were brought in winter to be out of the weather. These barns, with haylofts in them for winter feed, are used much less these days as farming methods have changed and big prefabricated cattle

The lower falls in summer

houses nearer the farms have taken over the job. Sadly, many of the laithes are in a bad way now, missing roofs and walls, and some have collapsed entirely. It seems tragic that they, like many of the dry-stone walls in the Dales, should be allowed to decay, but unless somebody is prepared to put money into the area it is likely that they will continue to deteriorate. The maintenance of barns, like good dry-stone walling, is expensive, and though courses are being run by local authorities to teach dry-stone walling to young people, there are almost certainly millions of man-hours of work already there in the repair work   and who can afford to pay for it? My argument, for what it's worth, is that if we as a nation want National Parks, then we must be prepared to pay for them, but it's not an argument that is very popular with many; dry-stone walls don't win votes, national opera companies it seems do.

An hour's walking through the snow brought me to a footbridge across the Rawthey to the first set of falls where the breeze shaking the branches of the trees above me in the gill showered me with snow as I looked upstream. The lower falls were gentle tumbles over stone ledges like some of the falls in upper Dentdale, running below the bridge and on into a darker and deeper cleft in the rocks that in ice and snow looked definitely out of bounds. In summer the place would be alive with dippers and wag-tails, the banks in flower with marsh marigold, celandine and herb robert. Now, held fast in the grip of winter, the world was turned into mono-chrome and the only moving things were the water, the snow gently flaking from the branches of the trees, and

me as I strode along at a good pace to keep warm in the sharp, chill air.

The path above the falls was icy, so I walked off it upwards on to the snow where the footing was firmer and, kicking footsteps as I went, I headed upstream again. Now the gill was

ABOVE: *Primroses*   BELOW: *Celandine* (left)   *Water avens* (right)

ABOVE: *Uldale upper falls* FACING PAGE: *Sheep, Uldale Beck*

I have the escape routes well sorted out. In case you think that is over-cautious, a water board official whose house was on the Pennine Way near Top Withins died in snowdrifts less than a quarter of a mile from his home in easy walking country, and he was a man who knew the moors about him well.

Ahead of me now I could see the gillside becoming shaley and steep. I pushed on and climbed above the beck on to more open land. I could hear coming towards me from the south the noise of roaring water and after a little more walking I came to the main falls of Uldale, an impressive rock lip with the infant Rawthey plunging over it, its spray coating the branches of the overhanging trees with ice and turning the fringes of grass at the bankside into organ pipes. Further upstream great sheets of icicles had joined to form a wall below the overhang of the valley sides. I scrambled through a gap in them and struck up on to the fell, climbing hard.

Below West Baugh Fell Tarn I sat and had my brew and looked out at the Howgills to my left as regal and possessing as ever and the slopes of Swarth Fell and Wild Boar Fell ahead of me. It is said that it was on Wild Boar Fell that Sir Richard de Musgrave killed the last wild boar in England in the fourteenth century. A lot of people said the idea was just a load of rubbish until in 1847 they opened his grave while repairing the church at Kirkby Stephen. There by his side was the tusk of a wild boar, which just goes to show that either the legend was correct or Sir Richard was waiting for the tooth fairy to call.

I sat for a while in bright sunlight watching the landscape, until the light began to fade as the sun sank below the crest of Baugh Fell. Then, with the afternoon mellowing towards dusk, I struck off towards Bluecaster, having stood looking about me one last time, the newly risen moon crisp in the sky over my shoulder, the Howgills spread out before me cloaked with a mantle of snow. I walked back to the car with six good hours of snow walking behind me and then, as school children always used to write at the end of essays entitled 'My Day Out', I went home and told my mum what had happened and had my tea.

narrowing and in places the path seemed to vanish entirely. I picked my way through and walked on. On a good day and pushing myself I know that carrying a full pack I can cover three miles an hour in the hills; taking my time to look round and take pictures I reckon two miles an hour is realistic. When there is snow on the fell I take every precaution necessary, reckon a mile and a half an hour gives me plenty of leeway, and make sure that

GRISEDALE AND THE PIKE

WINTER is one of my favourite times for walking. I like the clearness that you get on good frosty days and the sharp bite that the air has to it. I like it when the wind is raging across the tops and the ground is frozen hard beneath your feet and, best of all in winter, I like walking in snow when the skies are blue and clear and the fells are white over. Such days are hard to find, however, and often I have had to do with second best or less than second best when the snow's been there in plenty but the sky has been grey and threatening.

A few winters ago, I went to one of my favourite dales, Grisedale, a quiet valley tributary to Garsdale near Garsdale Head. It is flanked by Baugh Fell and White Birks Common and dominated at its head by Swarth Fell and Wild Boar Fell. All around are the open fells and crags of Mallerstang and the Upper Eden Valley.

Warm and lovely in summer, wild and woolly in winter, Grisedale ('The Valley of the Pigs' in Old Norse) is known to many as 'The Dale That Died', after a television documentary of that name made by Barry Cockcroft of Yorkshire Television. Had the upland farming subsidies come in time, Grisedale might have been saved, but they didn't, and one after another the farming families of the dale left the land and the elements turned in and began the slow but steady process of destruction, so that what were once family homes where folk were born, worked and died, became dark ruins, brooding in an empty dale. At one time sixteen families farmed this dale, sixteen farmhouses with children, hired maidservants and the Irishmen that came to Hawes hiring fair every year to be hired for the haytime. Now, only one house is permanently lived in, by a writer and his family. Many of the rest have fallen, in less than thirty years, into ruin, and the old chapel is now a holiday home.

It was a few weeks into the New Year when I parked the car by Beck House, near where the old Grisedale chapel stood, and walked through deep snow towards Moor Rigg. I had the Old Series two-and-a-half-inch Ordance Survey map as my guide and it showed a clear footpath from Moor Rigg, by a footbridge, over Grisedale Beck, along Butter Beck, by High Lathe to the open fell. The footpath was hidden by snow and the footbridge had vanished completely. I crossed the beck by jumping from ice-skinned stone to ice-skinned stone and just about made it to the other side. Unmarked on the two-and-a-half-inch map, although, as I later discovered, marked on the new Pathfinder Series, a forestry plantation closed in around me, until by High Lathe I was forced to climb fences and work my way through young spruce to the open fell.

I'm not a great fan of conifer afforestation, whether Forestry Commission or otherwise. The forests change the look

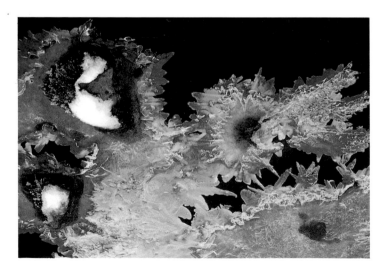

LEFT: *Frozen beck, Grisedale*   FACING PAGE: *Looking northwards from Grisedale, summer*

of the landscape, their regular boxed patterns impose hard edges on the countryside, and they change the drainage patterns of the land considerably. Deciduous broad-leaved trees absorb wet and lose it through their leaves – in fact, one of the best ways of draining marshland is to plant alders. With deciduous trees, the leaves fall in the autumn creating a good mulch for other growths and the ultimate self-renewal of the forest. Spruce drop no such leaves, their needles provide next to nothing in the way of nourishment, and the system of planting by machine produces ditches that cause a quick run-off of rain with the result that rivers rise and fall overnight, producing flooding in the valley plain.

Broad-leaved trees provide shelter and homes for animals, birds, insects and flowers. You'll hear little birdsong in a spruce plantation. The old argument is that it provides jobs and money. It provides money for the investment groups that plant forests and get grants for doing it, such as tax-avoidance schemes or pension schemes, but provides nowhere near the numbers of jobs that the management of broad-leaved woodland or coppicing provides. The basic cynical truth is that it provides a relatively quick turn round on capital investment. Twenty years is nothing in the lifetime of a pension fund and foreknowledge of a world timber shortage comes in handy too.

From the edge of the woodland I climbed upfell, following the beck, to the Pike. Grisedale Pike, like the Megger Stones, is a group of cairns lining the edge of a fell, and for what reason no one is sure. However, something I have read recently has made me think of one possible function for the cairns.

Reading in a history book about the tumulus of Seaty Hill near Malham, I came across a description of how when the tumulus was excavated two chambers were found in the interior of the burial mound. In one there sat upright the richly dressed skeleton of a Celtic chieftain staring across into the second compartment, which contained a beautifully made and well-

LEFT: *'Beware of the bull', Grisedale*

preserved cairn. Obviously, then, in Celtic times, the cairn had some religious significance. Certainly the fact that such an important chieftain was buried with a model cairn facing him on his trip to the underworld would indicate that this is the case. Accepting this, and the fact that nobody seems to know the age of the many cairns that line the edges of the Dales summits, there is, in my unlettered opinion, good reason to believe that these cairns are far older than we think, perhaps dating back to Celtic times, and that they may even have a religious significance.

I stopped at the Pike for a while; a cold wind blew and grey clouds were racing across the sky. To the south-east were Dandrymire Viaduct and the flanks of the fells of Abbotside Common, Ure Head and Lovely Seat with Shunner Fell in between them. In the far distance, Pen-y-ghent and Ingleborough were just visible in the grey snowy light.

Grisedale Pike from the Coal Road into Garsdale

ABOVE: *The ruins of Round Ing, Grisedale* FACING PAGE: *Looking towards Dandrymire Viaduct from Grisedale Pike*

I struck off upfell through the wind, the snow making it heavy going, until I came at last to where in summer I'd seen the tarns of Tarn Rigg Hill. Now they were frozen solid and snowed over. All about me there was nothing but a plateau of white and the solitary cairn. My finger ends felt like frozen sausages and my body was crying out for hot tea, so I looked about me for somewhere to shelter out of the wind. Eventually I found a hollow near the wall where I snuggled down and made a pig of myself with garlic sausage sandwiches and hot strong tea.

A lot of people shake their heads when I tell them I go fell-walking. They tap their temples and wink knowingly at each other as though to say, 'They're not all locked up, you know.' I must admit it is hard to explain to somebody the sense of achievement I get from a long hard walk completed, or the sense of the smallness and insignificance of man in the face of nature that I feel when I'm on the tops in a storm or when I stand on a crag edge and look at the world below me. I think it's something you either love or hate – like bagpipe music, there's nothing in between.

So I put my bagpipes away, took a compass bearing, and walked off the tops looking for a gill, either Cartmire Gill or Grisedale Gill, that would lead me down into Grisedale proper. So many gills spring up on the northern slopes of Baugh Fell that it would be easy to follow the wrong one and end up in Uldale, but luckily I struck a gill going in the right direction and as I followed it down, I saw ahead of me the ruins of Round Ing, the first of the sad relics of Grisedale.

In the still snowy afternoon with the grey light fading, there was something almost painfully sad in this ruined family house with its crumbling walls and its garden and outbuildings overgrown with nettles and weeds. Where are the men now who led horses and hay sleds out of these gates? Where now are the children who played in the beck beneath the house?

From Round Ing a footpath led to West Scale and East Scale along the frozen beck side to Moor Rigg. As I walked through the dying afternoon the wind that had followed me off the fell dropped and a stillness came over the dale. Nothing stirred, and through the silence I heard the muted sounds of the beck trapped beneath its skin of ice as it ran downdale. I walked slowly on past the sad empty farms of East and West Scale and the tumbled walls of outbuildings and fields. As I turned by a fallen dry-stone wall to follow the track back to my car I heard the only sound of life in the dale, the laughter of the children of East House skating on the frozen beck.

7. Wharfedale

WHARFEDALE is a big broad dale, the kind of all the dales whose river, like the Dee in Dentdale, is named after a Celtic goddess, the Dee being named after the goddess Deva, the Wharfe after Verbena.

From Grassington with its disused lead-mines and souvenir shops in the south, coming by Kettleswell and Buckden to Hubberholme and Yockenthwaite at its northern end, Wharfedale is a total delight.

Langstrothdale leads into Wharfedale by Beckermonds and the road from Wensleydale over Fleet Moss, while the road from Bishopdale comes in via the hamlet of Cray. Further downdale, the Littondale road winds by the lovely village of Arncliffe where the Falcon Inn still serves beer straight from the barrel into a jug without any pumps, and by Litton where the Queen's Arms does wonderful ham and eggs.

Wharfedale is full of interesting walks. Around Grassington are the remains of Iron Age villages and lead-mine workings. Grassington itself is a busy walking centre with many cafés, bed and breakfast places and, although it's a little bit touristy, is still an attractive place. Further up the dale is the limestone outcrop of Kilnsey Crag while above Arncliffe are vast expanses of limestone with the remains of Iron Age settlements upon them. Beyond, Kettlewell, where the Coverdale road comes over the saddle of the fells, is the old Iron Age defensive ditch of Tor Dike.

Hubberholme has a beautiful church and a smashing pub, while Buckden is still famous as the home of the Beresford Band, a traditional Dales dance band which plays round the Dales at village hops. In Wharfedale there are high hard routes over Great Whernside and Buckden Pike, cross-valley walks from Littondale by Horse Head Pass to Langstrothdale, lovely riverside walks along the Wharfe, and limestone edge walks above Hubberholme and Kettlewell.

RIGHT: *Bridge over the Wharfe near Yockenthwaite* FACING PAGE: *Yockenthwaite stone circle*

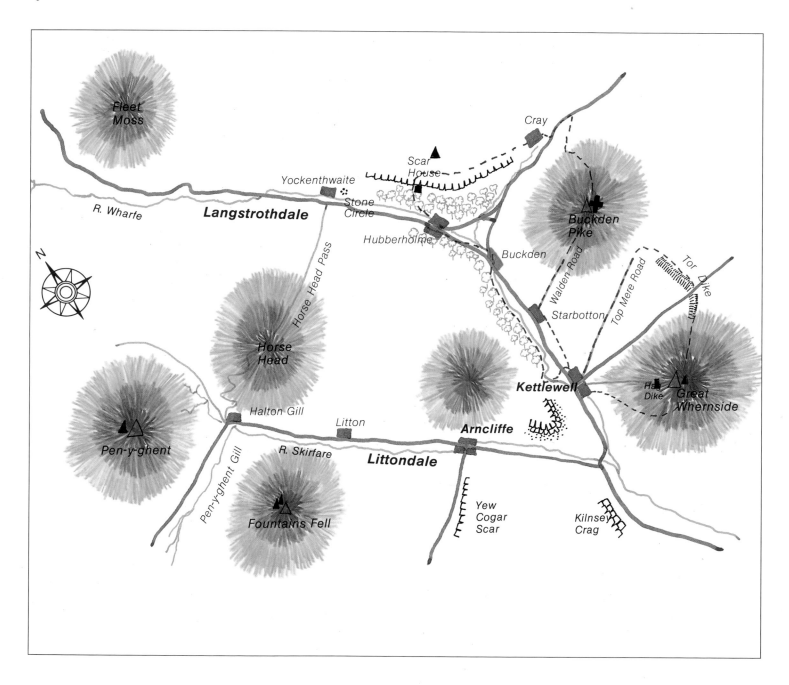

Fleet Moss

Cray

Scar House

Yockenthwaite

Stone Circle

R. Wharfe

Langstrothdale

Buckden Pike

Hubberholme

Buckden

Horse Head Pass

Walden Road

Top Mere Road

Tor Dike

N

Horse Head

Starbotton

Kettlewell

Halton Gill

Litton

Ha. Dike

Great Whernside

Pen-y-ghent

R. Skirfare

Arncliffe

Littondale

Pen-y-ghent Gill

Fountains Fell

Yew Cogar Scar

Kilnsey Crag

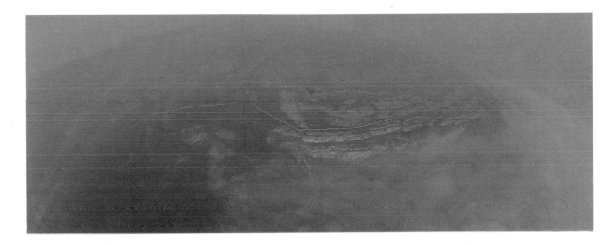

RIGHT: *The scars above Arncliffe from a hot-air balloon*   BELOW: *Kilnsey Crag, summer*

BUCKDEN PIKE AND HUBBERHOLME

IF you'd ventured into the bar of the Blue Bell Inn in Kettlewell not so many summers ago on a certain July night, you would have found me sitting by the window looking intently at a map tracing a route I was planning to take the next day from Kettlewell by Starbotton to Buckden Pike over into Hubberholme by Cray and back to Kettlewell by the Dales Way. Around the bar a number of farmers were stood discussing a land sale that had just taken place in one of the back rooms of the pub.

'Where are you off tomorrow?' one of them asked.

'Hubberholme,' I answered.

'Ubram! Well, you'll be passing my farm if you're doing that. What time will you be going past?'

I said I thought it would be about four o'clock.

'Reet then,' he said, 'knock on t'door as you're passing, an' we'll 'ave t'kettle on for you.'

It was warm and muggy the next morning as I left the village and walked through the fields following the well-worn path through close-cropped meadows and through the fringes of Cross Wood, where rabbits, disturbed by my coming, scattered for their burrows, white tails jigging behind them. High cloud and haze cast a pearly light over the dale and the July day was still and close, so that by the time I got to Starbotton, only a few miles into the walk, I was almost deliriously happy to find the shop by the pub open for the sale of lemonade and ice-cream. Having no children to spoil with me that day, I spoiled myself and bought a lemonade and an ice-cream to fortify myself for the long walk up the old green lane of Walden Road on to Buckden Pike.

On cold wintry days with a good strong wind the climb up Walden Road is grand. The wind cools you down, or if you're lucky and it's a westerly with a bit of south in it, it pushes behind you helping you on to the top. Today, with no wind, it was a

sweaty climb with many stops to admire the view behind and to mouth the air like a landed codfish before I made it to the boundary stone and turned north-west for the last climb to the top, feeling as I reached the summit like Tenzing on Everest.

On the summit of Buckden Pike, standing south of the trig point, close by the boundary wall, is one of the saddest monuments in the Dales. A stone cross with fragments of aircraft parts embedded in its concrete base stands as a memorial to the Polish crew of an RAF plane that crashed at this spot during a snowstorm in the Second World War. There was one survivor. Crawling from the wreckage with a broken leg, he found the prints of a fox in the snow. Reasoning that the fox would have been searching for food close to human habitation, he crawled through the snow following the footprints until they

FACING PAGE: *The sad monument on Buckden Pike*   BELOW: *Detail of the cross on Buckden Pike*

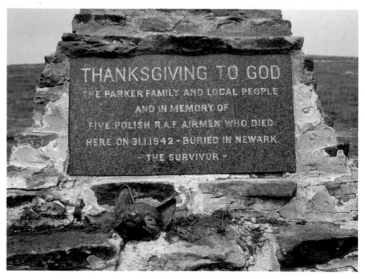

eventually led him down off the fell to a farm and safety. In thanksgiving for his own escape he later erected the cross and to commemorate the fox's part in the story set a bronze fox's head into the concrete. A few years ago, some twisted individual stole the fox's head but it has now been replaced and stands again, as it did before, at the foot of the cross.

I followed the boundary wall from the monument to the trig point on Buckden Gavel, then moved off down the fell towards Cray, following the footpath by Buckden Rake to Cray High Bridge. The high cloud began to break as I lost height, letting shafts of sunlight strike the little hamlet and the fields of freshly mown hay that were being turned by toy tractors and tiny people far below me down the dale.

When I got to Cray I had a row with a farmer that nearly spoilt the walk. He told me not only that the footpath I was on was not a right of way, though it was shown clearly on the map as such, but also that he didn't give a not-in-front-of-the-children what it said on the sorry-vicar map. It's rare that this happens, but when it does, you can either become as bloody-minded as the person concerned and force your way through, or you can do as I did: take another path and get in touch with a National Park warden or the local foot-paths officer of the Ramblers' Association.

Below Hay Close and that sorry-vicar farmer the footpath became a broad grass track,

TOP: *The George Inn and Hubberholme Bridge*   BOTTOM LEFT: *Hay timing above Cray*   BOTTOM RIGHT: *The well-known mark of Thompson, the wooden mouse*   FACING PAGE: *Interior of Hubberholme church*

following the line above Hubberholme Wood, with wonderful views down Upper Wharfedale towards Buckden. One of the great things about walking in the Dales is the fact that in a single day you can leave a dale behind and clamber through rough fell on to the tops, you can walk along the tops of limestone scars with the Dales spread out below you, and you can follow riverside paths in the valley bottom. It's this variety that makes the Dales such a fascinating place for me.

At Scar House I followed the track down to Hubberholme where the church is one of the bonniest and most unusual in the Dales. The interior walls of unplastered, rough local stone, the iron candelabra and the hand-painted rood loft where the cross was once stored, all give the church a medieval air. Rood lofts were destroyed during the Reformation as smacking of popery and this one, one of only two surviving in Yorkshire, dates from 1558 and is finely carved in oak and painted red, black and gold.

The church is visited by thousands of people and a favourite game amongst children is to try and count the number of mice in the church. The mice are wooden and were carved in the pew-ends by Robert Thompson the 'Mouse Man' of Kilburn in 1934. He was a fine furniture-maker and his signature was a wooden mouse which he carved into every piece he made. He's dead now, but the workshop he founded still turns out craftsman-made furniture, all of which carries somewhere a little mouse.

Across the road from the church is the George Inn where I have had many a fine sing-song in years past. It was originally the vicarage but has been a pub for some years now. Every New Year's Day a candle auction is held here in which a sixteen-acre field behind the inn is let for another year, proceeds of the letting of this 'poor pasture' going to help the old people of the parish. The sale has to take place before the candle, lit at the beginning of the auction, burns out. Needless to say, the auction is a scene of many old friendships being rekindled and 'the crack' is as important as the sale.

The parish of Hubberholme was served by the curates of

Halton Gill in Littondale, one of whom, the Revd Miles Wilson, wrote a novel that seems to be a cross between a space-age fantasy and 'The Goon Show'. In the book a cobbler climbs to the moon from the top of Pen-y-ghent. From the moon he makes a walking tour of the solar system, and the author uses the cobbler's experiences to introduce the reader to the science of astronomy.

The church was also the scene once of a curious baptism, when a child who should have been christened Ambrose Stanley

Hubberholme church and its not-wooden cat

instead received the name Amorous Stanley. The register couldn't be altered, the worried father was told when he tried to get the mistake rectified, and the child grew up with the name. Later on, in his business life he described himself as 'Amorous Stanley – licensed hawker'.

It was coming close to four o'clock by the time I reached the church and, remembering the offer of the previous evening, I called on the farm. Sure enough, the kettle was on and in the true Dales tradition of hospitality, the teapot was brought out by the farmer's wife on a tray loaded down with cups and piled high with slices of cake. Some men were clipping sheep in the barn behind us and as the last few sheep were clipped and the wool was wound and bundled we had a few minutes' crack. We talked of this and that, of the weather and of people that we knew in common, and then we talked of this and that again before I waved 'Thank you and goodbye' and toddled off full of tea and cake, along the road to follow the Dales Way to Kettlewell.

The Dales Way, devised by Colin Speakman, follows the

The Dales Way, Wharfedale

ABOVE: *Bridge over Crook Gill, which falls into Cray Gill*
RIGHT: *A waterfall in Cray Gill*

river Wharfe from Ilkley through Wharfedale, crosses the head of the valley by Cam, passes via Dentdale to Sedbergh, finally ending at Bowness-in-Windermere. Here in Wharfedale the Dales Way follows some of the most beautiful of riverside paths, and as I walked along it, the afternoon drew on, shadows lengthened and the river shone in the sunlight. Two herons took to the air at my passing, curving round about the Wharfe as they headed upstream, and the sun turned the tunnel of trees I was walking through into a green corridor with walls of yellow vetch and crimson campion.

I strolled through the magic of the afternoon 'toddling whom', as they say in Lancashire, content with a good day's walking and doing harm to no one: a day marred slightly by one farmer and made much more pleasant by another – because, as they say in Lancashire, 'There's nowt wrong wi' reet folk.'

Great Whernside from kettlewell

ON the eastern edge of Wharfedale between Kilnsey and Buckden the mound of Great Whernside looks down the dale. On its upper eastern slopes the river Nidd rises, while to the north the river Cover springs to run below Little Whernside down lovely Coverdale. Great Whernside itself is a little uninteresting as a hill, a gently swelling hump with a gritstone outcrop marking its summit, but it's worth the climb for the views down into Wharfedale and for a look at the remains of Tor Dike.

I set off from Kettlewell late one summer's morning under a cloudy July sky, the sort of sky that July in the Dales can sometimes bring which, although it doesn't herald rain, seems to lie on the landscape, rolling across it an ocean of dull iron-grey clouds. The forecast was for a break in the weather later, though I hardly dared to believe it.

I left Kettlewell by the lane beside the youth hostel and followed the rough track on to the sweet turf that lies on the limestone shelf above the dale. It was a good pull and in spite of the cloudy day the air was warm, so that by the time I climbed away from the good meadows across the rough peaty land

Looking across Wharfedale from the summit of Great Whernside

towards the boundary fence that would lead to the summit I felt as though I were climbing in a sauna.

Despite the dry weather of the last few weeks the land was still boggy and crossing the wet shoulder below the summit ridge bcame at times a matter of bog-hopping before I began to ascend again through Whernside Pasture towards Sweet Hill. Below me the isolated farm of Hag Dike clung to the fell beneath the scars but further views were muted by the leaden light. The farm looked a terribly lonely spot.

At the trig point on Long Crags I changed my sodden shirt for a spare I always carry with me in my rucksack and sat and had my lunch amongst the jumble of gritstones, fighting off a greedy sheep who was busy teaching her lamb how to beg.

The day brightened slightly but not enough to show up the landscape below in its true beauty. I know that many people will argue that a landscape is a landscape and is beautiful in all its moods, and to some extent I agree, but I find that the quality of light produced at either end of the day or at spring or fall of the year or in certain weather conditions can all make the landscape into something special. A grey mid-day with no detail in the sky and little in the landscape means that I usually leave my camera in the rucksack and my tripod in the bag.

Along the edge of Little Crag the path led down to Nidd Head and then turned west off the hill towards Great Hunters Sleets. Below, the fell stretched steeply towards the road from Coverdale where it made its way over the pass into Kettlewell and Wharfedale. On either side of the road I could make out the line of Tor Dike, an Iron Age ditch and mound built by the rebel Brigante chief Venutius, sometime around AD 70, as part of a defensive system to close off the heads of the river valleys and prevent a Roman attack advancing beyond them.

By commanding the high ground and by closing and fortifying the heads of the passes, Venutius hoped to contain the power of the Romans southwards of his main fort at Stanwick. His efforts were considerable and for the time his achievements are impressive. As well as the massive fort at Stanwick, he built

forts on Ingleborough, Gregory Scar (north of Grassington) and on Addleborough in Wensleydale, and a second line of ramparts made up of earthworks at Tor Dike and Fremington Edge. All these defences required a massive workforce and a considerable degree of social organisation, a different picture from that of the woad-painted savages handed to us by Roman historians.

The efforts, however, came to nothing. The Ninth Legion under Petilius Cerialis marched from York and destroyed the Brigantes' seat of power at Stanwick, after which the name of Venutius disappears from history. All that remains of his brave

FACING PAGE: *The ditch of Tor Dyke looking towards Nidd Head*
LEFT: *Campion*
BELOW: *Thyme*

stand are the forts and dikes left behind crumbling in the winds and rains of the ages, the haunts now of sheep, rabbit, hare and curlew, while the Ninth Spanish Legion under Petilius Cerialis disappeared mysteriously from the face of the earth and came to be known as the legendary Lost Legion.

By the time I reached the Coverdale road the clouds had started to break and sunlight was streaking the fells – the forecast for once had been right. I lingered by Diamond Hill looking at the remains of the dike, now a ditch in parts, with an

enclosure wall on what must have been at one time the line of a pallisade. Although so little remains of the earthworks, it is still possible to sense what it must have been like to have stood there looking down the dale waiting for the gongs and trumpets and other noises of the Ninth Legion on the march to be carried updale on the breeze.

From Diamond Hill I was faced with two choices: I could either take the Starbotton Road, as the rough track was called, to Starbotton and walk back to Kettlewell by Calfhalls and the

ABOVE: *Top Mere Road looking towards Kettlewell*

FACING PAGE: *Kettlewell – looking like a plump landlady*

LEFT: *Kilnsey Crag in the mist*

woods, or I could take the shorter way back along Top Mere Road (another green lane). I chose the Top Mere way back, hoping that the light would change enough for me to get one of the classic views of the Dales, the view down Wharfedale from the lane as it drops down Cam Pasture, a view second only to that of Wharfedale from above Hubberholme Wood.

I was in luck and the view was wonderful, the valley spread below me in the late afternoon light with Kettlewell looking snug as a plump landlady in the valley bottom. I leaned on the wall for a good half-hour watching the light play on Cote Scar and the blurred outline of Kilnsey Crag appear and disappear in the heat haze before I walked down through warm sunshine to the Blue Bell Hotel, my resting place for the night.

8. the upper eden valley

THE Upper Eden Valley runs from Garsdale Head northwards to Kirkby Stephen and on by Brough to Appleby and the Solway Firth. The northern outriders of the Eden are Knock Fell, Little and Great Dun Fell and the highest of all Pennine hills, Cross Fell, which is unique in all England in that it is the only one to have its own wind, the Helm, a peculiar wild wind that can rage for days around Cross Fell trailing behind it from the hill's broad summit a cloud called the Helm Cloud.

Appleby is a fine market town and famous throughout Europe for its annual gypsy fair when true Romanies and other travelling people from the British Isles and beyond gather on the hill above the town to buy and sell horses and tackle, and above all to meet up again with old friends and relations. Appleby is really beyond the subject matter of this book since the Dales end naturally at the boundary formed by the Stainmore Gap and the A685 Kirkby Stephen to Tebay road; but geographical boundaries are never that rigid and though the walks in this chapter are both set south of Kirkby Stephen, the world doesn't end there. As J. R. R. Tolkien says, 'The road goes ever on', and Appleby, as you'll see later, has some bearing on one at least of the walks.

Kirkby Stephen is built largely of brockram, a strange natural stone made up of chippings of limestone embedded in a sort of red sandstone cement. It stands at the head of the Mallerstang end of the Eden Valley and is a plain, some say

dour, town. One of the earliest travellers to write about the town certainly didn't like it. In 1831 Gideon Maude wrote, 'On entering Kirkby Stephen we saw one of the most disgraceful scenes that ever was witnessed by man. Two men and a group of boys were trying to bury a horse alive.'

Things are nothing like as bad as that now, and though the town does still crown a temperance goddess and often has a Sunday afternoon atmosphere about it on a Saturday night, it's not a bad place and seen on a summer's evening when the brockram stone is shining pink in the westering sun, it even looks quite pretty. But I don't suppose it would thank you for calling it pretty, for Kirkby Stephen is a working North Country town and none the worse for that.

South of Kirkby Stephen, below Nateby and Nine

FACING PAGE: *Wild Boar Fell and Mallerstang*   RIGHT: *Mallerstang, winter*

ABOVE: *Hot shoeing, Appleby horse fair*   TOP LEFT: *Fortune teller, Appleby*   BOTTOM LEFT: *Lady waiting for her fortune to be read, Appleby horse fair*

VE: Travelling people, Appleby   TOP RIGHT: *A little boy for
om it's all been a bit too much*   BOTTOM RIGHT: *Gypsies washing
ses in the river at Sedbergh*

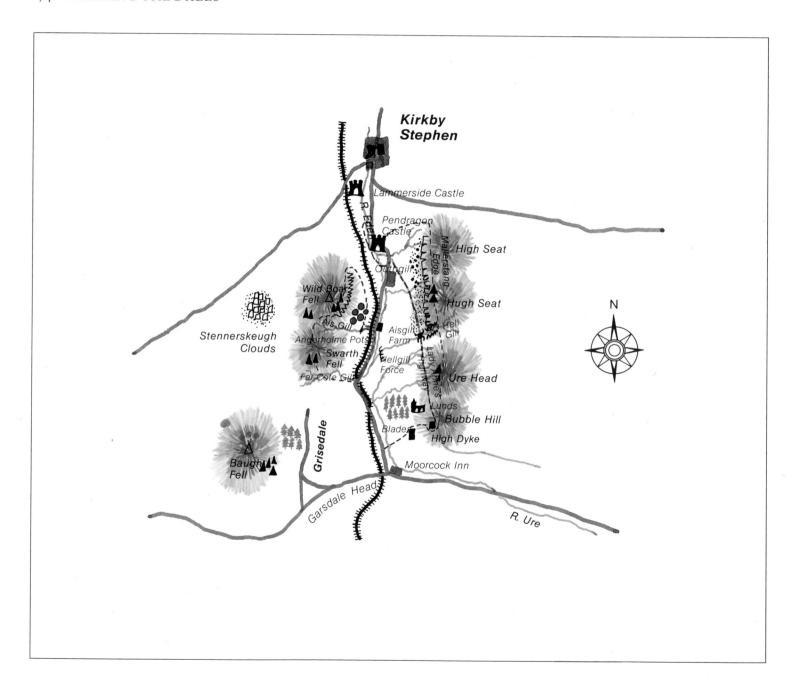

Lammerside Castle

Standards Rigg, runs a wild and lovely valley dominated by the crags of Mallerstang Edge and the nab of Wild Boar Fell. At its southern end rises the river Ure to flow by Hawes and Wensley to the North Sea, while only a cock-stride away springs the beck of Hell Gill which falls through a steep-sided ravine to the valley floor where it becomes the river Eden and begins its journey towards the Irish Sea.

It can be a blear and stormy valley at times; in fact the one hamlet of any size in the dale, Outhgill, owes its name to the Old Norse for 'desolate ravine'. It must have been wilder still at times, for running southwards from Kirkby Stephen is a line of three castles whose presence means that defence, whether against Roman legions, Scots raiders, robber cousins, or Cromwellian troops, was an ever-present need.

Of the four castles in the area, Croglam Castle is little more than an earthmound and a name on the map now, both Lammerside Castle and Pendragon Castle are in ruins, while Wharton Hall, the earliest fortified building still standing in the area, has been incorporated into a farmhouse. Changed they may be, but so many in so few miles? – here was border country indeed.

The dale is one of my favourite walking areas; it's little visited and the walks along Mallerstang Edge and the crags of Wild Boar Fell are marvellous, while from Nine Standards Rigg there is a wonderful view over the Eden Valley to Cross Fell and far beyond. Nine Standards Rigg isn't included in this book for the simple reason that there isn't enough space, but if there's a *Son of Walking the Dales* or *Walking the Dales Rides Again*, then it will certainly be there in red letters because it's 'a little cracker'.

mallerstang edge and lady anne's highway

RUNNING from the flanks of Abbottside Common at the head of Wensleydale and curving into the Upper Eden Valley, following the valley side to Pendragon Castle, is a wild and lovely track. It was once a prehistoric route, later a Roman marching road and finally the way used by that remarkable woman Lady Anne Clifford to travel from her castle in Skipton to Pendragon.

Lady Anne was born in Skipton Castle in 1590; her father, George Clifford, was an Elizabethan adventurer who made eleven expeditions to plunder the ports and rob the fleets of Portugal and Spain. It would appear that Lady Anne inherited her father's temperament, for after two unhappy marriages, and having been widowed for a second time, she set her mind to recovering her estates in Yorkshire which had been taken from her by her uncle and his heirs. At that time, estates passed through the male line so that on the death of her father, her uncles and cousins had inherited all Lady Anne's most beloved lands.

She waited patiently until they had all died; then, in her fifty-third year, she received back into her hands the castles and estates of Skipton, Barden, Appleby, Brough, Brougham and Pendragon. Lady Anne spent the rest of her life travelling the North, altering, repairing and improving her castles, all of which, with the exception of Skipton, her family later allowed to fall into ruins. Pendragon Castle, the supposed birthplace of Uther Pendragon (father of the most famous king of England, Arthur of Round Table fame) is now a sad ruin looking down Mallerstang above the river Eden.

One windy day in late spring I left the car at the roadside near the milestone north of the Moorcock Inn and followed the farm track to Blades, where the chickens and geese at the farm looked down their beaks at me as I passed by, obviously used to a better class of walker. High clouds were rolling in from the north-west, scurrying across the dale chasing shadows from Swarth Fell to Sails, and with the wind behind my back, I left the farm and began climbing towards High Dyke.

High Dyke, now a ruin, was once a fine house at which travellers would halt on their way along the old highway. In its time it has been a dame's school and an inn, and it was as an inn that it is said to have been a favourite haunt of the famous highwayman 'Swift Nick' Nevison, who, amongst other things, shooed his horse backwards so as to fool pursuers; he was reputed to be a perfect gentleman and is rumoured to have leapt the 'fearful ravine of Hell Gill' on horseback. Looking at the wind-battered and roofless ruin of High Dyke now, it is hard to imagine that not so very long ago these walls would have rung to

FACING PAGE: *Lady Anne's Highway*   BELOW: *The ruins of High Dyke Farm*

the sound of laughter, singing and fiddle music and the clanking of pots of ale.

It was quite a long slog from High Dyke up the open fell to Sails and Ure Head and the wind was more than welcome as I pulled up on to Bubble Hill, heading north to the broad mossy top of Sails. It is below here that the river Ure springs, its waters travelling by Cobbles Hill and Mossdale Head to Wensleydale. From Ure Head, I cut across the boundary fence where a boulder at the corner marks the strangely named Scarth of Scaithes. There was nothing there to tell me why it was called that, just a large boulder at the corner of the boundary fence.

On previous occasions, I have carried on by the fence to Hugh Seat and then on to High Seat, but now I wanted to walk the Edge. To do that I had to follow the fence to where it began to drop near Hell Gill, then, cutting well north, follow the contour to Hangingstone Scar.

From here the walk north along the Edge was one of the most impressive I have ever done. Wild Boar Fell across the valley looked bleak and threatening under a line of thick cloud that was forming beyond it in the west, while below, the Eden, in flood after the heavy rains of the previous week, shone a dull silver in the broken light. From the scars above Goodwife Stones I dropped down through a maze of tumbled boulders, some as big as garden sheds, that stretched my non-existent sense of balance to the limit. Once down I followed Gale Sike to the footpath that led to the road, Pendragon Castle and lunch among the ruins.

Pendragon Castle is on private land and has had little in the way of restoration work carried out on it so that it stands forlorn and uncared for, perhaps as real ruins should be, in the corner of a field by a river, surrounded by chewing sheep and one chewing walker. I must have sat in more ruins and eaten my lunch on more gravestones than anyone else I know. But I always say a sort of silent prayer in my own non-believer's way for those who lie beneath the stones and feel less guilty when I think that in the years to come some other rambler's

ABOVE: *Pendragon Castle and Mallerstang Edge*   FACING PAGE: *Pendragon Castle with Wild Boar Fell in the background*

ABOVE: *Hell Gill Falls* FACING PAGE: *Pendragon Castle, summer*

backside will rest itself above my mouldering bones.

From one of the few remaining windows of the ruins of Pendragon Castle, I could see in the fleeting sunlight the nab of Wild Boar Fell and the Eden flowing swollen in flood by the foot of the castle, very much as Lady Anne Clifford herself would have seen it, the whole landscape little changed save for the dry-stone walls and the meadows that now stand where stood the trees of Mallerstang Forest.

From Pendragon I crossed the road by Castle Bridge and followed the riverside path to Thrang Bridge. It was difficult at times because, as is the way with footpaths that are not very heavily walked, stiles had been blocked or had disappeared entirely, and though I had a good map, I still had to backtrack and climb over a few fences in order to make my way through.

By Thrang Bridge, Lady Anne's Highway joins the modern road and from here on I took the old track and the walking was glorious. The carriageway along which Lady Anne travelled is still evident on the fellside. It fords gills that thunder when they are in full spate and clings under the cheek of the fell, curving round towards Hell Gill.

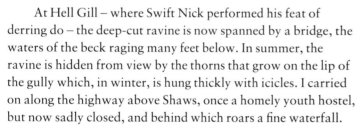

Lunds Chapel, Mallerstang

ABOVE: *Sheep taxi, Mallerstang*   FACING PAGE: *Mallerstang Edge*

At Hell Gill – where Swift Nick performed his feat of derring do – the deep-cut ravine is now spanned by a bridge, the waters of the beck raging many feet below. In summer, the ravine is hidden from view by the thorns that grow on the lip of the gully which, in winter, is hung thickly with icicles. I carried on along the highway above Shaws, once a homely youth hostel, but now sadly closed, and behind which roars a fine waterfall.

One winter, I walked the old highway when the ground was thick with snow and the trees around Shaws were bent down with its weight. When I looked back down the track, I saw in the distance Wild Boar Fell with a mantle of snow brooding above Mallerstang. Plodding through thick drifts, I came down to Lunds, a small hamlet of two or three houses and a little church, from which the old corpse road leads by High Dyke to Cotterdale.

Along this route bodies were brought over the fell for burial from Cotterdale to Lunds, where the graveyard sits at the side of the settlement. Standing in the graveyard that cold February day,

with grey skies above me and evening coming on, Lunds, deserted and silent, seemed the loneliest place on earth.

Now, in the stormy sunshine above Shaws, I ate the last of my sandwiches and threw an apple core to a sheep that was looking threateningly in my direction. I'm not frightened of sheep when they are on their own but this one had his brothers with him.

I reached High Dyke as the first drops of rain fell and the clouds that had been swirling over the tops all day bunched and darkened; then coming over from Wild Boar Fell I heard the first rumbles of thunder and saw in the west flashes that meant that a storm was brewing. By the time I came to Blades, the rain was bouncing off the track which itself was turning into a river, and I reached the road just as the afternoon turned black night. As I sat in my car with wipers swishing I could see ahead of me, lit up by a jagged tear in the thunderous sky, the long scar of Mallerstang Edge where I'd walked in broken sunlight only a few hours before, now shimmering behind a curtain of rain.

WILD BOAR FELL FROM AISGILL

WILD Boar Fell stands massive and grand at the northern head of Mallerstang. Seen from the eastern flanks of Swarth Fell it has the typical shape of those other big Dales hills, Ingleborough and Pen-y-ghent. When describing those Ribbleside hills writers will often use the word 'majestic', and if the word can be applied to them then I feel that Wild Boar Fell certainly deserves the title too. It's a big hill, at 1942 feet, a little below Whernside in height. However, it's not its height which fascinates me but its shape.

Wild Boar Fell is a great hulk of a hill with sheer crags on its eastern flank and the jutting Nab that stands out dramatically above Angerholme Pots to the west and the Dale of Mallerstang down below with the infant river Eden flowing through it. Wild Boar Fell is crazily excluded from the National Park because, it

BELOW: *Wild Boar Fell in winter*   FACING PAGE: *Looking down Lady Anne's Highway towards Wild Boar Fell*

seems, the political boundary which was accepted as the northern limits of the park excludes it. In the west Nidderdale and Washburndale are excluded also, though common sense plants them fair and square within the Dales. However, common sense and politicians are strange bedfellows.

One easy way up Wild Boar Fell is from the north-west via the limestone outcroppings at Stennersheugh Clouds from the old Roman road called The Street. It is a gentle walk and takes you up by Sand Tarn, where millstones were quarried and scythes were sharpened in days gone by, until a last pull brings you on to the level summit. But the best way of all to climb Wild Boar Fell is from Aisgill, where the Settle–Carlisle Railway, threading Mallerstang, reaches its highest point.

It's a bit of a pull in parts but the views of the fell are worth the effort and the route takes in the potholes of Angerholme Pots and the airy ridge walk along White Walls above the crags of Scriddles. Below you on your left the cliffs fall away sheer in a jumble of fractures and fallen gritstone, while ahead of you, marking the end of the climb, is a cairn that stands on a slight mound on the Nab. Excavations have showed the mound to be the grave of a Celtic warrior or chieftain. A fine place to be buried, but it's a pity that he won't be able to enjoy the views, because they are really impressive.

Mallerstang can be a wild and lonely place even in high summer. Seen on a wet, windy November day when storm clouds are racing over Wild Boar Fell from the west, it looks harsh and bleak and it is easy to see how the Victorian engineers who drove the Settle–Carlisle Railway up here thought it one of the most godforsaken spots on earth. It always seems untamed and remote, perhaps because it's higher above sea level and has less treecover than many of the other dales (except for an ugly

RIGHT: *The Nab of Wild Boar Fell from Angerholme Pots* FACING PAGE: *The burial mound on Wild Boar Fell* (top) *Cumbrian Mountain Express southbound below Mallerstang* (bottom)

pocket of sitka spruce at Lunds, courtesy of the Economic Forestry Group) and perhaps also because on either side of the dale the cliffs of Swarth Fell, Wild Boar Fell and Mallerstang Edge look broodingly down over the dale.

I've walked Wild Boar Fell several times in summer and winter and a few winters ago I decided to walk the fell while it was still under snow. It was a week or so into the New Year and

Cairn on Wild Boar Fell in a white-out

I was due to start an eighty-one-night concert tour of the UK early in February, so I was trying to get as many days in the hills as I could. A few days before, Pat and I had walked in bright sunshine across snow-cloaked fells to Great Knoutberry Hill and Arten Gill. Today, however, the sun was nowhere to be seen.

Low clouds hung over the dale as we ran the car off the road into the old quarry near Aisgill. Tony and Matt were walking with us, old companions from many a walk: Matt is a fine caver and hillman, a straight-faced South Yorkshireman with a laconic turn of phrase; Tony is an addictive scrambler and braver on ridges than I am but suffers from 'bosophobia', that is, he's terrified of bulls and cows. He leads me up scrambles that have me gibbering, I in revenge lead him through fields full of walking milk-bars.

From Aisgill we walked under the viaduct, past frozen pillars of ice in the beck and twisted hawthorns that were thick with frozen spray and cut off then towards Angerholme Pots. Any path there had been was now covered in snow, so we steered off to the left aiming to come to the Nab well away from the pots.

On days like this it's quite likely that they'd be covered with a lid of snow. Some of the pots are deep-shafts, certainly deep enough for a fall down one of them to be fatal, so it seemed wise to steer as far away from the pots as possible. Only a few months before a young walker had been killed on Cross Fell when he walked over an old mine shaft that had been crusted over with snow like the lair of a trapdoor spider.

As we ploughed our way onwards the walk turned into something of a scramble. Deep drifts covered small gullies that all of us from time to time sank into waist-deep without warning. Tony and Matt are quite tall and didn't sink in as far as I did, while Pat proved the superior intelligence of women by walking in their footsteps. As we neared the base of Scriddles and began to climb on to the ridge the weather finally closed in. What had been a stiff wind became a gale, and cloud the colour of old porridge dropped a couple of hundred of feet in a matter of minutes, blotting out the light. We climbed on up the Nab, visibility down to ten yards or so, and the roaring wind was now driving a fine snow through the mist, classic 'white-out' conditions.

At the Nab cairn we took a compass bearing and walked, spread out in a line four abreast, in the direction of the trig point. We never found it. We spent twenty minutes zig-zagging through this white world, the plan being to grab a quick bite and a cup of tea at the trig point, take a bearing and walk off on it, leaving Swarth Fell for another day. I had a theory that the trig point kept moving to confuse us. 'Like Shangri-La?' Matt offered. Tony wanted to know what the name of a bungalow in Scarborough had got to do with a trig point and Pat just said she wanted to go home.

The cairns of High White Scar in summer

The travellers and their vans near Ais Gill

With visibility down to three or four yards now, we regrouped, took another reading, and walked on until through the mist the line of cairns which mark High White Scar appeared like long-lost friends to tell us that we weren't. We stopped for a quick bite before taking another bearing for the Band and the way off via Ais Gill. As we dropped down below the cloud the day cleared slightly, the sky now being the colour of an old vest.

I amused everybody by falling in several deep drifts while Matt tried to run on the top of the snow, and ended up swimming in it. We reached Ais Gill and followed it down to the viaduct, the road and the car, where, wet, cold, and some of us crosser than others, we argued over who was to sit nearest the heater.

Last summer after a week of cloudless skies I did the full walk again up by Angerholme Pots to the Nab and on to the elusive trig point, where I sat in the sun to eat my lunch. This time I walked the full circle, strolling over Swarth Fell and returning to the old quarry by Far Cote Gill. A light heat haze flattened the colours in the landscape making long-distance views a bit murky, but it was a grand day for lying on the top in the sun listening to larks and curlews going noisily about their business.

I stretched the walk out a bit, dawdling at the cairns and ambling at an easy pace over the flanks of the fell. It was the sort of day that makes you feel that time no longer matters, that nothing is important enough to hurry for and that the going is more valuable than the getting there.

Within yards of the quarry my thoughts were mirrored by

the sight of two horse-drawn gypsy vans pulled off the road on to a bit of green common land; they were travellers on their way to Appleby to the horse fair. There were just two of them sat in the sun, a woman and her young son. She was a comfortable, handsome lass from York who came to Appleby with her husband by horse and van every year to carry on the old traditions and to teach her children what the Romany life means.

Kirkby Stephen and the area round about have for long been well known to the Romanies who make their way by horse and cart along the old quiet roads to the horse fair. I like gypsy folk. They get a bad name from people often for things they haven't done. Crimes of robbery increase when the gypsies are around but it's not the gypsies who are doing it but local lads, and some not so local, taking advantage of the gypsies' presence, knowing they'll get blamed for it.

It'll be a sad day when there are no more travelling people and we've all settled down in Milton Keynes. The travellers with their vans and horses, fortune-telling and songs, lend a colour and vitality to life that will be missed when local councillors and state bureaucrats have driven them off the roads and commons.

There's a beautiful Irish song about travelling people being pushed around that has a poignant last verse in which the traveller sings of Christ as a traveller, saying:

> But the man above who died for Love
> And was nailed unto a tree
> Sure and wasn't he a traveller too
> The same as you and me,
> And please God in His own good time
> He'll ease the traveller's load,
> And we'll bid farewell to poverty
> And the blue tar road.
>   (Liam Weldon: 'The Blue Tar Road')

Another traditional song, 'The Lish Young Buy-a-broom', tells of a buy-a-broom (gypsy girl) stealing the heart of a northern Dales lad.

> As I was a-walking in the north country
> Up by Kirkby Stephen I happened for to be,
> As I was a-walking up and down the street
> A pretty lish young buy-a-broom I chanced for to meet.
> She was right, I was tight, everybody has their way,
> It was a lish young buy-a-broom that led me astray.

The song goes on to tell a tale of love and seduction that is perhaps too strong for your delicate ears – so back to the roadside in Mallerstang where the travelling woman and I talked for a good half-hour in the sunshine about life on the road. She was a Boswell and I was surprised to find that she was the daughter of the Boswell who wrote a fine book on his own gypsy life, *The Book of Boswell*. One episode tells how as a child playing on Southport Sand he saw and played with the fairies, 'the little people', he called them.

'There must be something in it,' she said, 'as me dad weren't a liar, he couldn't stand a liar and he never told a lie in his life.' She looked around her. 'Things is changing too fast, you know, folk have no time for things any more. No time for each other. They have lost their spirit. That's why we do this every year. We settled down seventeen years ago, but I've travelled this road every year since to keep in touch with where I belong.'

Then she looked down at Mallerstang.

'It's beautiful here, isn't it?' I said. 'It's wild but it's still beautiful.'

She looked up from the kettle that was hanging from a crane over the fire and shielded her eyes with her hands from the sun. 'Do you know what us travellers call this? God's country.'

9. kingsdale

KINGSDALE (the name means 'valley of the Vikings') is the smallest of all the dales in this book. From Thornton in Craven where it meets the Skipton–Kendal road, it stretches a bare five and a half miles to High Moss where it meets the Occupation Road out of Dentdale before dropping down into Deepdale and Dent Town.

It is a lonely dale with only two farmhouses along its main length, Kingsdale Head Farm and Braida Garth. Above its western side looms the ridge of West Fell leading to the summit of Whernside at the head of the dale, while to the east the scars of North End and Keld Head are overlooked by the steep slopes of Gragareth that lead in their turn to Great Coum and the watershed.

Yet, short as it is, the dale is a superb example of limestone scenery. Like all the dales it is a glaciated valley, the steep scars on the western side having been scoured out by the relentless ice.

FACING PAGE: *Looking along Kingsdale from Raven Ray; Braida Garth is in the middle distance*   BELOW: *Kingsdale Head Farm*

Clouds over Gragareth

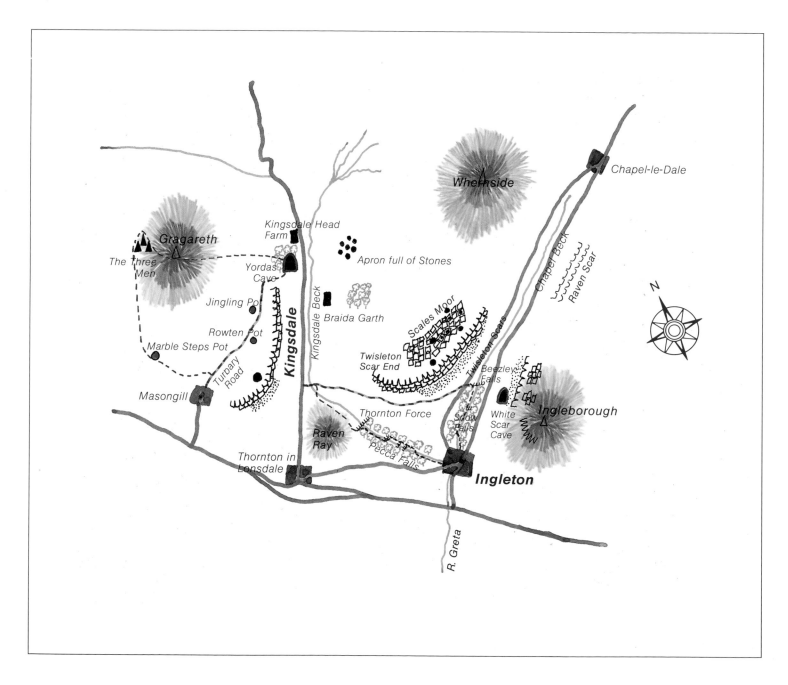

Sunset, Kingsdale

Kingsdale Beck in summer

Farm near Thornton-in-Craven

At its south-western end, the grassy hump of Raven Ray almost blocks the mouth of the dale. This is the remains of a terminal moraine that once dammed the neck of the valley causing a lake to form along its length, hence the flat-bottomed alluvial nature of Kingsdale.

Above the plain, the limestone scars on the western terrace contain some of the most exciting potholes in the area. Jingling Pot, a vertical shaft 141 feet deep, and Rowten Pot, whose 'eyehole' is a sheer fall of 213 feet, lie just yards from the Turbary Road, while a little further afield is Marble Steps Pot, a massive pot whose great limestone shelves drop a total of 197 feet under the fell. Back beside the main road in the valley bottom is the cave of Keld Head. It appears as a shallow pool, but beneath the rock wall of the pool is the entrance to a cave which is in fact the resurgence point for the water sinking into all the potholes on both sides of Kingsdale.

Man came early into Kingsdale. Braida Garth Farm is close by the site of an early Viking longhouse and nearby is the Apron Full of Stones, reputed to have been dropped by the Devil on his way home after building the church at Kirkby Lonsdale, but more probably the remains of an early settlement. Across from the Apron Full of Stones is Yordas Cave, about which more later.

Kingsdale makes a good starting point for the ascents of Whernside and Great Coum and for rambles across into Chapel le Dale, over Gragareth, and around the falls of Ingleton. It's a tiny dale but none the less interesting for that, particularly since its narrow road, gated at its northern end, keeps traffic on the low side. On a hot summer's afternoon it has an atmosphere of timelessness and peace.

LEFT: *Jingling Pot*

GRAGARETH FROM THE TURBARY ROAD

t HE Three Men of Gragareth stand sentinel on the north-western edge of Leck Fell, stone warriors looking out to Cumbria and the Lakes. Around them lies a mass of jumbled gritstone flakes and close by is a stone ringed hollow shelter thrown together by shepherds or walkers.

One blustery day in early spring, with bitterly cold winds rolling dark grey clouds over the fells, I left the car at Masongill and walked up Masongill Fell Lane out of the village. There was little prospect of sun but the going was pleasant enough and the hard winds kept me cool as I left the tarmac and hit the rough-walled track of the Turbary Road.

Turbary Rights, the right to cut peat for fuel on the fell, are ancient rights which go back in many cases to well before the enclosures, and lanes like the Turbary Road leading up on to the peat diggings are common in the Dales. This one, though, striking north-north-east above the limestone pavements of Keld Head Scar, may be a much older track than that in the valley bottom and may have been used by early man when the valley bottoms were dense swamps.

The views from the green lane of the Turbary Road down

Looking down Kingsdale across to Whernside from the Turbary Road

Looking from the shepherd's shelter and cairn to Ingleborough

Looking towards Whernside along Kingsdale

Kingsdale to Whernside were superb: the dale stretched out before me lonely and wild, Braida Garth just visible below the swelling fell that leads up to Cable Rake and the summit of Whernside.

On the right as I walked was the gaping hole of Rowten Pot. The narrow tree-ringed rift descends ultimately to a depth of 365 feet below the fell and is one of the finest potholes in the area. Further along the track on the left was Rowten Cave, said to be easily explorable, with care, but my path was taking me on a further three-quarters of a mile to a much more interesting cavern, Yordas Cave.

The cave was the haunt of a Norse giant called Yordas who dined on little boys for breakfast, dinner and tea, and probably elevenses as well. A. Wainwright in his classic book *Walks in Limestone Country* asks the very pertinent question, Why did the giant not eat little girls? Well, as the little girl said when somebody wanted to know why she'd asked in the sweet shop for boy jelly-babies and not girl jelly-babies, 'If you eat the boys you get a little bit more for your money.'

Yordas Cave was originally a show cave belonging to Braida Garth. At one time a fee had to be paid to view the cave which entitled you to a guide and candles. Both have gone and entry to the cavern is now free. You need a torch to see in the darkness, but it's quite safe and well worth the effort. The main chamber is thirty feet high and about 130 feet long. The floor is mud, gravel and cobbles and through it threads a small, shallow stream. In really bad weather the water, unable to get away, backs up and turns the floor into a lake. At the northern end of the cave there is a waterfall that falls more than thirty feet which, again in wet weather, is an impressive sight.

Other features of the cave are the Chapter House and a curious lump of stone called the Idol, which some people say looks like a Buddha but to me looks just like a curious lump of stone. If you do visit the cave, I have to warn you that the mud is

FACING PAGE: *Richard Chambers in the main chamber of Yordas Cave*   BELOW: *Yordas Cave, the waterfall*

ABOVE: *Rowten Pot with Whernside in the distance*   FACING PAGE: *The Three Men of Gragareth, the Lakeland fells in the background*

the most glutinous I've ever come across. It's like walking in Superglue.

As I came out of the cave the rain began to fall, not gently as it sometimes does here on what the Irish call 'the soft days', but heavily and malevolently so that after I'd put on my waterproof trousers and jacket I squeaked and rustled my way up the fell like a bright orange slug, and as I walked the world turned into grey soup all about me. Nobody has yet invented a device or chemical to keep spectacles from misting up on the inside as they get covered with rain on the outside, but if somebody does invent anything they'll get my money for a start.

It is only in weather like this when I'm fell-walking that I feel miserable. It makes me curse and kick things and when I'm alone I sometimes shout at the elements, wandering the moors like a short-sighted King Lear in a cagoule. Once, on the Langdale Pikes in the Lake District, I was cursing the elements

alone and aloud, doubting the parentage of the English weather system, when I rounded Pike o'Stickle to discover a dozen or so Girl Guides giggling before a red-faced and glaring leader. If any of them are reading this book now, then, gentle reader, you'll know it was I who was the wet madman wearing the misted-up jam-jar bottoms that staggered out of the murk that August day.

Slogging upwards like the boy in the poem 'Excelsior', I crossed the boundary wall at the summit of Gragareth, found the trig point, and in the mist and rain, cleaned my glasses, took a compass bearing, and walked downfell to the Three Men. There, with them alone for company, I made a hurried lunch, my thermos cup filling with rain faster than I could drink. But as I sat eating, the cloud shifted and the rain eased slightly, dark grey gave way to broken light and, as so often happens in these northern dales, the weather broke and a watery sun swept over the fell. Within half an hour the thick blanket of cloud had gone completely and the sky was a mass of high white clouds on a deep blue backcloth. I took off my cagoule, spread it on the stones to dry, and sat steaming in the suddenly warm afternoon sun.

As I sat back in the shelter I thought how strange it was and at the same time reassuring that we in the twentieth century are still using words that the Norsemen brought with them on their longboats all those centuries ago. All their other artefacts are preserved in museums, their boats, their tools, their weapons of war, but their language is still in everyday use. Braida Garth, Yordas, Gragareth, dale, beck, the tools we use to describe a landscape, are tools that a Norseman standing on this hill would have known. I never cease to be amazed by the flow and the flux of language.

As I sat musing thus, as the poet said, the afternoon turned towards evening and I came down to earth, packed my gear away and set off back down Ireby Fell to the sun-gilded roofs and smoking chimneys of Masongill with Morecambe Bay in the distance lit up in the late sunlight, looking like a helping of golden syrup on a slice of toast. It's amazing what you can see when you clean your glasses.

Ingleton and Beezley falls

THE waterfalls and glens of the rivers Twiss and Doe are amongst the most impressive in England, and the two sets of falls leading from Kingsdale and Chapel le Dale into the fine town of Ingleton have been visited by generations of folk from both Yorkshire and Lancashire ever since the Victorians decided that beauty need be no more than a charabanc-ride away.

Most people undertake the circular walk of the falls from the Ingleton end, but I, being an awkward devil, often walk in from Kingsdale and, after tootling round Twisleton Scars, follow Beezley Falls down for lunch in Ingleton. Then I walk back up the other falls towards the westering sun in the afternoon. This is perhaps the only tourist walk in the book, in the sense that the trails are artificial and there is a charge for admission at the Ingleton end. Touristy though they may be, the falls are nevertheless dangerous in parts and people have died (as many as three in one year alone) because they left the paths and slipped from the greasy rocks into the cataracts. If you fall in, particularly after heavy rain, the only way you'll get out again is when the divers of the Cave Rescue team pull you out of the pools and put you in your wooden overcoat.

One of the most amazing stories about the falls was told to me by Pete Roberts, a Settle ambulance driver, who was among the crew called out after a woman had fallen in while carrying a very small baby in her arms. The woman had managed to crawl out but unfortunately the baby had been swept out of her arms in the torrent.

Believing that there was little they could do other than look for a dead body at the other end of the falls, the rescue teams and ambulancemen donned waders and began marching upstream from the Ingleton end. Not long after they entered Swilla Glen they saw a small figure bobbing towards them on the current. Expecting to find nothing other than a tiny corpse, they were

ABOVE: *Pecca Twin Falls, Ingleton Glen*   FACING PAGE: *A friendly tup with Ingleborough behind, from the Beezleys*

amazed when they heard the baby crying and picked up a slightly bruised but otherwise unharmed infant. It had been kept afloat and alive by the quilted padding of its sleeping suit which had filled with air and acted like a life raft.

I don't know whether to believe this story or not because Pete Roberts also told me a story once which ended with a pig biting the head off a duck and I couldn't tell whether he was pulling my leg or not – but still, it makes a good story. If you take care and wear the right shoes (high heels, sling backs and Swedish backless clogs are not) then I think you'll find the walk easy and the waterfalls dramatic, particularly in autumn after heavy rain when the falls are thundering and the glen is a copper alleyway with a brittle carpet of frosty leaves.

Last autumn I got a lift to the end of Kingsdale and, travelling light, followed the lane by the side of Kingsdale Beck to Twisleton Scar End. It was a warm and golden late October day, windless and blue-skied, with just a few small clouds wandering across the Dales. I came down to Beezleys Farm crossing the old Roman road that leads to Chapel le Dale and is now called Oddies Lane. The view from above Beezleys looking over to Ingleborough and the scars of Raven Scar and White Scar are wonderful, only marred by the massive quarry below Skirwith. After the moon landscape of Helwith Bridge in Ribblesdale this has got to be one of the major eyesores in the Dales.

Below Beezleys, roaring in the sun, was the first of the Beezley Falls, where Chapel Beck, having become the river Doe below God's Bridge, falls down the first of a set of stairs that will take it down to Ingleton where it joins the one-time Kingsdale Beck that has now dropped through Ingleton Glens to become the river Twiss. Both rivers at this point become the river Greta, which in its turn goes on to join the river Lune – all very confusing, particularly for the river which by now must be suffering from several identity crises.

From the first set of falls the river drops steeply and very dramatically through narrow steep-sided glens, disappearing from sight at times between walls of high stone that fall away from the tree-lined path. Ash and beechwood were turning to yellow and the rowans were a deep metallic red beside the path as I walked. The colours of autumn in bright sunlight sometimes look so vivid and bright that it is hard to believe that they are natural and not produced in a test tube by some research chemist.

At Baxengill Gorge there is a footbridge that gives you a view of the river as it drops sharply through a narrow rift, thundering in spate. On wild days the gorge produces the very kind of scene that the Victorians liked to have engraved and hung over the antimacassar beside the glass bell full of stuffed natterjack toads. The path drops gently down, wandering through pleasant woodlands and past the ruins of a disused quarry into Ingleton village. As I said before, it is a fine little place, an honest-to-goodness working Dales town, a farming centre, a 'beauty spot' and a caving centre with shops, cafés and the best fish and chip shop in the Dales. The chip shop is run by a Lancastrian, but since Ingleton is so close to the Lancashire border nobody seems to mind.

The fish and chip shop was closed by the time I arrived, so I made do with some scones and tea at a nearby café before following the road down to the official starting point of the waterfalls walk. I paid my money and, almost alone now that the afternoon was wearing on, I followed the path to the falls of Twisleton Glen.

There is a rare beauty to be found in walking alone in autumn when the late sun is turning towards dusk and there is a stillness in the air. Mists rise and the sun silhouettes the far hills in graded tones of lilac and purple, and with nobody to disturb my thoughts I find this a great time for settling into my own pace and just strolling along letting my mind tick over like an engine in neutral. I often walk the fells with my wife and with other friends and companions because I enjoy their company, but I think there are also times when every one of us should go alone to the hills just to get away from all the noise and hassle of Silicon City.

Thornton Force – the point of unconformity at which a hand's breadth can span a million years

I remember one day in the Lake District I was filming a programme on walking for BBC television. I had flown in late the day before from New Orleans where I had been working on another BBC series. After five weeks of filming and 2000 miles of travel in America followed by 3000 miles in a jumbo jet, my head was still somewhere over the Atlantic by the time the day's filming had ended.

We'd finished the shoot near the Coppermines Valley below Coniston Old Man and as the crew turned back to Coniston at the end of the afternoon I headed up the Old Man to clear my head, planning to climb up by the tarn, cross the Old Man, and return by the miners' track. As I climbed up through the early evening I came across a lone tent pitched by the still waters of Low-water Tarn. In front of the tent, cooking his evening meal, was a lone figure sat by the stove staring out across the lake. I passed by quietly leaving him to his solitude and have never envied anybody so much, before or since.

As I walked through the woods of Swilla Glen I saw just before me a little owl doing a spot of early evening dinner-getting perched in the fork of a silver birch. It saw me coming and took off up the glen into the dark. When I lived in Ribblesdale I often used to see a little owl hunting at night on the verge by the roadside. I watched him many a night by moonlight hopping on and off the dry-stone wall into the long grass looking for mice and shrews. As someone who was once described by a journalist as a 'cuddly owl', I feel I have some affinity with the feathered hunters of the night.

There are two footbridges across the Twiss between Swilla Glen and the first of the Twiss falls, and at the last footbridge I

Thornton Force on a bank holiday

ABOVE: *Looking towards Ingleton, evening*   FACING PAGE: *Thornton Force, detail*

stopped for a little while to look at Pecca Falls and then followed the path by Pecca Twin Falls and Hollybush Spout to the tea hut at the head of the glen. Years ago the tea hut used to do marvellous glasses of homemade lemonade. I must have drunk gallons of it on hot summer days walking this route over the years. Now, alas, the lemonade is gone, although they still do good cups of tea, and what better way to warm yourself up on a late autumn afternoon than with a cup of Rosy Lee?

It was getting darker now, the autumn evenings closing in towards back-end, so I hurried on to Thornton Force where the river Twiss flows under Raven Ray and falls forty feet from its limestone bed on to the older Silurian rocks below. Dr Arthur Raistrick said it all beautifully when he remarked that at the point of unconformity below the waterfalls where the old slate rocks jutting up vertically meet the horizontal limestone strata which lie upon them, a person placing his hand across the junction of limestone and Silurian rock can span with his hand's breadth a million years.

Below Raven Ray I followed the path to the footbridge over Kingsdale Beck and tracked back to my car as the last rays of the westering sun tinged the lip of Keld Head Scar and the shoulder of Ireby Fell.

10. the howgill fells

IF somebody were to ask me where my favourite area for walking was then I would be badly torn between the Three Peaks, Swaledale, Dentdale and the Howgill Fells.

The Howgills have something about them that is not found anywhere else in the Dales, an openness, a sense of airiness and a sense of space that is totally unique. They are a vaguely strawberry-shaped mass of hills lying between the Tebay–Kirkby Stephen road in the north, the M6 in the west and the Kendal–Kirkby Stephen road in the south-east. They are composed almost entirely of Silurian rock of the Coniston Grit variety and are well drained and, since there are common grazing rights, they are largely unfenced so that walking their tops is a total pleasure.

The Howgills have been described variously as being 'elephant backs' and 'as though they've been draped in green velvet'. Both descriptions are fitting, though I would add that they are rugged and steep and in certain places, for example at Cautley and Black Force, exposed and wild.

FACING PAGE: *The Howgills from Fox's Pulpit*   BELOW: *Bram Rigg from White Fell*

The Howgills from Frostrow, looking like a range of 'elephant backs'

R. Lune

Tebay

Ravenstonedale

N

Langdale Fell

West Fell

Green Bell

Hare Shaw

Uldale Head

Docker Knott

Randygill Top

Carlingill Beck

The Spout

Bowderdale Beck

Kensgriff

Gibbet Hill

Black Force

Hazelgill Knott

R. Lune

Fell Head

Bush Howe

Yarlside

Castley Knotts

Cautley Spout

Ben End

Chapel Beck

White Fell

The Calf

Cautley Crag

Barkshin Gully

Howgill

Bram Rigg Top

Great Dummacks

Holme Beck

Crosedale Beck

Cautley

Cross Keys Hotel

Firbank Fell

Fox's Pulpit

Arant Haw

Knott

Sickerts Fell

Winder

Crook

R. Rawthey

Sedbergh

Crook of Lune Bridge near Beck Foot

Ravenstonedale and Kirkby Stephen where the Dales proper end and the beautiful country of the North Pennines begins, leading at length by Cross Fell and High Force to the Cheviots and the Border.

To the south of the Howgills Sedbergh with its famous boys' school is a good centre from which to walk many of the southern fells, while Ravenstonedale in the north-east is a bonny village with some accommodation. Generally, though, the Howgills are not a popular walking area and when I was putting this book together various people didn't want me to include the Howgill Fells because, as they said, 'We don't want people finding out about them.' I'd hate them to become overcrowded but, let's face it, if everybody adopted that attitude nobody would ever have found out about the joys of fell-walking and a million copies of A. Wainwright's wonderful handbooks would have remained unsold.

In any case, I think that the exclusive elitist dog-in-a-manger attitude some walkers and climbers have towards their favourite patches of hills or rocks goes against the whole spirit of fell-walking. The fells are there for all to enjoy. Who am I to say that the glorious walk to the Calf from Four Lane Ends or the ridge walk from Cautley to the head of Bowderdale shouldn't be enjoyed by everybody? I'd hate to see the Howgills end up like Blackpool on a Bank Holiday but I think that there's room for a lot more people yet. Mind you if they build a Pizza Hut on top of Winder I may live to regret my words.

As a footnote to this piece, can I say that it was only thanks to the hard work of Tom Stephenson that the southern end of the Howgills was included in the National Park in the first place.

From a central core around the Calf and Cautley in the north the fells fall away in ridges that fan out to create long steep-sided dales, and in the south are bunched up like a fist. Westwards, the Howgills look down on the Lune Valley and Gorge, and in fact many people see them from their cars on the M6 near Killington Lake Services without realising exactly what it is they're looking at. In the east the fells fall gently towards

RANDYGILL TOP BY BARKSHIN GULLY

tHERE are very few places in the Yorkshire Dales where the average walker stands much chance of causing himself any damage. Weather conditions can make the safest fell a death-trap at times to the unwary, the purely unlucky or the basically stupid. However, the Dales contain some of the safest though generally not some of the softest walking areas in the country.

There are a few places where a bit more care than normal is needed – the gritstone edge of Pen-y-ghent, for example, or the gullies of Ingleborough are neither of them areas I would recommend anybody to fool about in – but generally the death toll among walkers in the Dales is low. There have been deaths, but many of the deaths that have taken place have been older walkers suffering heart attacks. Still not a laughing matter, but if you've got to go it must be one of the better ways to shuffle off this mortal coil. I would rather go halfway up (or preferably on top of) Pen-y-ghent on a hot July day than senile in a wheelchair being pushed daft and dribbling from dining-room to sunlounge.

Though the Dales provide safe walking, there are still ways in which a walker can stretch himself if he wants to. One is by walking against the clock – not something I enjoy very much myself. I have walked the Three Peaks time after time in under eight hours in sun, rain, wind and sleet, and though I have enjoyed the challenge, the erosion of the route in the last few years has put me off doing it again.

I can never understand why people who otherwise never set foot in the Dales stream here in their thousands to walk the Three Peaks in organised sponsored walks for charity. You see them hobbling off the hills in all sorts of weather, clapped out and almost delirious with exhaustion, never to return again – why? I think they should leave the hills for those that enjoy them and if they want a challenge they should offer to walk a thousand times round their local duck pond, and that way the footpaths of the Dales would be in far better condition and at least the ducks in the pond would be kept amused. Sponsored walking has virtually brought about the closure of the Lyke Wake long-distance footpath. I would hate to see that happen to the Three Peaks.

If you don't want to walk against the clock and if you don't want to load your rucksack up with boulders or take your granny up on your back just to give yourself some more weight to carry, you can always set yourself a bit of gully-scrambling to do. On unexposed faces, gully-climbing can be about as close as a serious fell-walker will get to rock-climbing and, provided that you are not stupid, it needn't be any more dangerous than walking the well-trod paths.

You've got to be sensible about it, pick a gully that isn't just a waterfall in spate, make sure you can back down out of it if you scramble yourself into a corner, and you've got to be able to see where you are heading for and know that you can in fact scramble in at the bottom and out at the top. Having said all that, there is many a time I have set off to do the gully route to the top of somewhere or other and have had to retire gracefully having run out of things to hold on to, stand on, or get my teeth round.

One bright day in mid-October I set off from the Cross Keys at Cautley to walk Yarlside and Randygill Top. I think the name of the latter pike held some attraction for me as well as the fact that I hoped to get a good picture of Cautley Crag and the Spout from the opposite side of the valley. It was while I was walking towards the saddle at Cautley that a gully on the flanks of Ben End caught my eye. It looked a stiff climb but not at all risky, stretching from a screeslope at the valley floor to the first shoulder of Ben End. It narrowed considerably in its last

FACING PAGE: *Cautley Crag*

hundred feet or so but it looked climbable so I ventured onwards.

The gradient stiffened after the first hundred feet and the gully started to close round me as I walked up into it. There were plenty of places for hands and feet and it was nowhere near vertical yet. There was a bit of water flowing down the gully, but nothing like the amount flowing down Cautley Spout on the valley side opposite. Another hundred feet of climbing and the gully had become in parts the bed of a stream flowing in a series of miniature falls over Silurian gritstone, giving me plenty of opportunity to remember the old equation $H_2O + ROk = SOS$.

As usual in gullies such as this, the stones on and around the beck-bed were mixed with shale and larger rocks, ranging in size from pebbles to lumps as big as footballs. Frost and their friable nature meant that the rocks had been split and riven until in places they could be pulled apart. I came to a tricky spot where I had to toe-balance on a ledge with one foot while moving the other foot up on to a clump of grass and shale. My arms, meanwhile, were outstretched, one hand firmly round a tussock

FACING PAGE: *Backside Beck below Yarlside*   RIGHT: *Cautley Spout, detail*   BELOW:*Wild fell ponies below Calders*

to the right and the other grabbing for a spar up and above me to the left. As I shifted my weight I reached up and grabbed the spar of stone. It came away in my hand and I watched helplessly as a rock the size of a garden gnome and sharpened at all its edges like a parrot's beak rolled in slow motion past my face and gently but firmly as a smoothing plane took a fair length of skin and hair off my shin.

I didn't let go. To do so would have been foolish – there

wasn't much below me but space. I knew my mother was eighty miles away in Manchester, so it was no use calling for her. I just did what every butch macho son of a gun would have done, and shouted good old Anglo-Saxon words into the soil four inches from my face – then I had a bit of a weep. Well, it does you good to get it off your chest and somebody did once say it takes a real man to cry.

The rest of the gully was a hard pull and in places a serious scramble, but passed without incident except that, near the top, a buzzard gracefully riding a thermal hung above me in the still

RIGHT: *Looking down towards Dentdale from Ben End*
BELOW: *Looking out of Barkshin Gully*

The peaks of the Lake District from Yarlside

air. He reminded me of the lines of Gerard Manley Hopkins' beautiful poem about the falcon 'The Windhover':

I caught this morning morning's minion, king-
        dom of daylight's dauphin, dapple-dawn-drawn Falcon, in
                his riding

I love birds and hate to see them in cages. I know very little about them, to my shame, and can only identify ten or so species at sight, but I find their presence in our world, like that of all wild creatures, a reassurance that man is not having it all his own way and that in spite of the concrete and the glass and the cars and heavy lorries, the kestrels and crows still fly above it all while below, the worms and the moles undermine the foundations.

Whenever I see the ruined castles of the mighty like Bolton Castle and Pendragon Castle staring eyeless into the space about them, I often think of the men who built them and how they must have thought they would last for ever. Such thoughts give me a little encouragement when I look at the massive quarries of Cracoe and Helwith Bridge. Some day the machines will be

gone, Tilcon and Redland Roadstone will be no more, and the nettles and fireweed will turn in to begin the healing of the wound.

My wound, meanwhile, was not healing and was in fact throbbing like an egg with an oversize chick about to hatch from it. To make things worse, at the summit of Yarlside the cloud layer which until then I would have guessed as being at about 2500 feet dropped in a fit of pique and blocked out the light, making me reach for compass and map. I took a bearing and was walking down the fell to get under the cloud when I came on a group of wild fell ponies in the mist. They looked up as I appeared through the cloud. I slowed down and carefully drew closer to watch them and take some shots of them before they moved off. For a while they ignored me as I stood breathlessly watching them, then unconcernedly they slowly wandered off.

I walked below the summit of Kensgriff and climbed steadily up to Randygill Top where I sat and ate my lunch in the mist. It was a bit dark and I almost ate my fingers twice, so I packed up my stuff and slowly worked my way along one of the many becks and down the steep fellside to Bowderdale. Walking along the dale bottom, I passed the shoulder of fell where earlier that year I had watched a dog fox coursing away from me along the steep slopes. The noise of sheep on the move below the cloud drew my eyes up to some specks on the far hillside – men and dogs moving their flocks down the fell to be counted and sorted out.

Sheep are fairly territorial animals, usually keeping to their own stretch of the fell, but some do wander, and each back-end the farmers gather them in, bringing them down off the high tops to winter lower in the dale, at the same time sorting out any strays that may have chanced in among their own flocks.

I stopped to chat to one farmer and his dog who surprisingly I had seen only a matter of minutes before halfway up Kensgriff. It is incredible really how fast farmers can cover ground on the fell. With an old tweed jacket, a strong pair of breeches, a pair of wellies and a stick, there is many a farmer

Looking towards Four Lane Ends, winter

that can outpace a team of younger walkers in their dayglo cagoules and Italian walking boots. It must be something the farmers put in their wellies.

I sat below Cautley Crag for a while before I got up to walk the last half-mile to the road. Light was fading now, getting towards what they used to call in Lancashire 'th'edge o'dark'. Somewhere close at hand a blackbird was scolding in the bushes, going 'chuck, chuck, chuck'. Above me, the falls were dropping in a stairway of cascades nearly 700 feet long. I thought of how, earlier in the year at the end of a long hot summer, I had walked over Winder and the Calf the length of the ridge to

Ravenstonedale and how I had walked back down Bowderdale and sat here in the evening warmth watching what was then a rill trickling lazily down the gully, but which was now a torrent falling through the mist.

Evening drawing in fast and the lights of the farm at Cautley coming on in the dusk, I ambled back to the car, every bit of me feeling good – except my shin. I was going to have to bathe it in alcohol, the farmer had said when I told him what had happened as we talked below Kensgriff.

'Does that work?' I asked.

'Aye,' he said. 'But you've got to do it from the inside.'

black force by carlingill beck

OF the two places in the Howgills where the Silurian rocks of Coniston Grit outcrop, Black Force is undoubtedly the most dramatic. Cautley Crag, where the curve of the crag ends in the succession of stepped waterfalls that make up the Spout, is certainly wild and grand, but Black Force, hidden from view in the upper folds of Carlingill, a narrow gash in the flanks of a steep-sided valley, is away from the world, a remote and almost always lonely place.

I usually walk to Black Force from the bridge where the Fairmile road crosses Carlingill Beck, and one winter's day I drove out of Sedbergh past Four Lane Ends towards Tebay and down the old Howgill road (once a Roman marching road linking Castlehaw at Sedbergh with the Roman fort at Low Borrow Bridge near Tebay). I left the car at the hamlet of Howgill and walked along the road towards Carlingill Bridge. I don't like road walking much but this road is particularly quiet and since if I was to complete the circular route I would have to walk along it anyway, I thought it was better that I walked it now than at the end of the day, when my already sore feet would be further hammered by the hard road.

Coming over the last stretch of Carlingill, there opened up before me what must be one of the most beautiful views in England, now marred entirely by the motorway thundering through it. I have an old print in my house that came from a sale of railway paraphernalia. It's one of those prints that used to be fixed to the wall behind the seats in railway compartments to give your eyes something to look at above the heads of your fellow travellers, in the days when trains ran on time and British Rail pies did not bark at you. The print is entitled 'The Lune Gorge, Tebay, Westmorland', and shows as fine a view of a river valley as you'll get anywhere. Now, years later, the view is dominated by a concrete conveyor belt along which thunder fleets of juggernauts carrying spam for Sainsbury's, Kilmarnock, while below an underused railway line threads its way peacefully along the dale – madness, total madness.

Close by the road at Carlingill Bridge is Gibbet Hill, where heaps of bones were once found as evidence that here, by the old boundary stone between Westmorland and Yorkshire, the miscreants of both old counties were executed and hung on the gibbet to serve as a warning to all. Local legend still has it that men walking the Fairmile of a black wintry night have heard the ghostly rattling of chains and the wind moaning through the

RIGHT: *Gibbet Hill*

gibbet. Now all you'd be able to hear would be the crashing of gear boxes on the other side of the valley.

I left the road and followed the beck that was loud and angry and swollen with rain, and found an indistinct path that cut into the hillside above. On my left-hand side the quaintly named Weasel Gill cut deeply into the fell. I turned right and the valley narrowed round me as I pushed on, a wintry wind buffeting me below low cloud that at times dropped well below the level of the tops. At Haskhaw Gill and Small Gill the becks tumbled in a series of waterfalls that were a taste of things to come. The gillsides narrowed and the path petered out completely, the way ahead being a series of slippery scrambles across boulders and shale. I am always glad there's nobody around at times like this since I, who dream of climbing Everest, end up sliding down boulders on my bum in a very clumsy and very un-'hard man' style.

The last scramble brought me to what I had been able to hear but not see for the last few hundred yards or so, Black Force, where little Ulgill Beck drops in a series of cascades to the valley bottom. The cloud and mist had fallen again so that the force took on the aspect of a Chinese or Japanese landscape painting in muted and subdued tones. There is in fact a fine book called *The Silent Traveller in the Yorkshire Dales*, written and illustrated by a Chinese artist called Chiang Yee, and it is amazing to see in this book the different way in which an oriental eye sees the landscape of the Dales.

Beyond Black Force the path gets more difficult until finally at the Spout, another cascade, it becomes definitely impossible and I had to scramble up a hairy screeslope to the left and carry on climbing to the saddle between Uldale Head and Docker Knott. The cloud had dropped very low now and visibility was down to yards, so I followed the fellside up until it levelled off to

RIGHT: *Black Force: as in a Chinese landscape painting, the water tumbles through the misty crag* FACING PAGE: *Carlingill Beck*

ABOVE: *The folding of the rocks on the western face of Black Force*   FACING PAGE: *The Spout beyond Black Force* (left) *The summit of Fell Head* (top right) *The hamlet of Howgill* (bottom right)

the saddle and then looked for the rise that told me I was below Docker Knott.

There I sat and ate my lunch, alone in the mist, occasionally seeing the shapes of wild fell ponies coming and going in the fog. It was too cold for comfort, so I didn't linger long and set off through the pearly grey for Breaks Head, following a compass bearing to the cairn on Fell Head.

The snow still lay thick in drifts on Fell Head, much of it crusted with ice. Nothing stirred, the wind had dropped now and still mist hung and swirled around the fell. I took what looked like a reasonable way off Fell Head, dropping steeply and quickly down to Long Rigg Beck, and as I walked out of the low

clouds I saw the welcome sight of the valley below, drab as it was in its February colours.

The short winter day was failing as I climbed up from the beck to follow the footpath over the last rise above Howgill. Cottage chimneys were smoking and I hurried down to the village spurred on by the thought of my own fireside. On days like this in the fells, although its bleak and chill, it's nice to be up if it's not too misty and you're still out in the open fells, emptiness about you with the noise of the wind and the falling becks as your only companions. It's nice to be up, but when the light starts failing and night's coming on, it's nicer still to be down again.

winder to bowderdale end

EVERY schoolboy at Sedbergh School is supposed to climb Winder at least once in his career. I don't know if they do but the hill does feature in the school song.

It's Cautley, Calf and Winder
That make the Sedbergh man.

Winder is certainly one of the best introductions to the Howgills and was the first hill I climbed in these fells when I walked with Tony and Matt to the Calf and on through the rains of November to Cautley and back by the river. But one of the best, though longest, days in these fells took me up Winder and right across the ridges to Bowderdale End.

It was midsummer and a cloudless, warm morning when I left Sedbergh by the back lane from the car park with Pat and some friends, Rod, Sue, Robert and Cynthia. All of us together comprise a loose sort of walking club where I pick the route and get blamed if anything goes wrong. It makes you realise how difficult it must be being the president of a big country. Crocodile fashion we began the long grind up Winder, the landscape below unfolding as we climbed, Sedbergh and the Rawthey close at hand, Baugh Fell, Middleton Fell and Lunesdale further away in the morning heat haze.

We paused on the summit of Winder to get our breath back and to look at the views. It was a magnificent morning. Above us was a lark, a high black wisp in the sky, his song filling the fell, seeming too big for such a little bird so far away. From Winder we strolled off towards Arant Haw, the broad saddle of the fell

Walkers on the ascent of Winder

FACING PAGE: *A runner below Arant Haw*
BELOW: *Looking north from the Calf*

ABOVE: *Cautley, winter* RIGHT: *The Howgills from Firbank in winter*

falling on either side, until we came to just about the only piece of fencing in these hills. The view back towards Winder was superb. From the cairn on Calders, the hills folded away all about us in the morning light and further to the west we could see the fells of Firbank and Fox's Pulpit.

By the time we reached Bram Rigg top, most of the climbing had been done and the shouts of, 'How much further is it, *el presidente*?' had stopped. I whipped them back into line and we dawdled along to the Calf, the far fells of Lakeland coming into view as we reached the trig point. The last time I had been here the fells had been thick with snow; now the grass was thick and dry and I allowed the team to sit down for the regulation tea break and have a rest in the warm grass.

From the Calf to Hazelgill Knott a rough Land-rover track

School party below Arant Haw

was easy to follow by small pools where flies rode across the dusty surface and where, at Hazelgill itself, a group of wild ponies were grazing the steep fellsides. Langdale Fell and the steep-sided valley lay below us to the west as we reached our final point at West Fell. Northwards lay the hills of Eden and Crosby Garrett and below us Bowderdale and the path that would lead us south to Cautley. Coming down the fell a large dog fox loped across the path and scuttled for safety across the broad flanks of the fell running towards Cautley, looking behind him just the once to see if we were following him. The descent down the flanks of the fell to Bowderdale Beck was so steep that certain members of the team slid down on their backsides, which seems an undignified way of going fell-walking to me.

When we all reached Bowderdale Beck we regrouped and certain members of the party dusted themselves down before we followed the beck, stopping once or twice to drink its cool water in the hot sun. The walk back to Cautley was a gentle meander along the beautiful valley of Bowderdale, disturbed only by the appearance of what we took at first to be a mirage, but what was in fact a lady walking topless with a man and a dog, about which I am going to say absolutely nothing at all except that I can't remember what the dog looked like.

Bowderdale is a grand valley to stroll along on a hot summer's afternoon and the fact that it ends in the wild crag of Cautley makes it doubly delightful. Cautley is like a great stone bowl curving away from the stairway of fells that make up the Spout on the opposite fell, and facing the crag was the narrow path through the bracken that we took that day, the bracken

Looking down Bowderdale towards Cautley

smelling sweetly of peaches in the heat. Across the valley we could see the Spout, not really one waterfall but a series of broken falls over 700 feet in height, falling in what must be the most spectacular series of falls in England.

From Cautley, where the Cross Keys Hotel is the only temperance inn I know in the area, the field path leads back to Sedbergh below Knott. It's a pleasant walk back through fields and by farm lanes, although some of the party had become mutinous and one in particular was muttering about tea and thirst and dictatorships. It looked as though I would have to get my whistle out and blow for order when suddenly we were waylaid at Hollin Hill Farm by a little Brownie.

It is not in the usual nature of Brownies to hijack people but this little girl told us that as part of the Brownies' and Girl Guides' National Tea-making Week she had turned her garden into a tea garden and would we like some tea and scones? I was trodden to the ground in the rush as the thirsty five scrambled through the gate and plonked themselves on the grass shouting, 'Tea for five and the Führer' – ungrateful lot.

a note on walking

I'M not really sure that this piece is altogether necessary because walking is the second thing most of us learn to do after eating, but if it helps to save somebody's life or give the Fell and Cave Rescue lads a night in, then it will have been worth it. If you're not already an experienced fell-walker and if after reading this book you are planning anything more than a riverside stroll with the kids, then here are a few bits of advice.

Always dress for the occasion. In the hills that means you should always wear walking boots and socks and carry waterproofs and spare warm clothing with you. Of course you *can* do Pen-y-ghent on a good day in trainers and shorts, but what about the rain we get in our good old British summertime?

Always take a map and compass and make sure you know how to use them; don't just hang them round your neck to give you fell credibility. In winter take extra clothing, food and hot drinks, plan short walks and make sure you know *all* the escape routes. Always let people know where you're going and tell them that you've arrived safely when you get back.

Remember farmers have to live and work in what you and I think of as a playground, so please respect this. Close gates, don't let dogs chase animals, don't leave bottles and cans and plastic bags lying about, and take your muck home with you. The one thing that makes me feel like committing murder is the sight of a crushed Coca-Cola can or empty fag packet thrown down at the side of a path.

If you want to read further books on the subject then there are some excellent guides and maps to the Dales. Among them are Harry Rée's *Three Peaks of Yorkshire*, Colin Speakman's *Walking the Yorkshire Dales*, Gladys Sellars' *Walks in the Yorkshire Dales National Park*, Frank Duerden's *Great Walks of the Yorkshire Dales*. Forder and Raistrick's book *Open Fell, Hidden Dale* is a lovely pictorial record of the Dales and, of course, the classic walking books of all time are A. Wainwright's *Walks in Limestone Country* and *Walks on the Howgill Fells*.

As well as all these, there is a smashing range of walking books produced by *The Dalesman* publishing company who are based at Clapham in the Yorkshire Dales. The Ordnance Survey have now produced three excellent new maps of the Yorkshire Dales in their Leisure Series. With these three maps alone and a compass you've got almost everything you need.

If I can insert a little plug here, if you do like to go walking, whether it's alone or whether with a group of people, then you might like to consider joining the Ramblers' Association, a non-profit-making organisation whose members work hard and long to keep footpaths open, to protect the rights of walkers and to encourage walking in all its aspects.

Lastly, if you want to read more generally on the Yorkshire Dales then I must recommend Hartley and Ingliby's excellent books on the Yorkshire Dales and those of that most learned and readable of Dalesmen, Dr Arthur Raistrick.

a note on the photography

THE pictures in this book were taken over the last fifteen years of my life in the Dales. More than half were taken in the last twelve months for the simple reason that I'd judged my earlier work and found it wanting. Camera shake, poor focusing and, most importantly of all, the lack of stability of certain film emulsions, meant that I often had to go back and re-make shots that I had taken ten or twelve years ago.

The cameras I used were the Nikon F2 and FE2 with a range of lenses from 16 mm fish-eye to 500 mm telephoto; the Hasselblad CM2000 with 80 mm, 50 mm, 150 mm and 250 mm lenses; and the Fujika CSMCW Pro 6 × 9 cm camera – a wonderful camera for landscape work. If asked, I would have to say that the camera I used the most was the Nikon FE2. It's light, compact and, together with a few well-chosen lenses (the 35–105 mm zoom in particular), is my Number One camera.

I used polarising filters quite frequently to darken skies or take summer glare off grass and used graduated filters occasionally. The film I used was almost entirely Fujichrome Pro and I used mainly 50 ASA speed film, although I occasionally used 100 ASA. I find it quite simply the best lab-processed transparency film on the market for fine grain and colour quality.

I used a Pentax spot meter, a Weston Euromaster and a Minolta incident light meter as well as the internal metering on the FE2 and F2, and if it's any consolation to other budding photographers, I still made the occasional cock-up.

To transport my gear when I was walking I used a Camera Care System rucksack/'versatile' bag, a Warthog waist pouch and a tripod bag, all by the same firm. I used a tripod on seventy-five per cent of my shots, either a Kennett Benbow or a Baby Benbow, and at other times I almost always used a monopod, or at least a wall, a fence or a friend's shoulder to lean on.

I am not an equipment freak and though I used such a wide range of cameras I often found, and still find, that the shots that came most readily and seemed to work the best were those taken simply with my old 35 mm Nikon FE2 on a day out when I was expecting nothing to happen.

I once set up a shot of a brass band marching through the cobbled streets of Dent only to find that just as I was about to press the shutter of the Hasselblad a yellow mini pulled round the corner and stopped right in front of the camera, completely ruining a shot that had taken me half an hour to set up.

On the other hand, walking through Horton one afternoon in the rain, the clouds parted behind me and against a black sky a perfect double rainbow formed itself above Horton parish church. I had the Nikon FE2 with a 20 mm lens on in my hand and took a shot there and then that I couldn't have planned in a lifetime.

FACING PAGE: *Walkers descending Harber Scar Lane towards Horton, winter*

a final word

AS I said right at the beginning, this book isn't the sort of book you read as a guide and follow slavishly like the instructions in an assemble-it-yourself furniture kit. I wrote it so that people might know more about an area I love, and if, after reading this book, you take out a map and work out a walk for yourself and if you ramble along your chosen route either alone or with friends and, what's more important, if you enjoy it, then I think this book will have been worth the writing.

I would like at this last point to thank all my friends who have walked with me, carried the tripod with the minimum of moaning, and waited patiently while I jumped about from rock to rock changing lenses, pointing meters at the sky and muttering, 'A sixtieth at f8.'

Thanks to Pat, Sarah, Emma, Tony, Matt, Rod, Sue, Robert, Cynthia, Gordon, Jane, Mary, Geoff, Chris and Louise.

Thanks to Tom Stephenson for writing the foreword. Thanks to Richard, Jeff and Matt for the help in the caves and mines. Thanks to all the farmers whose lands I crossed – well, all but one. Thanks to all the publicans and café owners who fuelled the machine and thanks to Billy and Sam, two dogs who thought they were human and almost had me fooled.

FACING PAGE: *Haycocks, Dentdale*

INDEX

italics indicates illustration

The Kingfisher Book
of Living Worlds

The Kingfisher Book
of Living Worlds

Clive Gifford · Jerry Cadle

KING*f*ISHER

KINGFISHER
Kingfisher Publications Plc
New Penderel House
283–288 High Holborn
London WC1V 7HZ
www.kingfisherpub.com

Authors Clive Gifford, Jerry Cadle
Consultant Professor Philip Whitfield
Editors Russell Mclean, Jonathan Stroud
Designer Mark Bristow
Production controller Jo Blackmore
Picture manager Jane Lambert
Picture researcher Rachael Swann
DTP manager Nicky Studdart
Indexer Lynn Bresler

First published by Kingfisher Publications Plc 2002

2 4 6 8 10 9 7 5 3 1

1TR/0602/TWP/CLSN(CLSN)/150ENSOMA

A CIP catalogue record for this book is available
from the British Library.

ISBN 0 7534 0591 1

Printed in Singapore

Contents

Planet Earth

Earth is the only known planet in the universe which supports life. Every sea and continent has its own distinctive lifeforms, all adapted to the conditions around them. The millions of different living things which inhabit the planet are found in a narrow layer that extends down into the soil and rocks, and up into the lower parts of the Earth's atmosphere. This area is called the biosphere.

Seasons

The power of the Sun provides the Earth with the energy it requires to support life. The Earth orbits the Sun tilted at an angle, which creates the seasons. When the southern half – or hemisphere – of the Earth is tilted towards the Sun, it is summer in that hemisphere and winter in the northern hemisphere. As the Earth's journey around the Sun continues, the seasons change. Six months later, the northern hemisphere is tilted towards the Sun, creating summer in the north and winter in the south.

Temperature and climate

How the Sun's rays strike the curved surface of the Earth helps determine the temperature of an area. This, in turn, affects that area's weather patterns and what can live there. Around the centre of the Earth – the equator – the temperature is high and does not vary greatly. This is because the Sun's rays strike from almost directly overhead all year round. Further away from the equator, the Sun's rays strike the surface at a more slanting angle and their warming effect is less. This is why the poles – the furthest points from the equator – are also the coldest places on Earth. Temperature, along with height above sea level (altitude) and distance from the ocean, are major influences on a region's climate – the general weather conditions which an area experiences over a long period of time. Rainfall and the strength and types of wind also affect climate.

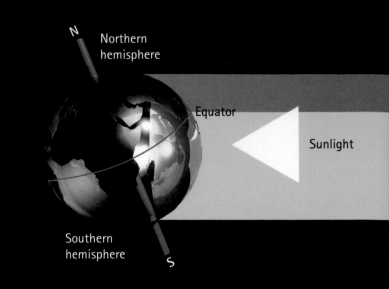

Northern hemisphere

Equator

Sunlight

Southern hemisphere

N

S

△ As the Earth orbits the Sun, it rotates on its axis at an angle of 23.5 degrees. This creates the seasons. Here, the southern hemisphere is tilted towards the Sun and experiences summer. The northern hemisphere experiences winter because it receives less of the Sun's energy. The rays have to travel through more energy-absorbing atmosphere and then hit the Earth's surface at a less direct angle.

▽ Hot, dry deserts where water is in short supply exist throughout the world, but still support much life. This horned devil lives in a desert in Australia.

▽ This underwater habitat off the west coast of Scotland contains kelp, a type of seaweed, which provides shelter for anemones, urchins and starfish.

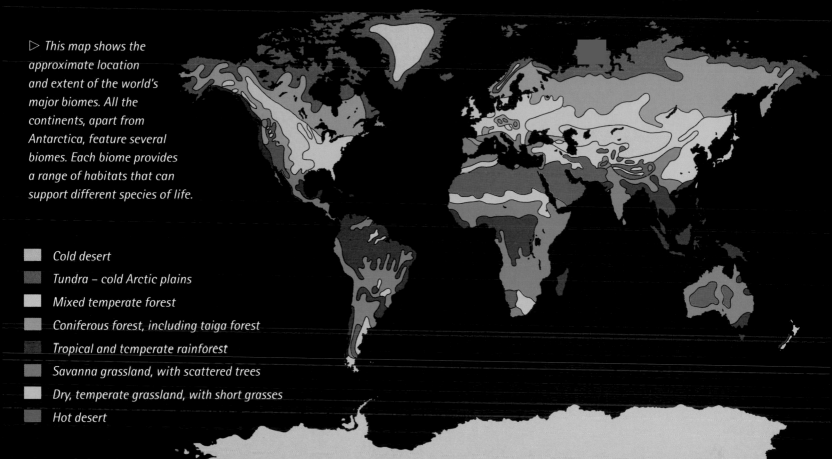

▷ This map shows the approximate location and extent of the world's major biomes. All the continents, apart from Antarctica, feature several biomes. Each biome provides a range of habitats that can support different species of life.

■ Cold desert

■ Tundra – cold Arctic plains

■ Mixed temperate forest

■ Coniferous forest, including taiga forest

■ Tropical and temperate rainforest

■ Savanna grassland, with scattered trees

■ Dry, temperate grassland, with short grasses

■ Hot desert

▽ The coldest parts of the world are its two polar regions, where less of the Sun's energy strikes. This icy habitat is in Canada's Northwestern Territories.

▽ Lush bamboo forests in China provide the giant panda with its one food source, bamboo shoots. Pandas may die out because they rely too heavily on a single food.

Biomes

The biosphere provides a large range of different surroundings and living conditions for plants and animals, called environments. These vary in temperature, moisture, light, and many other factors. The natural home of a plant or animal is called its habitat. Each habitat is a complex, well-balanced system which provides living things with all that they need for survival. A large, general habitat such as a desert or tropical rainforest is called a biome. The largest of all biomes are the oceans, which cover 71 percent of the Earth's surface.

◁ The air that surrounds Earth is constantly on the move in the form of air currents and winds. Clouds, formed of millions of droplets of water vapour, are blown around the Earth and bring rain and storms to the various regions.

7

Plants

Plants support all other life on Earth. They are autotrophs, which means they can survive on direct energy sources such as sunlight. They also take nutrients from soil, rocks and water. The types of plants growing in an area often define what sort of biome it is and what else can survive there, because they offer food, homes and shelter for many animals. Plants cannot move, but some of their parts are designed for travel. This means they can reproduce with other plants and then scatter their seeds, which will grow into the next generation of plants.

Ingredients of life

Plants need four basic things to grow and live – water, carbon dioxide, mineral salts and light. Water and minerals are drawn up through a plant's roots, its leaves take in carbon dioxide from the air and light is absorbed directly from the Sun. Water, carbon dioxide and light are used by plants to manufacture their own food in a process called photosynthesis. The energy from sunlight is used to convert the water and carbon dioxide into sugars which act as a plant's food. Photosynthesis also plays a vital role in recycling air – a waste product is the gas oxygen, which most animals need to breathe in order to survive.

▷ *The flower of a plant is where reproduction occurs.*

▷ *Carbon dioxide passes into a plant through tiny pores or holes, called stomata, in the leaf's surface.*

▷ *Chlorophyll, a chemical which gives plants their green colour, is stored in the leaves in packages called chloroplasts. Photosynthesis occurs in the chloroplasts.*

▷ *Water and the sugary sap created by photosynthesis are carried throughout a plant by veins in the stem and leaves.*

▽ *Plants which grow in soils that lack nutrients have evolved to obtain them from elsewhere. This sundew is a meat-eating plant. It traps and digests insects to get mineral nutrients.*

Nutrients

Most plants need extra nutrients besides those which they make themselves during photosynthesis. These include minerals, such as nitrogen and magnesium, which are taken up in water from the soil. Minerals in the soil are usually plentiful unless the same crop has been grown intensively for many years in a row. Farmers need to rotate their crops by growing plants such as lupins and clover in between their main crops. These plants enrich the soil by producing more nitrogen than they use.

▷ *Water is taken in through the root system of a plant.*

Flowers

Flowering plants produce male and female sex cells in different parts of their flowers. The flower's female cells lie at the base of a stalk called the style. Pollen is the male part of the flower. It grows on another stalk called the stamen and needs to reach the female sex cells of another plant in order for reproduction to take place. Grasses and many other plants rely on the wind to disperse their pollen, while plants with large flowers use them to attract insects and other creatures. These animals transport sticky pollen on their bodies from one plant's flowers to another.

◁ *Flowers are often brightly coloured to attract pollen carriers. Many contain sweet, sticky nectar, which provides food for birds, bats and insects, such as this bee.*

▽ *The seeds of dandelions are shaped like tiny parachutes, so they can be carried by the wind. A strong wind can blow the seeds several kilometres away from their parent plant.*

Seeds and spores

Seeds develop after a plant has been pollinated. They are often encased in a protective coating to form nuts, fruit or berries. If the coating is nutritious, it will be eaten by animals which disperse the seed in their droppings. Some seeds, such as winged sycamore seeds or dandelion parachutes, are shaped to catch the wind. Others are covered in small hooks which attach to an animal's fur. Ferns, mosses and liverworts don't create seeds at all. Instead, they have tiny spores which disperse in the wind.

Germination

Germination is the process by which a seed starts to grow into a plant. For a seed to germinate, it must come to rest in suitable soil with sufficient light and water. Seeds contain a food supply to sustain the seedling until it has grown enough to produce its own food through photosynthesis.

△ *This series of photographs shows the germination of a runner bean at three, four, seven, eight, nine and ten days. Growth is rapid, and starts with the root system.*

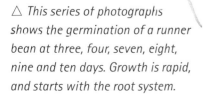

Animals

Like plants, animals can grow, sense changes in their environment and reproduce to make a new generation of young. Animals, however, cannot photosynthesize in order to create their own food from sunlight, water and gases. They are heterotrophs, which means they must eat something which is or was alive in order to refuel themselves. Most animals are equipped with muscles or other structures which allow them to move around. They also need to take in oxygen through respiration, or breathing.

△ Supported by water, which has a similar density to their bodies, this shoal of mullet swim by simply moving their tails back and forth. On land, animals use more energy and require stronger muscles, skeletons and hearts to move.

△ This grass snake shows great agility to plunge underwater and catch a fish.

Structure and movement

Animals whose bodies are supported by a backbone are called vertebrates. Invertebrates are animals without a backbone. Vertebrates include mammals, birds, reptiles and fish. They all have an internal skeleton made of bone or, in the case of sharks, a gristly substance called cartilage. Invertebrates such as worms, insects, crustaceans, spiders and jellyfish are far more common but are usually smaller and less complex animals. Most animals have muscles to power their movement – from the heart pumping blood around the body, to the movement of legs, wings or fins that propels an animal around.

▽ One of the largest predators on land is the female lion, or lioness, here seen stalking a herd of springbok antelopes in the grasslands of southern Africa.

Feeding

Most animals, from small insects to elephants, are herbivores – they eat plant matter. Others, called carnivores, are meat-eaters. Some animals, such as worms, bears, humans and some birds, are omnivores, able to eat both animals and plants. Food has to be broken down, or digested, for its nutrients to be absorbed. This is usually done inside an animal's body with the help of chemicals called enzymes. Carnivores have developed ingenious ways of catching prey – they use webs and traps, work in teams or rely on sheer speed or power. As protection from carnivores, many animals have evolved defences such as armour and stings. Others hide, use camouflage or live together in large groups to help avoid attack.

▷ Ospreys hunt for fish by hovering over the water, then diving with their wings swept back. At the last moment, they thrust their talons forwards to pluck the fish from below the water's surface. Adult ospreys are successful about once every four dives.

Senses

Animals need senses to find food, shelter and others of the same species, as well as to avoid danger. Just like humans, most animals are equipped with five senses – sound, smell, touch, taste and sight. In many cases, creatures have one or two senses that are more highly developed than the others. For example, high-flying turkey vultures have powerful long-distance sight and smell, enabling them to detect dead animals while flying hundreds of metres above the ground. Many creatures lack or have a poorly-developed sense which is compensated by other, more sensitive ones. Nocturnal animals – which feed and are most active at night – often have poor vision but enhanced senses of smell, hearing and touch.

◁ A spider uses sensitive hairs on its body as touch and taste receptors. The hairs also sense air currents and humidity. Most spiders have eight eyes. This jumping spider has four eyes on the front of its head and four on the top.

Communication

Animals communicate for many reasons – from calling a lost baby or attracting a mate, to sounding the alarm about an approaching predator. They communicate in a great variety of ways. Sound is used by animals on land, sea and air. Birdsong often marks out a bird's territory or keeps it in touch with the rest of its flock. The haunting and complex 'songs' of the humpback whale can be heard by another humpback hundreds of kilometres away. Many mammals use a combination of body language and sounds to communicate a threat or show they are ready to mate, while bees perform a dance to let others know the location of a food source. Scents and smells are very important to many creatures, from ants to big cats, to help them find food and communicate with others.

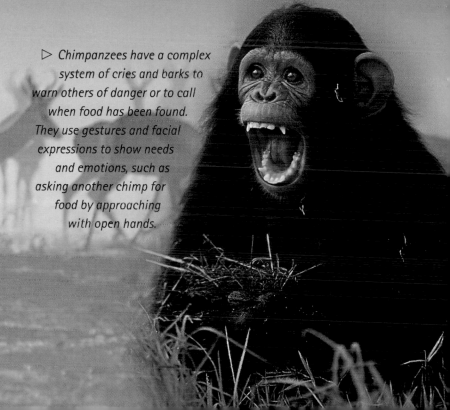

▷ Chimpanzees have a complex system of cries and barks to warn others of danger or to call when food has been found. They use gestures and facial expressions to show needs and emotions, such as asking another chimp for food by approaching with open hands.

Seas and oceans

Life on Earth began in water, and today water covers nearly three quarters of the planet's surface. There are five oceans – the Pacific, the Atlantic, the Indian, the Antarctic and the Arctic. Smaller bodies of water, such as the Mediterranean and the Caribbean, are called seas. The waters contain many different habitats – from the dark and hostile ocean depths to the teeming coral reefs – and support a huge variety of life. Seas and oceans have a level of species diversity as high as the rainforests.

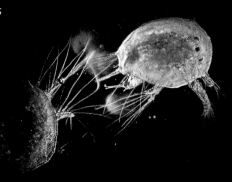

▷ Plankton, such as these examples from the waters around Britain, are divided into animal plankton and plant plankton. Plant plankton produce almost 70 percent of the world's oxygen.

▽ Anglerfish are named after an extension of their dorsal fin which can be wiggled like a fishing lure to attract prey. Usually living in water more than 15 metres deep, anglerfish have been known to leave the sea bed and attack seabirds on the water's surface.

Plankton

Food chains in seas and oceans start with primary producers called plant plankton or phytoplankton. They live near enough to the water's surface to take in sunlight. They use the light to make food through photosynthesis. Plankton also exist in animal form, called zooplankton. These cannot photosynthesize and feed off other animal plankton or plant plankton. Unlike phytoplankton, many zooplankton can swim rather than merely drift in the water. The different types of plankton form the crucial first stage of marine food chains which support sea plants, crustaceans, fish and water mammals such as seals.

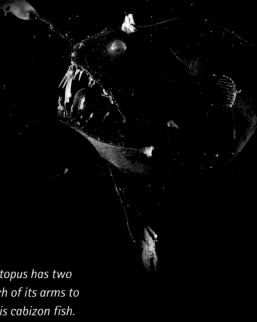

◁ This giant Pacific octopus has two rows of suckers on each of its arms to catch prey such as this cabizon fish. The octopus kills the prey with its beak and bites it into pieces.

Fish

Fish breathe by swallowing water and passing it over their gills – feathery tissues lined with blood vessels which absorb oxygen from the water. Most fish – over 20,000 species – are bony. Many bony fish, such as mackerel and herring, are streamlined and live in large shoals near the water's surface. They are called pelagic fish. Other bony fish, such as the sole and the halibut, are flattened and live on the sea bed. They are known as demersal fish. A bony fish has a gas-filled sac inside its body, called a swim bladder, which enables it to float. About 600 species of fish have no bones, but a skeleton made of gristly cartilage. These cartilaginous fish, such as sharks, tend to sink unless they keep swimming.

▷ *Deep-sea tube worms grow up to three metres long. Their tail ends are fixed to the ocean floor. The red plumes at the top contain blood which transports hydrogen sulphide from deep-sea vents to the bacteria inside their bodies.*

◁ *Manta rays are the largest species of ray, averaging 6.7 metres in width. They eat plankton, tiny fish and small crustaceans. A shoal of fish swims beneath this ray for protection.*

Into the deep

Most marine life exists in the top 100 metres of water, where light and plankton are plentiful. Yet the average ocean depth is 3,700 metres. At such great depths, there is no light, little food and extreme pressure. The animals which live there are specially adapted to the extreme conditions and many rely on food falling from the water above. Many deep-water animals produce their own light in order to communicate, catch prey or deter predators. This light, known as bioluminescence, is often generated by bacteria living inside the animals.

Black smokers

In 1977, new forms of life were discovered in the ocean depths, based around rocky chimneys on the sea bed called black smokers. Rocks beneath the Earth's crust heat water which seeps down through cracks in the sea bed to temperatures of 400°C. The water blasts back up to the sea floor, carrying minerals from the crust which are deposited to form chimneys. Bacteria thrive in the sulphur-rich waters of these hot spots and provide the crucial first stage in a food web which supports blind white crabs, sea anemones more than a metre wide, giant clams and tube worms.

▷ *Giant clams cluster around a deep-sea vent in the ocean floor, 2,600 metres below sea level. Little is known about their life cycle, but it is believed that, like tube worms, they rely on bacteria to break down the nutrients on which they feed.*

Coral reefs

In the kaleidoscopic world of the coral reef there is a greater variety of life than anywhere else in the sea. Over a third of all the world's fish species live there. Many animals, including seaslugs, starfish and small fish, come to eat the coral, and they in turn attract predators such as sharks and barracuda. With so many predators around, some of the reef creatures are camouflaged, but most have bright displays to warn that they are poisonous or to help them find a mate, making the reef a riot of different colours.

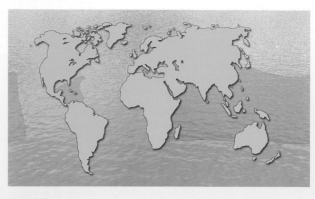

△ Reefs grow only under certain conditions. They need strong sunlight and water temperatures of 20°C or above, which can usually only be found in tropical waters less than 40 metres deep. The orange areas on this map show the regions where reefs can grow.

How reefs are formed

Coral is made by large colonies of small creatures called polyps. Ranging in size from one to ten millimetres, individual polyps consist of a central mouth and stomach, surrounded by a ring of plankton-catching tentacles. The polyps grow hard external skeletons for protection, and when they die these remain as a stony mass on the sea bed. A coral reef gradually builds up, as successive generations of polyps live on top of the growing pile of skeletons of their predecessors. It is a very slow process – the reefs grow no more than a few centimetres every year. Many reefs are thousands of years old.

△ A polyp's hard outer skeleton helps protect it from predators, while its tentacles trap passing plankton. The corals' bright colours are caused by algae growing within their tissues. In return for a place to live, the algae provide the corals with some of the food they make for themselves during photosynthesis.

▽ The living surface of the reef is formed of many different coral species, including the brain coral (below centre). Nooks and crannies within the layers of dead and living coral create perfect lairs for predators, such as this moray eel.

The Great Barrier Reef

The largest reef of all is the Great Barrier Reef, which lies off the north-east coast of Australia. It stretches for 2,000 kilometres, and is home to over 1,500 species of fish. Big enough to be seen from space, parts of it are over two million years old – the oldest structure made by living organisms. Today, the Barrier Reef is threatened by a coral-eating starfish called the crown-of-thorns. Since the 1970s, a plague of crown-of-thorns has swept the reef, devouring the coral and leaving vast regions barren and empty.

A threatened future

More than 90 percent of coral reefs are being damaged in some way. Heavy tropical storms break up the coral, as do fishermen when they drag their nets. Coral can be poisoned by pollution from shipping and industry, and the algae living within the coral are killed if the sea temperature changes. As global warming increases, the algae in more and more corals will be destroyed, bleaching them of colour and depriving them of a valuable food source.

▷ The crown-of-thorns starfish multiplied rapidly when its natural predators, large marine snails, were collected by humans. The sale of the snail shells has now been banned in an effort to halt the starfish plague.

△ Parrotfish are a natural predator of coral, although they do not cause serious damage. They eat the polyps and the algae in them, using special, chisel-shaped teeth that grind away the coral's protective skeleton.

▽ Many of the animals that thrive on a coral reef are among the oldest creatures on Earth. Corals, sponges and starfish have existed together for 500 million years, 100 million years longer than the fish that now swim past them.

▽ Shoals of fish browse the gentle, nutrient-rich waters of the reef. Its maze-like structure provides the fish with some protection from predators, such as the reef shark, which patrols the open waters of the reef at night.

Coasts and wetlands

Coastlines are found on every continent. Ranging from towering cliffs and jagged rocks to shingle or sand beaches, they are unusual habitats that alternate between wet and dry. The animals that live there must adapt to conditions both underwater and in the drying sun in order to survive. Much coastal life also has to contend with the problem of pounding waves. Yet, for the plants and animals which manage to exist there, the coastal environment can be ideal for growth, with plenty of sunlight, water and mineral salts from the sea.

△ A mixture of different seaweeds in a rockpool on the French coast.

Intertidal zone

The area where the sea meets the land is called the intertidal zone. Sometimes the zone is submerged under saltwater, at other times it is exposed to the air, as the tides come in and out. On rocky coasts, the intertidal zone is divided into three habitats. At the top, where only the highest tides reach, less life exists – mainly algae and molluscs. The areas always covered by high tide support a greater range of animals, including small fish, plant-eating snails and crabs. The bottom of the intertidal zone is exposed only during the lowest tides. Many fish, seaweeds, sea anemones, starfish and sea urchins are found here. On sandier shores, the intertidal zone is not so strictly divided. Mud and sand is always on the move, which makes it hard for algae or plants to establish themselves. Worms, clams, crustaceans, crabs and shorebirds occupy this area.

▽ The rocky Farne Islands provide homes for large colonies of guillemots, puffins and terns.

△ Low tide attracts predators, particularly seabirds such as these oystercatchers. They are drawn by the wealth of small animals hidden just below the sand's surface.

◁ Sea otters are one of the few animals to use tools. This sea otter is opening a shell by smashing it against a rock balanced on its belly.

Avoiding exposure

When the tide starts to go out, many coastal animals hide to avoid drying out in the sun. Wet, heavy seaweed or damp crevices in rocks are a retreat for shore-dwelling crabs. Many animals with shells simply burrow into the sand, emerging when the water returns. Others, such as cockles and razor shells, stay buried and extend a tube called a feeding siphon to pull in food-rich water. For animals which are anchored to the rocks, burying themselves is not an option. The sea anemone, for example, withdraws its tentacles and covers itself with a protective, jelly-like mucus. This prevents it from drying out and dying.

◁ A sea anemone has tentacles which trap, sting and draw prey, such as this fish, to its central mouth.

▽ Mudskippers are fish found in wetlands and mangrove swamps. They can live out of water, using their strong pectoral fins to skip along.

Wetlands

Wetlands are boggy areas where water lies on the land in pools, or where plants have grown out into open water to form marshes or swamps. The still water supports a great range of aquatic plants and animals. Wetlands often have the highest species diversity of all ecosystems. They are home to many species of amphibians, reptiles and birds, such as ducks and waders. Estuaries are areas where freshwater streams or rivers merge with saltwater from the ocean. Worms, oysters, crabs, waterfowl, algae, seaweeds, marsh grasses and, in the tropics, mangrove trees, can all be found in estuaries.

▽ The cliffs at Hunstanton on Britain's East Anglian coast are formed of brown carstone topped with white chalk. The cliffs have been heavily eroded to form a stony shoreline.

19

Rivers and lakes

When rain falls on high ground, some of the water soaks into the soil or seeps between cracks in the rocks. Water that remains on the surface is drawn by gravity towards sea level as a stream. Streams join together to become rivers. These huge bodies of moving water carve and erode rocks and land, creating valleys and gorges. Lakes form where water collects and doesn't drain away. Both rivers and lakes are homes to a wide range of plants and animals.

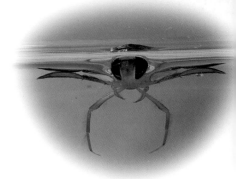

△ Some insects have adapted to life underwater in lakes and ponds. The water boatman stores air beneath its wings, so it can stay submerged for long periods as it feeds on plants.

The river ecosystem

A river offers more than one habitat. Different living things are found on the river bed, at the water's surface and at the water's edge. Plant life at the river's edge is both a home and a food source for many animals. Rivers also change along their length – flowing fast in their early stages and meandering slowly as they empty into the sea. In fast-flowing sections the fish are very strong swimmers, while some insects have developed ways of coping with the rushing water. Caddisfly larvae, for example, create a case of sticks and sand to weigh themselves down. Many animals spend only part of their lives in rivers. Salmon and trout are born and die in rivers, but in between they live at sea. Amphibians such as toads and frogs develop in freshwater as larvae and tadpoles, but spend much of their adult lives on land.

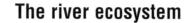

◁ Kingfishers feed on small fish, such as this stickleback. They dive into the water to catch their prey, then swallow it head first. Kingfishers live in lowland areas around clear, slow-moving rivers.

▷ Rainbow trout are migratory fish, starting and ending their lives in rivers. They can swim strongly against the current of a fast-flowing river, and even leap upstream.

The Amazon

The Amazon river begins in the snow-capped Andes mountains, in South America, then winds through the Amazon basin before reaching the Atlantic Ocean. At 6,500 kilometres long, it is slightly shorter than the Nile, but the thousand tributaries that run into the Amazon ensure that it contains more water than any other river. One fifth of the freshwater that enters the sea every year comes from the Amazon.

△ *The huge leaves of the Amazon water lily float on the water's surface. Each plant can grow as many as 50 leaves.*

▽ *The Amazon is home to one of the world's largest and heaviest snakes, the anaconda. Anacondas lie in wait for prey such as turtles, capybara – the world's largest rodent – and, as shown here, iguanas. They kill by suffocation, wrapping their coils around a victim to squeeze out its breath.*

Giant wildlife

The Amazon river's food-rich habitats have allowed giant versions of some animals and plants to evolve. The world's largest otter, the giant otter, can grow up to 2.5 metres long. It emerges from its den on the river bank to hunt for fish and crabs during the day. The vast Amazon water lily anchors its roots in the mud of the river bed and grows quickly. Each of its leaves can grow to 180 centimetres across.

▽ *The Cononaco river winds through the Yasuni National Park in Ecuador. Surrounded by lush rainforest, the river is one of the homes of the Amazon river dolphin.*

▽ *Lakes make up a very small percentage of all the freshwater on Earth, but they are rich habitats for life. This lake in Rwanda has formed in the crater of an extinct volcano.*

Lakes

Lakes form in different ways. Many, such as the Great Lakes of North America, were carved out by glaciers during ice ages. Others occur due to movement of the Earth's plates or develop in the craters of extinct volcanoes. The action of humans and animals, such as beavers, can also create lakes. Shallow lakes and ponds are often rich in nutrients and wildlife. Plankton – the microscopic organisms which float in water – are food for small insects and crustaceans. Aquatic plants are vital for the health of most lakes. They provide food and a place to live and breed, as well as releasing oxygen into the water.

People and water

Water is the most precious resource on Earth. It is essential for life and the habitat for many of the world's living things. People rely on water for many reasons beyond drinking it to survive – they hunt sea and freshwater animals for food, they use water in industry, and channel it to irrigate agricultural fields and provide power. People also damage sea and freshwater environments through pollution and by overexploiting their contents.

△ Viewed from space, the Nile river winds through Egypt, providing a ribbon of fertile land either side of its banks. This fertile zone supports industry, agriculture and over 95 percent of Egypt's human population.

Tourism

Tourism is one of the world's biggest and fastest-growing industries. Coastal areas are often the target of this trillion-dollar business. Unspoilt coastal regions on every continent except Antarctica have been developed into high-rise resorts, often with little thought to the ecological consequences. Natural wetlands, lagoons and coastline habitats are cleared or drained to make way for hotels and roads. Tourist facilities may pump unclean waste water into the sea, creating further damage. The massive increase in tourist numbers can destroy delicate habitats such as coral reefs, while the high demand for local foods can lead to a decline in stocks of shellfish and fish.

◁ Cancun, in Mexico, took just 20 years to develop into a resort with 1.5 million visitors every year. Around 60,000 hectares of rainforest were cleared and parts of Cancun's lagoon were destroyed or contaminated – affecting habitats for native plants, marine turtles, fish and other animals.

Pollution

Many substances dissolve easily in water, making it highly vulnerable to pollution from many sources – domestic sewage, dumped industrial chemicals and agricultural pesticides which can be washed from soil into streams and rivers. Oil spills have been especially devastating to marine and coastal habitats, injuring and killing much marine life. The *Exxon Valdez* supertanker spilled over 50 million litres of crude oil on to the coast of Alaska in 1989. Some of the species and the fishing communities living there have still not fully recovered.

△ *Oil slicks clog the fur of animals and the feathers of birds, such as this kittiwake. Oil can block the gills of fish, preventing them from breathing, and poisons animals which accidentally swallow it.*

Fishing

Fish have been a primary source of food for people in coastal areas and on islands for thousands of years. Modern sea fishing uses giant trawlers to haul in millions of tonnes of fish every year, at a rate which nature cannot keep up with. Many species, such as cod, haddock and certain shellfish, have been overfished. In some places, fish populations will recover only if fishing is limited by quotas or even halted altogether. At some fishing grounds, species have been overfished to local extinction. The animals which rely on these species for food have also suffered a decline, damaging the entire marine ecosystem. Modern fishing can also be extremely wasteful, with many unwanted sea creatures caught and killed in nets, including turtles, dolphins, diving seabirds and certain species of fish.

△ *These fishermen are hauling in a catch of herring. Of the world's 13 million fishermen, one million crew the 30,000 large fishing vessels which bring in half of all the fish caught in a year.*

▽ *Hydro-electric power stations need large dams, such as the Glen Canyon dam on the Colorado river, to hold back a giant reservoir of water. Building dams may cause rivers to be diverted and valleys flooded, destroying habitats and many animals.*

Water power

Moving water can be exploited to produce electricity. A hydro-electric power station uses a large dam to create a reservoir of water, then lets some surge through a tunnel to machinery called turbines. The turbines are turned by the falling water, powering generators which create electricity. Although dams offer a renewable source of energy, they are expensive to build and can seriously disrupt local ecosystems. Another water power system harnesses the energy in tides. Tidal barriers stretch across part of a shoreline or estuary, and their turbines are turned by the tide flowing in and out. The barriers are expensive to build, threaten certain habitats and prevent fish, such as salmon, from swimming up estuaries.

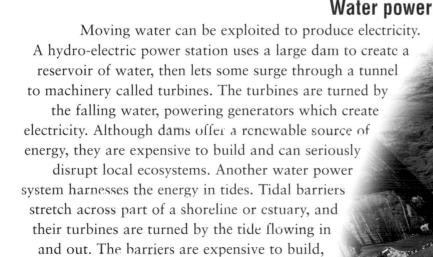

Rainforests

Rainforests are the most complex and productive biomes on Earth. They consist of huge trees growing closely together, interlocking and rising up to 40 metres from the ground. Rainforests thrive on sunlight and very heavy rain – between 200 and 1,000 centimetres of rainfall per year. The rain produces lush plant growth which, in turn, supports an enormous number of animals. Although rainforests make up under ten percent of the Earth's land surface, scientists estimate that they are home to as much as 90 percent of the world's animal and plant species.

▷ The temperate rainforests on the west coast of New Zealand receive up to 700 centimetres of rainfall every year. The forests teem with plant and animal life.

△ Rainforests are home to huge numbers of bird species, such as these scarlet ibis in Venezuela. In the rainforests of Costa Rica, for example, there are 845 different bird species, as well as 205 kinds of mammal and more than 10,000 varieties of plant.

Where are rainforests?

Rainforests are divided into two types: tropical and temperate. Tropical rainforests are hot (at least 20–25°C) and are found close to the equator. Over 50 percent of all tropical rainforests are in Latin America. Southeast Asia, the Pacific Islands, and west and central Africa are home to approximately 43 percent. Temperate rainforests are also wet but have a milder climate. They are found further from the equator, near the coast, and once covered large parts of Scotland, Iceland, Norway and Ireland. Today, Chile, New Zealand and the Pacific coast of North America are homes to the largest remaining temperate rainforests.

Rainforest layers

Rainforests are made up of four basic layers or strata: the forest floor, the understorey, the canopy and the emergent layer. The plants and animals which live in each layer are specifically adapted to life there. Each layer has its own particular microclimate according to the level of light and water it receives. The canopy is a rainforest's powerhouse – it receives up to 90 percent of all sunlight falling on the rainforest. Here photosynthesis is most productive, producing rapid plant growth. For example, a hectare of tropical rainforest produces more than 60 tonnes of new plant growth every year, twice that of a temperate oak forest.

40 m

▷ *The emergents are the tallest trees, scattered through the rainforest. Their tops poke out above the canopy.*

30 m

▷ *The canopy comprises the interlocking tops of the main forest trees. The majority of rainforest animals live here.*

20 m

▷ *The understorey is made up of small trees, shrubs, bushes, ferns and vines which can survive in shady conditions.*

10 m

▷ *The forest floor is damp, dark and still, as the plants above protect it from winds. Humidity is at 90 percent or above.*

◁ *Climbing plants, such as this vine in Peru, are common in rainforests. They snake up and round tree trunks, tying many trees together so that if one falls, many fall with it.*

Rainforests and the world's weather

Rainforests have a major impact on the wellbeing of the entire planet. As well as generating vast amounts of oxygen through photosynthesis, rainforests also help maintain global rain and weather patterns. The dense plant foliage acts like a giant sponge, soaking up vast quantities of falling rain before it can seep away. Much of the water returns to the air as water vapour given off by leaves. The vapour condenses to form rain clouds both over the forest and on lands far away.

▽ *Epipyhtes are types of hanging plants. By growing on the branches of canopy trees, they receive sunlight without having to grow up from the forest floor.*

◁ *Clouds form quickly above the dense, green canopy of a tropical rainforest in Venezuela. Without rainforests, many areas of the world would be affected by droughts.*

The forest floor

Far below the rainforest canopy lies the dark world of the forest floor. Only two percent of the light that hits the topmost branches reaches the ground, so few plants are able to grow among the fungi and twisting roots that cover its surface. Yet the leaf litter around the roots teems with life. Insects – from giant beetles to poisonous centipedes – are everywhere, and it is so wet that frogs, crabs and even fish are able to flourish in the gloom.

Releasing the nutrients

Rainforest soils are very poor. They contain few nutrients, and what little they do have is easily washed away by the rains that drench the forests. The main source of nutrition for the trees is the layer of leaf litter and dead plant and animal debris that covers the forest floor. Here, huge numbers of decomposers, such as bacteria, fungi and insects, break down the litter into nutrients. These are then taken up by the trees through their vast networks of roots. Special fungi, called mycorrhizae, cover the root tips and work with the trees, helping them to absorb the precious nutrients before they are washed away.

▽ *Many of the forest trees have huge buttress roots to prop them up in the thin soil. Around them, small seedlings wait in suspended animation for a hole to appear in the canopy above. They will then grow rapidly, racing each other to fill the gap.*

▽▷ *The lush conditions of the forest allow many species to grow to a giant size. Carnivorous centipedes (right) can reach 28 centimetres long. Land crabs (below) live in the moist leaf litter, as well as in the water that collects at the bottom of bromeliad plants.*

Down in the litter

The leaf litter is so damp and humid that creatures normally found in aquatic habitats live here. Frogs and land crabs scuttle among the leaves. The warm, wet conditions allow invertebrates to grow to gigantic sizes. Giant centipedes hunt at night for prey that includes rodents and snakes, while huge maggots of the world's largest beetle, the goliath beetle, pupate in the rotting leaves.

△ Big cats, such as this South American jaguar, are perfectly adapted to hunt on the forest floor. They are silent, superbly camouflaged and have excellent vision.

The single life

The vegetation of the forest floor is too sparse to support large herds of big herbivores. Those that live here tend to be solitary creatures. Tiny deer and large rodents, such as the agoutis and pacas, forage for smaller plants in the forests of South America. Taller plants are reached by animals such as the tapir, forest rhino and, in Africa, the okapi. Their predators – mostly the big cats – are also very few in number.

▷ The okapi is a relative of the giraffe. This extremely shy creature was first discovered in the African rainforest in 1901.

Odd adaptations

To get around the extreme lack of light, some forest floor plants, such as rafflesia, tap into the trunks of trees whose leaves reach into the light of the canopy – and steal their food. Others have giant leaves, or ingenious systems like lenses in their foliage to make the most of the dim light. Nearly all have special 'drip tips' on their leaves to drain off the constant moisture and prevent them going mouldy.

◁ Rafflesia is a parasitic plant that steals the food and water supplies of the vines that grow on the trees above it. Its huge flower – at one metre wide, the largest in the world – smells like rotting flesh. This attracts the flies that spread its pollen.

27

The canopy

The majority of life in a rainforest is found in its canopy, high above the ground. Unlike the forest floor, the canopy basks in sunlight – ideal for rapid plant growth. Leaves, flowers, fruit, nuts and seeds are valuable food sources for a great variety of animals – from butterflies, ants and other insects to frogs, lizards and larger creatures such as fruit-eating monkeys. Many of these have evolved and adapted to life in the canopy, finding ways to move, build homes, feed and reproduce high off the ground.

▷ The canopy food web involves thousands of different living things. The lush plant life provides a rich food source for insects and some birds, monkeys and mammals. These animals, in turn, are food for predators such as snakes and large birds of prey.

△ Rainforest canopies support many small, aquatic micro-communities. These tadpoles are living in a pool of water that has formed in the leaves of a bromeliad, a type of epiphyte.

Eagles

Snakes

Birds

Bats

Frogs

Sloths

Monkeys

Squirrels

Insects

Leaves

Fruit

PLANTS

Flowers

▽ A northern blossom bat feeds on a banksia flower in Australia. Bats are major pollinators of flowering plants.

An interconnected world

Over millions of years, animals and plants have evolved to fill different niches in the rainforest. Each living thing relies on the presence of others in order to survive. This interconnected world has a delicate balance. If one species of plant or animal becomes scarce, it can affect the survival of many others.

Pollination

Little wind enters through the top of the canopy, so trees and other plants need other ways of having their flowers pollinated. Many rely on insects and birds, such as the hummingbird, to carry away pollen that sticks to their bodies as they feed on nectar. Bats pollinate flowers at night. The flowers of some trees grow on the trunk, well away from the leaves, making it easier for bats to find them.

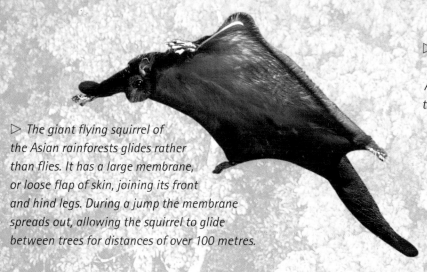

▷ The giant flying squirrel of the Asian rainforests glides rather than flies. It has a large membrane, or loose flap of skin, joining its front and hind legs. During a jump the membrane spreads out, allowing the squirrel to glide between trees for distances of over 100 metres.

▷ The slow-moving two-toed sloth of South and Central America relies on camouflage to avoid predators such as the jaguar. Green algae grows in its fur, allowing the sloth to blend into the leafy canopy.

▽ Like many hummingbirds, the rufous-breasted hermit hummingbird uses cobwebs to build a tiny nest in the shelter of a leaf.

Moving through the canopy

For animals which cannot fly, moving around the canopy calls for great skill. Sloths and tree anteaters have sharp, powerful claws which they use to ease their way up to and through the canopy. The flying fox and some species of flying squirrel glide between trees. Monkeys are the most agile of the larger canopy dwellers. With their grasping hands and feet, they grip branches as they leap between trees. The monkeys of the Americas also have a prehensile tail – this means the tail can grip, making a fifth hand.

Rainforest birds

Rainforests are home to over half of the world's bird species. Many birds are equipped with short, stubby wings to help them dart between the trunks and branches. Different-shaped beaks are specially adapted for different feeding habits. For example, the long, hollow and lightweight beak of the toucan is ideal for reaching dangling fruits, while the strong, hooked bills of parrots and macaws are designed to break through nut and seed casings.

Predators of the canopy

The animals of the canopy are vulnerable to attack from all directions. Predatory birds such as the powerful South American harpy eagle swoop down from above to grab monkeys and sloths. Insects and small animals are potential prey for birds, and many are camouflaged to blend into the leafy background. The most common predators are the different species of snakes, many of which are highly poisonous. From below, cats such as the margay and ocelot make occasional attacks. The cats live on the forest floor but climb up into the lower canopy at night to hunt.

▽ At 35 centimetres long, the eyelash viper is one of the smallest poisonous snakes of the Central American rainforest. It feeds on frogs, lizards, small mammals and birds.

Taiga forests

Taiga or boreal forests stretch through North America, Europe and Asia, covering around 11 percent of the Earth's land surface. During the long and intensely cold winters, much of the groundwater in rivers, lakes and ponds is frozen. Summers are short and there may only be between 50 and 100 frost-free days in a year. Many birds and some land animal species migrate from the taiga during winter, while others manage to live there all year round, coping in different ways with the extreme cold and the relative lack of food.

△ The capercaillie eats buds, shoots, berries and seeds in summer. In winter, it eats conifer shoots. Its chicks are often eaten by foxes, pine martens and sparrowhawks.

▽ The wolverine is a hunter with powerful jaws and teeth. Its varied diet ranges from wasp larvae and eggs to lemmings, hares and squirrels.

Coniferous forests

Forests of evergreen conifer trees dominate the vegetation of the taiga, and provide homes as well as food for many animals. The conifers are cone-shaped, so they can easily shed snow before their branches break under the weight. Their narrow, tough leaves can withstand strong winds and long periods of sub-zero temperatures. The waxy pine needles of many conifers protect the trees from the extreme cold, but are very slow to decay once they have fallen to the floor. Coniferous forests rely on fungi to slowly break down the needles and release nutrients back into the soil.

△ Moose are the world's largest deer, with adult males – shown here rutting – weighing over half a tonne. Moose eat twigs and bark in winter, and wade into thawed rivers and lakes in summer to eat water plants.

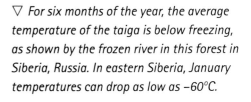

▽ For six months of the year, the average temperature of the taiga is below freezing, as shown by the frozen river in this forest in Siberia, Russia. In eastern Siberia, January temperatures can drop as low as −60°C.

△ *Beavers work together in well-organized family groups to fell trees and build dams and lodges. These provide shelter from the cold winters and a place to give birth to young.*

Protection from cold

Animal life in the taiga is limited by the severe winter. Some mammals hibernate, or sleep deeply, through the coldest months, while many bird species such as the wood warbler migrate south to a less harsh climate. Those animals which don't hibernate are usually covered with a thick insulating layer of fur or feathers. Many species are larger than relatives found in warmer climates, as their greater size helps them conserve body heat. The taiga is home to the world's largest deer (the moose) and weasel (the wolverine). The male capercaillie bird weighs up to four kilogrammes, making it the biggest member of the grouse family.

▽ *Some animals have evolved specific adaptations to let them reach cone seeds and use them as food. The crossbill's twisted beak allows it to break in to closed cones to get at the seeds before the cones open and the seeds are dispersed.*

▷ *A giant wood wasp drills a hole deep into the bark of a tree, before laying its eggs in the hole. When the larvae emerge from their eggs, they spend two to three years maturing under the bark, while feeding on the wood of the tree.*

Searching for food

Insect-feeding animals and birds usually migrate away from the taiga in winter. They return when warmer temperatures melt the groundwater and allow millions of insects to breed. Birds that feed on cones and seeds, such as red crossbills and pine siskins, stay in the taiga all year round. Some, such as the nutcracker, a member of the crow family, hide pine cone seeds in many different locations as a winter store. Predators such as the lynx and members of the weasel family – including wolverines, minks and ermine – hunt snowshoe rabbits, voles, red squirrels and other herbivores.

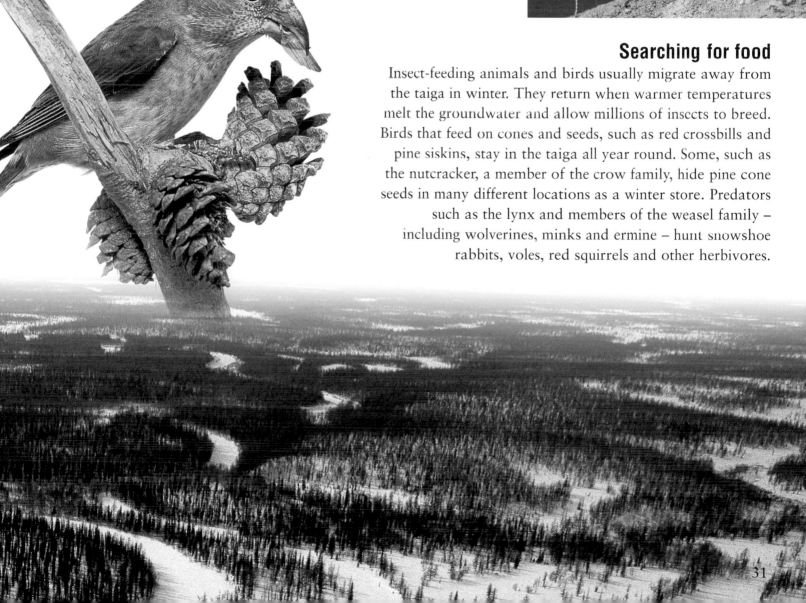

31

Temperate forests

Temperate forests and woodlands are found away from the heat of the equator and the extreme cold of the polar regions. They lie mainly above the Tropic of Cancer and below the Tropic of Capricorn, in regions with a great variation between summer and winter climates. Much of Europe and North America were covered by temperate forest until trees were cleared to make room for farmland, houses and industry. At one time, 80 percent of Britain was covered by trees. That figure is now only ten percent.

△ *Some animals, such as this hazel dormouse, survive winter by using up their reserves of fat during hibernation. To use less energy, the animal's body temperature and heart rate drop.*

◁ *A forest of deciduous aspen trees show their spectacular autumn colours in the Rocky mountains, Colorado. Aspens provide valuable food for elk and deer herds.*

Surviving winter

In temperate forests, the short days of winter provide too little sunlight for trees to photosynthesize much, while their roots struggle to absorb water from the cold, often frozen, ground. So trees rest during winter and protect themselves in different ways. Coniferous trees such as pines and firs have needle-shaped leaves with a waxy coating. This keeps moisture within the tree. Conifers also have a built-in antifreeze to protect them from frost. This means they can keep their leaves through winter and start to photosynthesize as soon as spring arrives.

Deciduous trees

Most broad-leaved trees are deciduous. This means they shed their leaves in winter to prevent damage from the cold, and to stop water evaporating from the leaves which their roots could not easily replace. In autumn, the trees take back nutrients from their leaves, which change colour from green to yellow and red. Then the leaves fall. The fallen leaves are broken down by decomposers such as fungi and earthworms to create a rich humus. The humus begins to decay and release nutrients into the soil in time for spring, when the growing season begins.

▽ *This rotting tree log is home to a range of fungi and green mosses. As it decomposes, a rotting log can provide a home or breeding ground for toads and salamanders, as well as worms and millipedes which attract moles, shrews and other insect-hunting animals. Eventually, the log will fall apart and decay into humus, enriching the soil.*

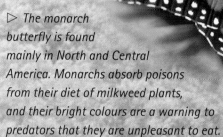

▷ The monarch
butterfly is found
mainly in North and Central
America. Monarchs absorb poisons
from their diet of milkweed plants,
and their bright colours are a warning to
predators that they are unpleasant to eat.

◁ Insects are a valuable
food source for many bird
species in deciduous
temperate forests. Here,
a garden warbler feeds
a caterpillar to its chicks.

▽ Monkey puzzle trees in Conquillio National
Park, Chile. The monkey puzzle is an evergreen
tree with stiff, overlapping leaves, growing to a
height of 45 metres. Its seeds are an important
food source for people and some animals.

Woodland wildlife

Temperate woodlands provide rich sources of food
in spring, summer and autumn. Most of the food
that comes from trees, in the form of leaves, nuts,
flowers and fruits, is high in the branches. This
attracts birds and squirrels. Trees also provide
a home and food source for a vast number of
insects. A single mature oak tree, for example, can
support over 35,000 caterpillars eating its leaves
at one time. Other insects eat bark or bore and
chew their way into a tree's trunk. The millions
of insects in a temperate forest are a vital part
of the food web. They are eaten by predatory
insects such as ladybirds and other beetles,
as well as many species of insect-eating birds.

The forest floor

In spring, the forest floor is carpeted by flowering plants
such as the snowdrop, crocus and primrose. They grow
in the sunlight that streams through the bare trees above
them. In summer, plants adapted to life in the shade –
ferns and mosses – thrive in the damp and relatively
dark conditions on the forest floor. These plants, and
the insects they attract, are food for small mammals
such as mice, voles and, in North America, chipmunks.
Predators which feed on these animals include foxes and
some owls and weasels. In many temperate forests, deer
browse on the leaves of shrubs and bushes.

◁ Bluebells flower from early April to June, making
full use of the sunlight before the deciduous trees
above them are fully covered with adult leaves.

33

People and forests

Forests, particularly tropical rainforests, are home to many tribes of people and provide the world with many important products, from foods to timber. As well as balancing the levels of carbon dioxide in the atmosphere, they provide habitats for hundreds of thousands of plant and animal species which might perish elsewhere. Yet forests are constantly under threat because of a range of human activities – from harvesting trees for timber, pulp and paper to converting the land they stand on to other uses.

△ Many roads are carved through forests to improve transport links. This road runs through the largely unspoilt taiga forests of Kuusamo in Finland.

Rainforest peoples

Over a thousand tribes of forest peoples live in the rainforests. They obtain all they need from the forest, often live in small groups, yet need a large area of forest to support them. The Pygmies are Central African forest dwellers. Their small size allows them to move easily through the dense tree growth as they hunt monkeys and gather honey and fruit. The Yamomami live in the Amazon. As well as hunting animals, they cultivate gardens in the forest, growing plants for medicine, food and building materials. The Yamomami were only discovered by outsiders in the 1950s, yet already their numbers have plummeted. Their habitat is being destroyed by foresters, while tribespeople are killed by outside diseases such as measles and influenza, against which they have no natural defence.

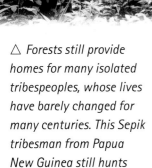

△ Forests still provide homes for many isolated tribespeoples, whose lives have barely changed for many centuries. This Sepik tribesman from Papua New Guinea still hunts using a bow and arrow.

▽ In Chile, almost half a million hectares of native forest have been cut down and replaced by plantations of fast-growing imported trees, such as Monterey pine and eucalyptus. Native animals have trouble surviving in these single-species, or monoculture, plantations.

Forest destruction

Forests have long been ravaged for their timber and to convert the land they stand on into farming fields, mining territories or new settlements. Many of the large temperate forests of the USA, Europe and New Zealand have disappeared as the human population has grown. Large areas of taiga and rainforest are under threat from modern timber gathering techniques which reach further into the most isolated areas. The forests of southern Canada are being harmed by acid rain from the industrial northern United States, while Scandinavian forests are suffering the same fate from pollution generated in western Europe. Fires, occurring naturally in a dry summer or caused by thoughtless human visitors, can also destroy large tracts of forest.

◁ *These trees in northern Europe have been damaged by acid rain. This is created when industrial pollution and motor vehicle emissions mix with oxygen and water vapour in the air.*

Forest products

For people who live outside forests, wood has been the prime forest product for thousands of years. Different timbers are used for different jobs. Elm, resistant to rotting in water, is used for harbour piers and lock gates. Mahogany and rosewood have beautiful colours and are used for decorative furniture. Many plants, such as coffee, rubber, avocado and the kola nuts used in cola drinks, all originated in rainforests.

◁ *Rainforest plants and trees are used in 20 percent of the world's medicines. This Madagascar periwinkle contains a large number of useful substances, including vincristine and vinblastine. These are used in the manufacture of drugs to fight cancer.*

▽ *Christmas Island, 360 kilometres south of Java, is home to a number of rare bird species. Phosphate mining has devastated parts of the forest, but now most of the island has been designated a national park and trees are being replanted.*

Saving forests

There are many ways in which the impact of deforestation – the destruction of forests – can be reduced, from recycling paper to protecting endangered forest species. Preserving the remaining forest areas and growing new trees to replace those already lost are the priorities. Many countries have turned large forests into protected national parks, while hundreds of initiatives are returning trees to urban wastelands and areas affected by drought or the spread of deserts. The Green Belt Movement in Kenya, for example, has planted over ten million trees in 20 years. Poorer countries often rely on their forests to generate money for their people. Sustainable forestry – planting new trees to replace those cut down – is one way to protect this source of income.

African grasslands

The tropical grasslands, or savanna, of Africa support bushes, scattered trees and an abundance of grasses. They are hot all year round, but with long dry seasons and shorter wet seasons. The grasslands are a food-rich environment for insects, some birds and large herds of plant-eating creatures such as wildebeest, zebra, gazelles and giraffes. Different animals feed on different plants, enabling the grasslands to support a vast array of grazers, which in turn are an ample food source for predators including big cats, crocodiles and birds of prey.

△ The black-headed weaverbird builds a nest from grass and twigs, hanging it high in a tree.

▽ A giraffe's extremely long neck allows it to reach the high branches of acacia trees.

△ As well as wild herds, the African grasslands support some domesticated animals. The Masai people of Kenya rely on herds of cattle, goats and sheep for food. Sometimes, cattle blood is a major food source for the Masai.

Safety from predators

The wide open grasslands of Africa provide no hiding places from predators. Grazing animals have developed three main methods of defence. Some, such as the elephant and hippopotamus, have evolved to a large size and have thick skin, making them hard to attack and wound. Animals such as the zebra and wildebeest live in large herds. Herds provide greater protection for the young, more sets of eyes to keep a lookout for danger, and the sheer mass of bodies can confuse a predator. Many herd animals use speed to escape attacks. They have long legs and hooves instead of toes, allowing them to run for long periods at full speed.

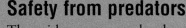

▷ Migrating herds of zebras and wildebeest drink at the Mara river in Kenya.

Megafauna

African grasslands are home to the largest land animals on Earth – hippos, rhinoceroses and the largest of them all, the African elephant. An adult male elephant stands four metres tall and can weigh seven tonnes. It uses its flexible trunk to pass roots, grass and trees to its mouth. White rhinos are grass-eaters, weighing up to three tonnes. Living in small groups, they mark out their territory with piles of dung and urine. With their immense size and power, plus a thick protective skin, megafauna have few predators and do not need to move fast. Their most serious threat comes from humans. Elephants are killed for their ivory tusks, while rhinoceros horn is prized as a medicine in Asia. Populations of both animals have been slashed, with only 5,000 white rhinos left in the wild by the year 2000.

▷ *African elephant numbers have been greatly reduced by ivory poachers. Here, tusks collected from poachers are burned.*

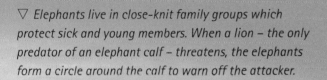

▽ *Elephants live in close-knit family groups which protect sick and young members. When a lion – the only predator of an elephant calf – threatens, the elephants form a circle around the calf to warn off the attacker.*

Great migrations

Living in giant herds provides some safety from predators, but it also poses problems for grazers. With herd sizes in their tens of thousands, land cannot support such grazing for long and the herds have to travel to different places to feed. In the Serengeti grasslands, wildebeest herds start an annual migration in May as the dry season arrives and food runs out. They head north to the long grasses of Lake Victoria and then move again to fresh grazing lands across the Mara river. By November, they return to their starting point, where new grass will support them until they begin another migration the following year.

African predators

The grazing animals of Africa's grasslands are at risk of attack from a range of powerful hunters. On land, the big cats are the most well-known predators, while crocodiles lurk in waterholes, lakes and rivers and birds of prey are a threat from the air. These animals all have strong claws or jaws to grab and bring down their prey, and sharp teeth to slice through hides and flesh – but catching prey calls for raw speed, teamwork or great ingenuity.

Overlapping roles

The predators of the African grasslands would struggle if they all hunted the same creatures and ate in the same way. So lions and crocodiles attack larger grazing animals, while cheetahs and leopards target smaller ones such as Thomson's gazelle. Rodents, insects, small birds and amphibians are hunted by the zorilla (a relative of the skunk), wild dogs and birds of prey such as the eagle and secretary bird. Once a kill is made, a series of creatures benefit. The predator takes its share but other animals may force it away to feed as well. Scavengers such as jackals, hyenas and vultures feed on carrion – the dead, rotting remains of other animal's kills. In their role as decomposers, scavengers play a vital part in the grasslands ecosystem.

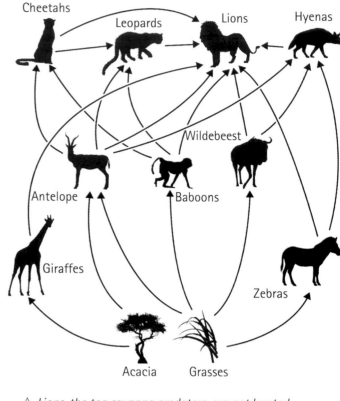

△ Lions, the top savanna predators, are not hunted by other animals, but they are threatened by drought, habitat destruction, a lack of food and killing by humans.

▽ The Nile crocodile lies in wait for drinking animals such as this wildebeest, then drags its prey underwater to drown it.

△ A lioness forces down a waterbuck in the Kruger National Park, South Africa.

Cheetahs

Smaller and lighter than other big cats, cheetahs are built for speed. They sit on rocky outcrops called kopjes, on the lookout for young wildebeest and smaller gazelles. Cheetahs hunt alone, or sometimes in groups of two or three, keeping low in the grasses to get as close as possible without alerting their prey. Their phenomenal burst of speed can be kept up only over short distances. Cheetahs eat quickly after a kill, because they are small enough to be driven off prey by scavengers such as vultures and hyenas.

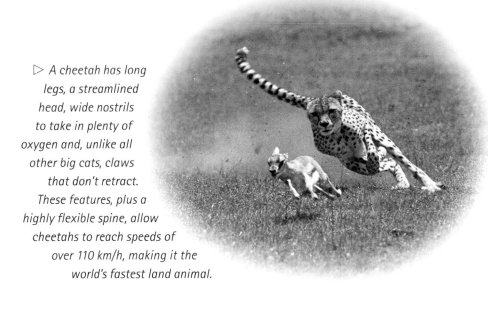

▷ A cheetah has long legs, a streamlined head, wide nostrils to take in plenty of oxygen and, unlike all other big cats, claws that don't retract. These features, plus a highly flexible spine, allow cheetahs to reach speeds of over 110 km/h, making it the world's fastest land animal.

Hyenas

Hyenas look ungainly, with oversized heads and short back legs, but they can reach speeds of 65 km/h. They spend most of the day in underground dens, then hunt their own prey and scavenge the kills of other animals at night. Hyenas hunt in large packs which harass herds of zebra or wildebeest until one is separated and brought down by sheer weight of numbers. A hyena's jaws are so powerful they can shear through a zebra's thigh bone. After a kill, individuals tear off a chunk of meat to eat away from the others.

△ Hyenas are successful hunters and scavengers, capable of defending food from other animals. This spotted hyena is chasing away a vulture.

▽ Lions live in family groups called prides, which include several females and up to four males. Although the male lions don't take part in the hunt, they are the first to feed. They are followed by the adult females and then the cubs. In hard times, the cubs are the first to starve.

Lions

Lions are the largest of the African big cats, but they are slower than some of their prey, with a top speed of 58 km/h. Only female lions hunt, both in the day and at night, relying on teamwork to ambush their prey. Up to ten lionesses approach a herd, single out an individual and fan out. One or two of the team charge the prey, forcing it towards the other lionesses hiding in the grass. The prey is usually killed by suffocation – a lioness clamps its mouth over the animal's mouth and nostrils, or bites its windpipe.

Temperate grasslands

Grasslands develop in areas which are too dry for forests to form and too wet to be deserts. Temperate grasslands have warm summers and cold winters, yet overall they tend to be cooler than savanna grasslands. Temperate grasslands include the veldt in South Africa, the pampas of South America and the central Asia steppes region. Grasslands once covered a quarter of the planet's land, but much of this is now used for agriculture. Grasslands still cover wide areas, but they can be extremely delicate and easily disrupted, as has been the case in North America.

△ The bison is the largest animal on the plains of North America. Adults weigh up to 650 kilogrammes.

▽ Burrowing owls use old prairie dog burrows as an underground nest for their chicks. They line the burrow with animal dung. The dung generates heat as it decomposes, helps mask the scent of the owls from predators, and also attracts dung beetles – a source of food for the chicks.

Bison and the plains

The North American plains and prairies once occupied 2.5 million square kilometres and were home to over 50 million bison. This large grazing mammal feeds heavily on tough grasses which are relatively low in nutrients. Bison were the main food source for native Americans, who hunted them selectively and used every piece of their prey for tools, food, clothing and shelter. With the arrival of European settlers, an ecosystem which had lasted thousands of years was severely disrupted. The settlers used horses and guns to hunt large numbers of bison. In the early 1870s, 2.5 million bison were killed each year. By 1880, only hundreds were left. A programme of conservation saved the bison from extinction and herd numbers are now around 200,000 across North America.

△ The prairie rattlesnake needs an underground refuge for the winter months. Snakes cannot dig their own holes, so they find a rock crevice or use the burrows of prairie dogs as a winter home.

A changing ecosystem

The loss of bison herds was just one of many changes to the grasslands ecosystem. Farmers began to heavily exploit the rich, fertile soil of many grassland areas. They grew wheat and other cereal crops, removing the habitat that local plants and animals needed to survive. The wheat was not as hardy as the native grasses it replaced, nor did its roots bind the soil in place as well.

Dust bowl

A period of drought in the 1930s left the soil of the North American grasslands exposed and then blown away by strong winds, creating a giant 'dust bowl'. Today, the plains and prairies have returned to intensive agriculture thanks to modern farming and irrigation techniques. Three quarters of the United States' wheat exports now come from this area, but many species of wild plants and animals have suffered as a result.

▽ Prairie dogs live in an enormous network of burrows, in family groups called cotteries. They mark the entrance to each burrow with mounds of earth, and post lookouts to keep watch for predators such as eagles and coyotes.

▽ America's Yellowstone National Park is home to around 3,500 bison. Although they appear big and slow, adult bison can gallop at speeds of up to 45 km/h.

Prairie dogs

The lack of trees on the plains means that many animals need to look elsewhere for a home. Without a deep network of tree roots, the ground is ideal for burrowing animals such as prairie dogs, a species of ground squirrel. They dig enormous systems of burrows with separate toilet, sleeping and birth chambers. Each system can extend over tens of kilometres. Old burrows are used as homes by other animals such as owls, black-legged ferrets and swift foxes. At one time, it was estimated that over 800 million prairie dogs existed in North America. Numbers are now closer to two million, after a poisoning campaign by farmers in the early 20th century, and the turning of over 98 percent of their habitat into farmland.

Grasslands

People and grasslands

Grasslands are highly productive ecosystems, providing habitats and food for a great range of plant and wild animal species. They also support large human populations all over the world through the products they can provide. A balanced grassland region recycles its water and keeps its fertile soil in place, allowing many different organisms to live there. Grasslands are also a major store of carbon – over one third of the Earth's carbon is found in grasslands, mainly in the soil. Unfortunately, the activities of humans have had a devastating effect on some grassland areas.

△ Unspoilt grassland areas are home to large numbers of wild flowering plants. The California poppy is native to grasslands which stretch along the western side of North America, from British Columbia to southern California. Native Americans in some parts of California used to boil and eat the poppy's leaves and stems.

◁ The state of Montana is part of the Great Plains region of the USA. It contains around two million hectares of wheat fields, which produced 2.62 million tonnes of wheat in 2001. Only the states of North Dakota and Kansas produce more wheat.

▽ Most of the North American prairies were ploughed up to produce farmland for growing cereal crops such as wheat and corn. In the 1930s, poor farmland management, a long drought and strong winds eroded much of the fertile soil, creating a dust bowl.

Threats to grasslands

Grasslands face a number of threats, including overgrazing and desertification – the spread of desert areas. The most common threat is their conversion by humans to other uses, such as new urban areas and, in particular, agriculture. Converting huge areas to crop-growing removes the natural habitat of many living things. New roads divide and fragment any remaining habitats, which can also be disrupted by the introduction of non-native species. Wild animals and plants are suddenly seen as pests and are eradicated by hunting and the use of pesticides, herbicides and poisons. As farming is conducted on an ever larger scale, the diversity of life in a region tends to fall.

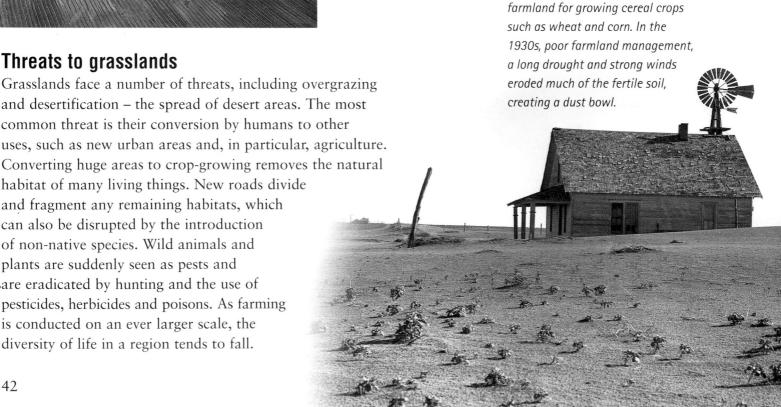

The pampas

Argentina and part of Uruguay are home to wide, largely flat, grassy plains called the pampas. Covering approximately 760,000 square kilometres, the pampas have undergone great changes since the introduction of cattle by Spanish colonial rulers. By the 19th century, large cattle herds roamed much of the pampas. Today, huge cattle ranches called estancias are run by cowhands known as gauchos. Much of the remaining pampas grasslands have been converted to growing crops such as wheat, corn, soybeans and fruits. Apart from losing their natural homes and feeding grounds, many wild animals such as rheas, the pampas deer and several species of wild cat have been hunted for their skins or killed because they are pests.

△ Geoffroy's cat is found in isolated forests and grasslands in Bolivia, Paraguay, Uruguay and southern Argentina. Until the late 1980s, it was heavily hunted for its fur, with 25 cat pelts needed to make a single fur coat.

▷ The skilled cattle herders of the pampas are known as gauchos. They immobilize and catch cattle using a boleadoras, three stones tied together with a rope, which when thrown accurately, wraps itself around the legs of a cow.

Mongolian steppes

The large central Asian country of Mongolia is one of the most sparsely populated countries in the world. Yet, because it is poor, has little industry and much of its land is barren desert, the pressures on its grasslands, known as the Mongolian steppes, are severe. Livestock products such as meat, milk and hides make up a third of its economy and with a population that is rising by two percent every year, the pressures on Mongolia's fertile land to feed everyone are growing. As a result, overgrazing is widespread. In addition, around 23 percent of Mongolia's land is at risk of desertification. This forces wildlife into over-competition for remaining food and habitat space.

▽ Mongolian herders move their livestock to summer grazing ground near Lake Hovsgol, in north-western Mongolia. Mongolian nomads sometimes have to contend with harsh conditions. In 2001, an extremely dry summer followed by a severe winter caused the loss of more than three million livestock.

☙ Deserts

With less than 250 millimetres of rainfall every year, deserts are the driest places on the planet, and occupy over 20 percent of the land surface. Of all the world's environments, deserts offer the greatest challenge to life. The soils are so poor that few plants can grow and there is little shelter from the strong winds which blow soil and sand across the surface. In some deserts, temperatures can fluctuate from extremely hot (over 40°C) in the day to below freezing at night. Deserts are often inhabited by unusual plants and animals which have adapted to the tough conditions.

△ Seen from space, the Atacama desert of Chile is a cloudless strip, running for 950 kilometres between the Pacific Ocean and the Andes mountains. In some parts of the desert, rain may not fall for a year or more.

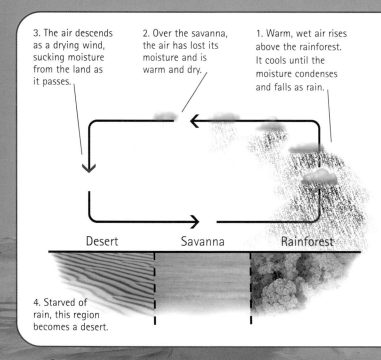

3. The air descends as a drying wind, sucking moisture from the land as it passes.

2. Over the savanna, the air has lost its moisture and is warm and dry.

1. Warm, wet air rises above the rainforest. It cools until the moisture condenses and falls as rain.

Desert   Savanna   Rainforest

4. Starved of rain, this region becomes a desert.

◁ Tropical deserts form approximately 1,500 kilometres either side of the equator – in the Tropics of Cancer to the north and in the Tropics of Capricorn to the south. The Sahara desert of north Africa, the Thar desert of the Indian subcontinent and the Victoria desert of Australia are all tropical deserts.

Continental deserts

Different types of desert are created in different ways. Continental deserts, such as the Gobi in Mongolia and China, form because they are so far from the sea that little rain ever reaches them.

Coastal deserts and rain shadow deserts

Coastal deserts form near cold seas. Air passing over the sea is cooled down, creating clouds which drop their moisture over the sea as rain or mist before reaching land. Africa's Namib desert is an example of a coastal desert. A rain shadow desert occurs where a range of mountains lies in the path of rain-carrying winds from the sea. The winds cool down over the mountains and release almost all the water they carry as rain. The land on the other side of the mountains receives little rainfall and becomes a desert. The Rocky mountains of North America and the Great Dividing Range of Australia have created deserts in this way.

△ The shovel-snouted lizard lives in the Namib desert, which stretches for 2,000 kilometres along the west coast of southern Africa. When the temperature soars into the high thirties, the lizard uses its wide snout to burrow below the surface.

Desert surfaces

People think of deserts as sandy wildernesses, but not all deserts are covered in sand. Desert winds can blow sand and other light materials away, exposing the heavier gravel, rocks and stone below. The sand is often deposited in one area as a great sea of sand dunes. These seas are called ergs, and individual dunes can be hundreds of metres high. Sometimes, a strong, turbulent wind scoops up the surface sand, generating a sandstorm which may travel hundreds of kilometres.

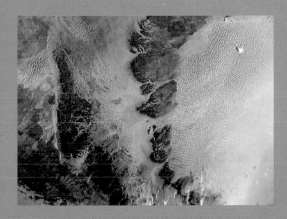

◁ Areas of sand, stony ground and rocky outcrops can all be found in the same desert. This picture from space shows part of the Sahara desert. The sandy area is a vast expanse of sand dunes, called the Murzuk Sand Sea, in the north African country of Libya. Both the sand dunes and the rocky outcrops support little life.

△ The surface of this desert on the Colorado plateau in the USA is made of sandstone – the remains of desert sand dunes which have hardened into rock over millions of years.

Water in the desert

Rainfall is not the only source of water in a desert. Coastal deserts receive moisture from mists that roll in from the sea. Mists occur regularly in the Namib desert in Africa and in the western deserts of Peru and California. Oases are another water source. Deep underground, layers of rock trap water and stop it draining away. Where these rock layers reach the surface and are eroded to form a hollow, the water is exposed. Life tends to spring up around the water, forming an oasis.

▽ An oasis is an area of fertile land in a desert, supplied all year round with fresh water. Some oases form naturally around underground springs, others are created by humans. They are often the only source of surface water for hundreds of kilometres.

✛ Water of life

Deserts are defined by their lack of water. It can be years between rains and the key to survival is making the most of the tiny amount of existing water. Desert plants are the masters here – by gathering and storing water they then make it available to animals further up the food chain. Because of the water contained in the plants, many desert animals never drink at all – the herbivores eat the plants and the carnivores eat the herbivores. However, for those animals which must drink, some ingenious solutions are required if they are to survive.

△ In times of drought, African quiver trees can shed some of their branches to reduce water loss and ensure their survival.

Gathering and keeping water

Desert plants suck up water from a wide area, using enormous webs of fine roots. Many plants store the water in a large underground tap root, out of reach of the withering sun. Others store it in their stems, which are often covered in a waxy, waterproof coating to reduce water loss by evaporation. Because of their large surface area, leaves lose a lot of water through evaporation, so in desert plants they are often small or non-existent. During droughts, some plants can actually shed their leaves – or even whole branches – to minimize their water loss.

▽ The welwitschia plant of the Namib desert has two 7-metre-long leaves that collect fog droplets and funnel them to a buried tap root at the centre of the plant.

△ Cacti have special concertina-shaped stems that can swell with water without splitting. To minimize water loss by evaporation, they have spines instead of leaves and photosynthesize through their stems. The spines also prevent attack by thirsty animals.

Animals and water

For those animals that need to drink, the desert poses huge challenges. They must be able to travel long distances between water sources, and store water efficiently in the meantime. Camels can hold up to 40 litres of water in the fat of their humps, enabling them to travel up to 1,000 kilometres without drinking. By contrast, the sandgrouse must drink every day, but while adults can fly far to find water, their flightless chicks cannot. The adults solve this problem by sitting in water holes, soaking up water into their sponge-like feathers, and then carrying it to the chicks. Another ingenious adaptation is that of the fogstand beetle, which collects water from mist by allowing it to condense on its body.

▷ When sea mists roll in across the Namib desert, the fogstand beetle rushes to the tops of sand dunes, lifts its back into the air and waits for fog to condense on its shell. The water droplets then run down its raised back and into its mouth.

△ The sandgrouse's feathers are specially adapted to retain water. They must absorb a large amount, because much of it will be lost on the flight back to their nest.

▽ The spadefoot toad emerges from the ground after the rains to mate and lay eggs. The eggs hatch, and the young frogs retreat underground before drought returns.

The coming of the rains

If rain eventually comes, the desert bursts into life. Amphibians emerge from hibernation to breed in the temporary desert pools. Seeds that have lain dormant, or inactive, begin to grow – but only if there is sufficient water. Many seeds are covered in a chemical that stops them growing unless it is completely washed off, which only a large amount of rain will do. The seeds grow quickly, flowering within days to attract the insects that follow the rains. After pollination, the plants set seed, wither and die, having lived only a few weeks.

▽ For a brief period after the annual rains, the desert is full of life. Plants and animals take advantage of the season to reproduce and store up food and water.

🌵 Surviving the heat

If animals become too hot, they die. Overheating is a major threat to survival in the extreme temperatures of some deserts. Animals in other biomes cool down by sweating or panting. Water evaporates from their bodies, taking away heat as it leaves. But in the desert, where every drop of water is vital, animals stay cool in other ways. Many desert animals are pale in colour, because pale shades reflect more heat than darker colours. Other ways to avoid the heat are burrowing underground, sheltering in shade and foraging for food at night.

△ Scorpions are mainly found in desert areas, although some live in other habitats. Female scorpions give birth to many young, who spend the first week or two of their lives on their mother's back. Once they climb down, they lead an independent life.

△ A gemsbok oryx in the Kalahari desert, South Africa. Oryx spend the day seeking shade. They never drink and rely on obtaining water from the plants they eat at night.

The cool night

Most desert animals are active at night, when the desert is much cooler. Spiders and scorpions scuttle out of their lairs to hunt. Scorpions use hairs which are highly sensitive to air movements to track down insects, small rodents and lizards. Scorpions grip their prey with powerful pincers, then rip it apart with strong jaws. A scorpion only uses its sting on large prey. Night is also the best time for plant-eating creatures to feed. Dew forms on the plants, increasing their water content from a few percent to as much as 40 percent.

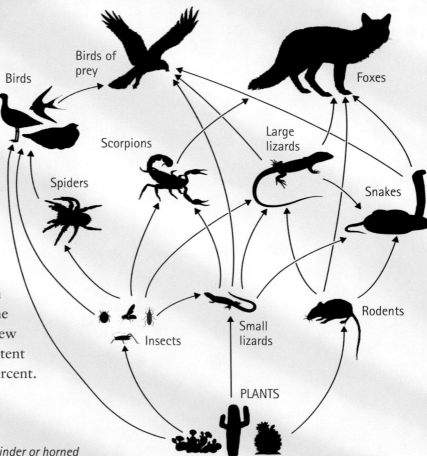

◁ The sidewinder or horned rattlesnake moves in S-shaped waves. This means that only a tiny part of the snake's body touches the baking ground.

△ The food web in the desert is smaller and less complex than in other biomes. Foxes, birds of prey and snakes are at the top of the food chains.

Going underground

The surface of the desert can reach temperatures of over 70°C, yet just a few centimetres below ground it is much cooler. Many animals live underground to avoid the potentially lethal heat on the surface. The sandfish is a lizard with small, close-fitting scales which allow it to wriggle through the sand with a side-to-side movement similar to a fish. Some desert animals, such as desert toads, remain dormant deep underground until the summer rains fill ponds. Then they climb to the surface, breed, lay eggs and replenish their body reserves of food and water before returning underground.

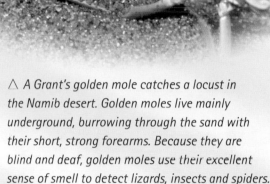

△ A Grant's golden mole catches a locust in the Namib desert. Golden moles live mainly underground, burrowing through the sand with their short, strong forearms. Because they are blind and deaf, golden moles use their excellent sense of smell to detect lizards, insects and spiders.

△ Elf owls are the smallest owls, about the size of a sparrow. They live in deserts, dry grasslands and savanna, nesting in holes in cacti or trees and hunting insects at night. These elf owls are sheltering in a saguaro cactus. The hole was made by a woodpecker for its own nest in the past.

Desert homes

For many desert animals, home is a burrow dug into the sand which protects them from the sun. A fennec fox's burrow is a tunnel up to ten metres long, while the kangaroo rat's burrow contains storage areas for food. Camel spiders and wind scorpions block their burrow entrances with plugs of sand to keep out the heat. The giant saguaro cacti of America's Sonoran desert are home to several bird species. Ladderback woodpeckers chisel out holes in a cactus high above the ground, where it is cooler. When the woodpeckers move on, desert owls inhabit their old nesting holes.

▷ The fennec fox lives in deserts in northern Africa and the Middle East. It is the smallest fox, but has large ears which act as cooling devices. The fennec spends most of the day in an underground burrow. It hunts at night, using its large ears to detect insects and rodents.

49

4 People and deserts

Just as animals have found ways to survive in the world's deserts, so have people. Some people live near oases, farming and living off the fertile land close to the water supply. Other desert peoples live as nomads, moving from place to place with herds of animals or eking out an existence by hunting, gathering and trading. The harsh environment has a great impact on how desert people live, but the human impact on deserts is even more dramatic. Many deserts are growing larger as neighbouring areas have been overfarmed and poorly managed.

▽ A Mongolian nomad and his tented home, or yurt. Traditional yurts have a wooden frame covered with felt or animal skin. The yurt is pitched wherever the nomad finds good pasture for his herds.

△ Bedouin peoples live a nomadic existence in the Sahara, Syrian and Arabian deserts. They herd their animals across the desert, following the rains in search of grazing land. Flowing robes and head-dresses shield the Bedouin from the fierce sun and wind-driven sands.

Desert nomads

In the past, most desert dwellers were nomads who herded goats, camels and cattle, or they were hunter-gatherers, such as the San peoples of the Kalahari desert. Others, like the Tuareg, controlled the trade routes of the Sahara. They carried gold and ivory in large caravans of camels. Today, life is very different. Droughts have reduced the size of the nomads' herds, and national borders make it impossible to wander as freely as in the past. New roads have restricted the importance of camel caravans, which now carry mainly salt rather than the riches of before. Many desert peoples have been forced to settle and seek work in oases or in towns away from the desert.

◁ For thousands of years, people have used camels to travel across desert regions. These Bactrian camels can carry a heavy load on average 50 kilometres per day. All camels store food as fat in their humps and can go without water for more than two weeks.

Desertification

Desertification is the spread of desert environments. It is a growing problem in many parts of the world – as much as 60,000 square kilometres of new desert are created every year. These lands are less able to support life of any kind – wild species, livestock, crops and people. Desertification is caused by the planet becoming warmer and drier, which means there is less water to support plants and animals. Human activity also has a major effect. Deforestation, overgrazing and certain types of farming result in ground losing its covering of plants. The exposed topsoil, which is vital to plant growth, may be blown away. Without topsoil, water runs away, wells and springs dry up and what plant life remains is threatened.

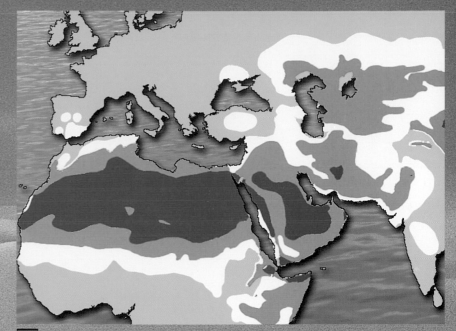

■ Extreme desert
□ Arid zone at risk of further desertification
□ Semi-arid zone at risk of desertification

△ This map shows the spread of deserts in northern Africa and Eurasia .

Desert management

Stopping a desert from spreading is difficult and costly. Animals and people are moved from land under threat to avoid overgrazing and allow plants to recover or be reseeded. Keeping the soil in place is vital. Windbreaks reduce the amount of soil blown away. Covering the soil with a layer of leaves, straw and sawdust is called mulching. This enriches the soil, keeps it in place and cuts down water loss due to evaporation. Irrigation is the channelling of water to a dry area. One technique is called centre-pivot irrigation. Water is pumped up to the surface from deep underground and distributed over a large circular area.

△ The Sahel is a dry savanna region south of the Sahara desert. Severe droughts and an increase in the number of people and grazing animals have caused major desertification. In places, the Sahara desert has spread south by more than 100 kilometres since the 1950s.

▽ A rock painting from AD300 shows a cow and herder in the Sahara region, suggesting that the Sahara once supported grazing animals.

▽ Seen from space, the desert near the Tuwayq mountains in Saudi Arabia shows the effects of centre-pivot irrigation. Dark circles are watered areas where crops are being grown. Lighter circles are fields currently without crops.

The tundra

In the far north, where the trees end and the Arctic ice begins, lies the tundra. This bleak, windswept biome makes up 15 percent of the Earth's land area. The soil under the surface is permanently frozen, and mosses, lichens and a few shrubs are the only plants that can survive the long, snowbound winter. But during the brief summer, flowers bloom in their millions and migrating creatures arrive to eat and breed before the winter sets in again.

△ *The Arctic fox's pure white winter coat provides perfect camouflage. It preys mainly on lemmings, storing some of its kills in ice caverns for when times are hard.*

▽ *In the short summer, which begins in June, the surface temperature can reach 25°C and the tundra bursts into life. Plants such as these lupins carpet the landscape, while insects thrive in the warm conditions, attracting thousands of migrating birds.*

Hardy survivors

During the dark winter, when temperatures can fall as low as −60°C, the tundra is one of the most inhospitable places on Earth. However, there are creatures that live here all year round. Lemmings survive the bitter cold in complex underground tunnels, feeding on the roots of plants above them. In turn, the lemmings provide food for hunters such as the Arctic fox and snowy owl.

▷ *Wolf packs appear from the taiga forests in summer, following the herds of caribou (below). Using teamwork, they pick off weak members of the herds, then harass them for hours until the weary beasts can be attacked safely. Flocks of ravens follow the wolves, stealing titbits from their kills.*

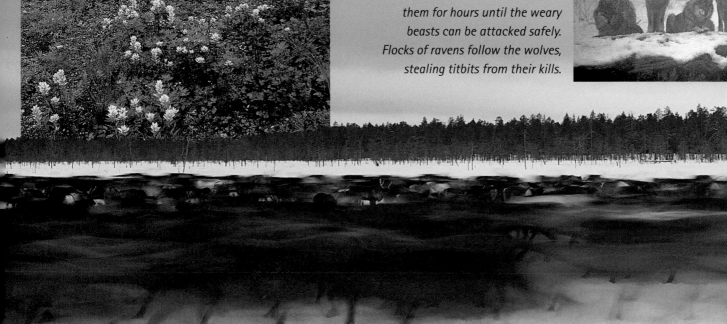

◁ Lemmings are a key part of the tundra food web. Remaining active in burrows under the winter snows, lemmings can produce eight litters of nine young each year. This huge population sustains many of the tundra's predators.

Migration routes

Millions of migrating birds flock to the tundra to breed in summer, attracted by the vast number of insects with which to feed their young. The tundra has relatively few predators, making it an inviting place for birds such as the Arctic tern. These long-distance travellers fly 35,000 kilometres each year, journeying from summer in the Antarctic to summer in the Arctic and back again. They navigate by the Sun and stars, and by an inbuilt compass that is sensitive to changes in the Earth's magnetic field.

The land reborn

With the coming of summer, the snow melts and the soil at the surface unfreezes. The ground beneath is still frozen, however, and prevents the meltwater from draining away. This makes the tundra in summer a boggy place, ideal for insect life such as mosquitoes, blackflies and springtails.

Safety in numbers

Every summer, huge herds of caribou head north, leaving the forests in which they have spent the winter, to graze on the rich vegetation that blooms briefly over the tundra. The caribou move constantly, never overgrazing the delicate lichens, which can take up to 40 years to regrow. Wolves shadow them at all times – if they attack, the caribou form a circle around their calves. In winter, hunters and hunted return to the forests.

▽ Snowy owls catch lemmings by using their highly developed hearing to pinpoint tiny rustling sounds under the snow.

△ Large numbers of caribou return to the relative safety of the forests during the winter months. They migrate in herds of up to 10,000 animals.

The Arctic ice

Further north of the taiga forests and the Arctic tundra lies the Arctic ice cap. This area of sea and ice is intensely cold. During winter, which lasts almost six months, the Sun does not rise in the Arctic skies, sending temperatures plummeting as low as –60°C. This icy world supports almost no plant growth, but the waters around and beneath it teem with life. Mammals such as the polar bear, Arctic fox, walrus and seal have adapted to the bitter cold, insulated by thick layers of fat called blubber.

Growing and shrinking

The North Pole is covered by an immense ice sheet, most of which floats on the Arctic Ocean. This is a polar ice cap, forming an area larger than Europe. The boundaries of the sheet are constantly changing. In spring, the edges of the ice cap start to melt, causing large chunks of ice to break away from the main mass. By mid-summer, the polar ice cap has almost halved in size. The ice returns to its full extent in winter, but scientists have noted that overall the ice cap appears to be shrinking greatly – both in thickness and area. Many scientists believe that global warming is to blame.

△ The Arctic ice sheet grows and shrinks with the seasons. This map shows its average extent over a year.

▽ The orca, or killer whale, uses echolocation – a type of sonar – to detect prey. It emits high-pitched clicks and senses the sounds as they bounce back off solid objects such as fish, sea turtles, seals and even other whales.

▷ Ice breaking off from the edge of the Arctic ice sheet can form floating icebergs. They are much larger than they look, because most of the ice floats below the water surface. Some icebergs may weigh hundreds of thousands of tonnes.

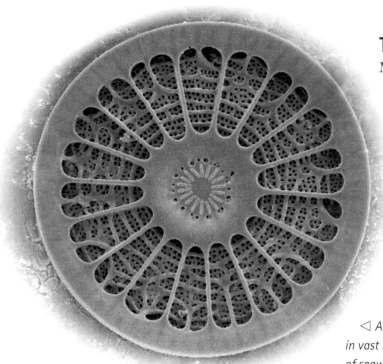

The basis for life

Many animals, including three quarters of a million whales and other sea mammals, migrate to the Arctic in summer, when the feeding conditions and climate are less hostile. Others spend their whole lives there, supported by the rich food sources of the Arctic Ocean. Food chains start with diatoms, which are types of plant plankton – microscopic organisms which float in the water. The plankton provide ample food for crustaceans and smaller marine animals which, in turn, support huge shoals of fish and shellfish. These are preyed upon by a range of hunters, including seals and walruses.

◁ A diatom viewed under a microscope. Diatoms live in vast numbers in both seas and freshwater. One glass of seawater can contain more than two million diatoms.

▽ Walruses grow up to 4.3 metres long and can weigh 900 kilogrammes. They use their metre-long tusks to haul themselves over the ice.

Walruses and seals

Each summer, when the pack ice breaks up and floats around in large chunks, walruses travel with it. They cover up to 5,000 kilometres before winter sets in and the ice locks together again. Walruses use these ice floes as bases from which to hunt mainly shellfish, but also snails, worms and sea cucumbers. They spend most of their life in the sea, surfacing with the aid of air sacs in their throat which act in a similar way to a lifejacket. Some species of seal, such as the ring seal, live deep inside the Arctic circle. Ring seals hunt fish under the ice, surfacing to breathe air at small holes. Seals are a vital part of the Arctic food web, as they are eaten by polar bears, killer whales and walruses.

▽ Polar bears ambush seals as they surface at breathing holes in the ice. Scavengers such as the Arctic fox may eat the remains of a kill.

Polar bears

Standing three metres tall and weighing up to 770 kilogrammes, polar bears are the world's largest land carnivores. They live and breed on the ice, but are excellent swimmers, hunting seals and, occasionally, walruses in the water. Their wide, partially webbed front paws are used as paddles, while they steer with their hind feet. On land, they are capable of short bursts of speed up to 40 km/h and are strong enough to smash in the heavy ice roofs which protect young seals in their nurseries. Polar bears rarely drink water – they get most of the moisture they need from seal blubber.

❄ Antarctica

Antarctica is the coldest and windiest place on Earth, with winter temperatures as low as –89°C and winds reaching 300 kilometres per hour. The continent only receives about as much water as the Sahara desert, but it falls as snow. Not all of Antarctica is covered in ice. A range of mountains almost 5,000 kilometres long splits it in two, leaving bare rock outcrops and valleys which support little life.

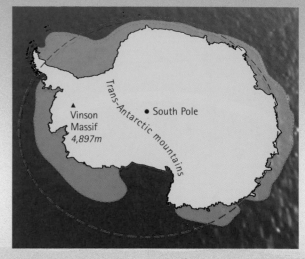

Vinson Massif 4,897m

● South Pole

Trans-Antarctic mountains

☐ Land mass

╱ Antarctic circle

☐ Minimum extent of ice sheet

△ Pack ice surrounds the Antarctic land mass and extends out into the southern oceans. The ice sheet grows and shrinks with the seasons.

Life on the continent

Antarctica's climate is so severe that little can live permanently on the land. Plant life consists mainly of simple algae, lichens and mosses. These provide food for some small insects and micro-organisms and, nearer the coast, certain seabirds. In contrast to the barren land, the seas around Antarctica teem with life. Krill, small shrimp-like animals that feed on plankton, live in massive swarms. Krill are a major food source for many animals, especially whales.

▽ Krill grow up to five centimetres long and live in swarms that can be several kilometres wide. In places, the krill live so closely together that as many as 20,000 occupy a single cubic metre.

△ The red tint in this aerial photograph of the McLeod glacier in Antarctica is caused by red snow algae.

Whales

Seals, penguins and fish all feed on krill, but the biggest consumer of all is the whale. A number of species of whale, including the blue whale and the humpback, migrate to Antarctica in summer especially to feed on krill. Krill-eating whales have horny plates in their mouths called baleen plates, which act as a filter. Whales take a mouthful of sea water and krill, close their mouths and force the water out through the plates with their tongue.

▷ The blue whale is the largest animal on Earth. It can measure up to 30 metres long and weigh up to 200 tonnes.

△ The ice fish is unique in the animal kingdom. It is the only vertebrate which does not contain haemoglobin – a substance that helps transport oxygen around the body – in its blood.

Ashore to breed

Antarctica has no large land predators, making it a safe environment to bring up young. Food can only be found on the shore, so most animals which come on to land to breed stay near the coast. Emperor penguins and petrels are two rare exceptions. Albatrosses breed on Antarctic islands, where the parents can leave their single chick for days as they hunt for food. Huge elephant seals only come ashore to breed and moult. The males arrive first and fight for space. The females join them, pregnant from the previous year's breeding. The pups are fed on rich milk to build up insulating blubber.

Cold seas

Despite the rich supply of food and oxygen, fish struggle to live in the intense cold of the southern oceans. Of the 21,000 species of fish in the world, only 120 can be found in Antarctica, including eel-pouts and the Patagonian toothfish. Most of these have chemicals in their blood called glycoproteins. These act as an antifreeze and lower the temperature at which the fish would normally freeze and die.

△ Emperor penguins come ashore in the autumn and journey up to 100 kilometres inland to their breeding grounds. The female lays a single egg which the male incubates in a pouch through the winter.

▷ This leopard seal has captured an Adélie penguin in the Antarctic waters.

Squid and penguins

Squid are abundant in the waters around the Antarctic. These relatives of the octopus have ten arms and move quickly, propelled by water jets. Yet they are easy prey for a variety of seabirds such as penguins and albatrosses. Penguins, in turn, are victims of leopard seals. Long, sleek and fast, the leopard seal confuses a penguin with its rapid movement before using powerful, wide-hinged jaws to catch it, bite the head and legs off and then consume the body whole.

People and the poles

The two polar regions have had very different histories of contact with humans. The Inuit people have long lived in the Arctic, carefully using its resources, but in the last 150 years, modern hunting and industry have exploited more and more of the Arctic tundra. Protected by pack ice, no one set foot on Antarctica at all until 1821, when seal hunters and whalers began to plunder its waters. Today, however, the frozen continent is used purely for scientific research.

▽ Although the Inuit of today use modern weapons to hunt, they still maintain many of their traditions. Their igloos, built from ice, are temporary shelters used during the winter seal-hunting season.

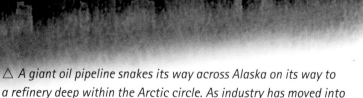

△ A giant oil pipeline snakes its way across Alaska on its way to a refinery deep within the Arctic circle. As industry has moved into the Arctic, it has disrupted the delicate ecosystems of this biome.

Inuits and the Arctic

Traditionally, the nomadic Inuits lived entirely by hunting, stalking Arctic animals in their kayak canoes and killing them with harpoons. They wasted no resources – their lamps and cooking stoves were powered by blubber, and they used huge whale bones to build their homes, lining them with seal skins for insulation.

Modern Arctic exploitation

European hunters brought disaster to the Inuit. By 1860, more than half their people had been wiped out by European diseases and, since then, their way of life has been steadily eroded. Today, many areas of the Arctic are under threat of pollution from giant industrial corporations which exploit its oil and gas reserves.

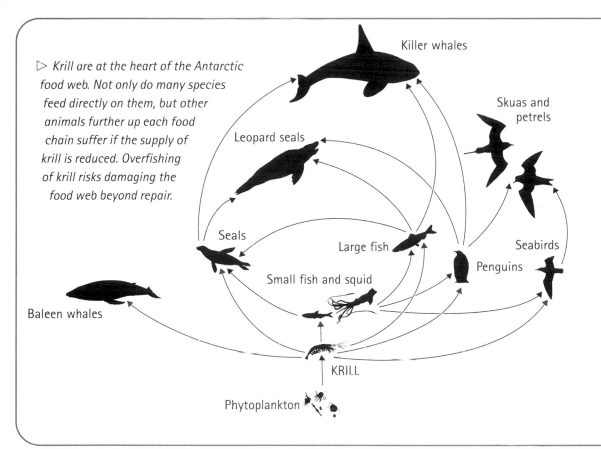

▷ Krill are at the heart of the Antarctic food web. Not only do many species feed directly on them, but other animals further up each food chain suffer if the supply of krill is reduced. Overfishing of krill risks damaging the food web beyond repair.

Killer whales

Skuas and petrels

Leopard seals

Seals

Large fish

Seabirds

Penguins

Small fish and squid

Baleen whales

KRILL

Phytoplankton

Modern dangers

Today's threats to the Antarctic biome focus on two key members of the food web. High radiation caused by the growing ozone hole above the Antarctic threatens the floating single-celled plants – phytoplankton – on which the entire biome depends. The vast shoals of shrimp-like krill, which provide food for much of the Antarctic ecosystem, are also in danger from modern commercial fishing.

Antarctic whaling

The Antarctic biome was most disrupted by whalers in the 19th and 20th centuries. They sought valuable baleen plates – the horny plates in many whales' mouths – and oil, which were used for everything from margarine to umbrellas. The whalers mainly hunted blue whales, the biggest of all, shooting them with exploding harpoons. When blue whales were almost wiped out, the hunters turned to fin, sei and minke whales. In 1988, with many whales on the brink of extinction, the whaling nations agreed a self-imposed ban. Today, whale numbers are increasing slowly, but they still total only 15 percent of the original population. Fortunately, this level of disruption has not occurred on land. A few scientists are the only people who have been allowed to make settlements on the Antarctic landmass.

△ In the early 20th century, whaling stations, such as this one on the island of South Georgia, were the centre of the industry. With the arrival of factory ships in the 1920s, whole whales could be processed at sea, and the speed of slaughter rose quickly. In 1930 alone, 30,000 blue whales were killed.

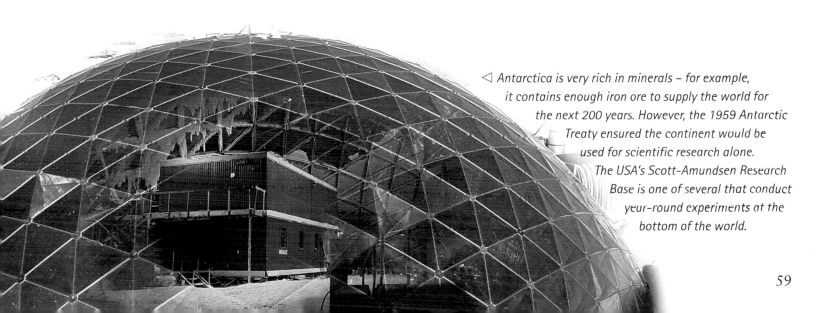

◁ Antarctica is very rich in minerals – for example, it contains enough iron ore to supply the world for the next 200 years. However, the 1959 Antarctic Treaty ensured the continent would be used for scientific research alone. The USA's Scott-Amundsen Research Base is one of several that conduct year-round experiments at the bottom of the world.

Islands

Islands are isolated land masses surrounded by water. Many were formed by volcanic activity causing new land to rise up from the sea bed. The Galapagos Islands, Iceland and Tahiti were created in this way. Other islands begin as a coral reef surrounding a volcanic island. The island gradually sinks under the weight of the volcano, until all that remains above the surface of the water is a ring-shaped reef of coral known as an atoll.

▽ *These are the fruit of the coco de mer, a palm tree unique to the Seychelles Islands in the Indian Ocean. Each fruit takes ten years to mature and can weigh over 22 kilogrammes.*

Special ecosystems

Island ecosystems may vary greatly from those found in mainland areas. Animals that have become extinct in the more competitive environments of the mainland may survive on islands. Isolated from the rest of the world, many island plants and animals have developed into new species which are endemic – unique to that island. Some island animals shrink over generations, as the limited resources are better able to support large numbers of smaller creatures. Fossils show that pygmy elephants once lived in the Mediterranean and the East Indies, for example. On islands which lack big predators, some species developed into larger versions – giant tortoises and crabs, three-metre-tall flightless birds and dog-sized rats, for example.

▷ *Christmas Island is home to an estimated 100 million red crabs. Every autumn, the crabs migrate to the coast to mate and lay their eggs.*

Reaching islands

Islands tend to support fewer species than an equivalent area on the mainland, because the sea acts as a barrier. Plants and animals overcome this in several ways. Sea mammals and birds have no problem reaching an island, sometimes carrying seeds or insects with them. The seeds of some plants, such as the coconut, can float and are dispersed by the sea. Very light seeds are carried long distances by winds, while small animals and plants reach islands by floating on rafts of vegetation.

◁ The Rock Islands of Palau, in the Pacific Ocean, are formed from the remains of coral. Wave action and coral-eating molluscs called chitons have eaten away at the islands, giving them their unusual shape.

▷ The top predator of the Galapagos Islands, the Galapagos hawk, sits on top of a giant Galapagos tortoise. The tortoise eats prickly pears, water ferns, cactus and fruits, but can live for up to a year without food or water.

The Galapagos Islands

The 19 islands that make up the Galapagos lie in the Pacific Ocean, approximately 1,000 kilometres from the South American coast. Undiscovered by humans until the 16th century, Galapagos is famous for its large number of endemic species. Most Galapagos animals are thought to have originated in South and Central America, but they have adapted and evolved into separate species. For example, the marine iguana is the only iguana lizard which swims and feeds on seaweeds, while giant tortoises, which can weigh over 200 kilogrammes, are believed to be the longest-living land animals. Plants are an equally important part of the Galapagos ecosystem – over a third of species are endemic.

▷ The coconut palm originated in Southeast Asia but has spread throughout much of the tropics. Its giant fruits – coconuts – float in water. This enables the tree to disperse its seeds over long distances, carried by the sea. Once a coconut floats ashore in a suitable place, such as this beach in the Seychelles, it can germinate.

Ecological niches

Most islands have limited resources, but offer a range of ecological niches. Island plants and animals seek to fill a niche in order to survive. Similar animals may evolve and adapt to avoid competing for the same food sources. In the Galapagos, for example, the many species of Darwin's finch are believed to share a common ancestor. Each type of bird has adapted to fill a different niche by evolving a particular beak size and shape suited to a certain diet. Some have long, thin bills to probe flowers for nectar, while others have strong, stout beaks for pecking wood or eating insects.

▷ Found in the Galapagos Islands, the woodpecker finch is one of the few birds in the world to use tools. The birds use cactus spines or twigs to pry insects and larvae from cacti or from beneath tree bark.

Large islands

Large islands tend to be formed by volcanic activity, by a rise in sea levels which cuts off a land mass from the mainland, or through continental drift – the moving apart of land continents. Sometimes, large islands are created by two of these processes. Australia was initially formed as a result of millions of years of continental drift. Then the partial melting of the polar ice caps about 10,000 years ago caused sea levels to rise, splitting New Zealand and Tasmania from the Australian mainland.

△ Mount Etna, on the large Mediterranean island of Sicily, is Europe's highest volcano and one of the most active in the world. Etna has erupted hundreds of times in recorded history.

Natural arks

Apart from being places where new species evolve, some isolated islands are natural arks. In other words, they preserve descendants of animals which have vanished elsewhere, for example Australia's marsupials – the pouched mammals such as the kangaroo and koala. The world's fourth largest island, Madagascar, in the Indian Ocean, is one of the most ecologically diverse places in the world. It has over 8,000 species of plants, including 1,000 different orchids and more types of palm – 175 species – than are found in the entire continent of Africa. Lemurs, tenrecs, two thirds of the world's chameleon species and many types of nesting bird are found only in Madagascar. Many familiar animals such as rabbits, moles, monkeys, apes, toads and newts are missing. These species never reached the island after it split from Africa.

△ About the size of a house cat, the ring-tailed lemur is found only on the large island of Madagascar. It spends up to 40 percent of the day on forest floors, seeking out fruit, leaves, flowers and occasionally insects.

◁ Koalas are unique to Australia. Their name comes from an Aboriginal saying which means 'no drink'. The koala rarely drinks water, usually obtaining enough moisture from the leaves of eucalyptus trees – its only source of food.

▽ One of the rarest of all flightless birds, the takahe was thought to be extinct, but was rediscovered in 1948. Its small wings are used only in courtship and in displays of aggression.

Flightless birds

For all its ecological diversity, Madagascar has only eight species of mammal carnivore – the striped civet, the fossa and six species of mongoose. Typically, large islands have few large predators, which explains why most of the 40 species of flightless bird still in existence today are found on islands. These include kiwis, takahes and kakapos in New Zealand, and the cassowary of New Guinea and Australia. They evolved from flying ancestors which settled on an island and, with little or no predatory threat, gradually lost their ability to fly. The arrival on many isolated islands of humans, along with introduced predators such as dogs, posed new threats to many flightless birds. Species including the dodo, from Mauritius, and the two-to three-metre-tall elephant bird of Madagascar have become extinct in the past 350 years.

▽ Uluru, a giant rocky monolith in Australia's Great Western desert, is a sacred site for the local Aboriginal peoples and a major tourist destination. Red kangaroos, several species of bats and many reptiles can be found in the national park surrounding Uluru.

Differing habitats

Small islands can offer a range of habitats, from coral reefs to lush woodland groves. Larger islands can feature dozens of habitats and sometimes completely different biomes. Australia, comprising 7.6 million square kilometres of land, has three major biomes. Tropical rainforest is found on the eastern coast while the centre is dominated by huge, dry deserts. Much of the remainder of Australia is savanna grassland. Each biome supports many different habitats, creating thousands of ecological niches for plants and animals to fill.

Australian wildlife

Australia was once part of a supercontinent known as Gondwanaland. Continental drift caused Australia to break away from the mainland and, over a period of between 55 and 60 million years, move gradually towards its current position. Isolated from evolutionary developments in the rest of the world, Australia has developed its own distinct ecosystems, habitats and wildlife. In many cases, Australian animals are quite unlike anything found elsewhere in the world.

△ The cassowary, a flightless bird, grows up to 1.75 metres tall. It eats fruits and occasionally dead birds and marsupials in the rainforests of northern Queensland.

Marsupials

Most female mammals have an organ called a placenta. This connects an unborn mammal to its mother's bloodstream, allowing the young to stay inside the mother until it is well developed. Placental mammals colonized Earth millions of years ago, but Australia, isolated from the rest of the world, provided a home for older, non-placental mammals. These included marsupials – mammals with pouches – such as the kangaroo, wallaby, koala, bandicoot and wombat. Like all mammals, marsupials bear live young, but the gestation period inside the mother is very short. Newborn young are very small and weak. For many months after birth they live inside their mother's pouch, suckling milk until they are more developed. Nearly all of Australia's 140 species of marsupial are not found anywhere else in the world.

△ An echidna is a monotreme that feeds on ants and termites. It tears into mounds or nests with its sharp front claws and pointed snout, catching the insects with its sticky tongue. An echidna does not have teeth. Instead, it crushes prey between horny pads in its mouth.

▷ A red kangaroo joey weighs little more than a gram at birth and is just two centimetres long. It remains in its mother's pouch for five to six months and then spends many more months in and out of the pouch before it is fully independent.

Monotremes

Another group of Australian mammals without a placenta are monotremes, such as the echidna and the duck-billed platypus. Instead of giving birth to live young, monotremes lay eggs. The echidna looks like a hedgehog, with sharp quills covering its body. Female echidnas lay a single egg in a burrow. After it hatches, the blind and hairless baby attaches itself to a milk patch on its mother for up to 12 weeks, until its spines start to grow. The duck-billed platypus lays two or three eggs in a grass-lined nest. Newly-hatched babies are under two centimetres long, but eventually grow to an adult size of around 50 centimetres.

△ The quoll is a nocturnal, meat-eating marsupial. During the day it retreats to a burrow, a rock pile or a hollow log. At night, it hunts for rats, birds, frogs, rabbits and insects.

Australian predators

Despite its large size, Australia, like most islands, supports relatively few large predators. In place of the big wild cats and wolves that exist elsewhere are carnivorous marsupials such as several species of quoll and the Tasmanian devil. About the size of a small dog but incredibly fierce and aggressive, the Tasmanian devil has powerful jaws and teeth capable of cutting through bone. It is one of the few animals which kills and eats its own species. Small mammals, birds and other animals are hunted by a number of other predators, including birds and venomous snakes. The taipan is believed to be the most deadly snake in the world – an adult carries enough poison to kill 200 sheep.

Introduced species

The first known peoples to reach Australia, the Aboriginals, arrived over 40,000 years ago. They brought with them a number of alien species, including a wild Asian dog called the dingo. From the 1780s onwards, British and then European settlers introduced a range of new species to Australia. Camels were imported in the 19th century as pack animals for the hot, dry desert interior. Other alien species have had a profound impact on Australian ecosystems. Cattle and sheep have altered large grassland areas, while water buffalo have damaged wetland habitats. The poisonous cane toad and the rabbit, both introduced in small numbers, have multiplied into populations of millions, disrupting fragile natural ecosystems and becoming major agricultural pests.

△ A wild dromedary camel in the Northern Territory of Australia. Today, between 60,000 and 90,000 wild camels roam the island's deserts and grasslands.

▷ Dingoes live alone or in small family groups. Their flexible diet includes rats, frogs, injured wallabies and even fruit. Dingoes' main effect on native ecosystems was to out-compete marsupial carnivores for food. The Tasmanian devil, for example, was once found throughout Australia but is now limited to Tasmania.

People and islands

Since the earliest times, humans have modified or transformed the environments in which they live. Islands are no exception. Set apart from mainland areas, smaller islands in particular can find their ecosystems dramatically changed by the arrival of human colonists. For example, although islands make up only a small fraction of the total land on Earth, approximately one third of the world's plants threatened with extinction grow on islands.

Historic human impact

Easter Island lies in the south Pacific, more than 3,000 kilometres from any other inhabited land. It is one of the most isolated islands in the world, yet Polynesian voyagers managed to reach it in around AD400. The first phase of their impact saw them introduce chickens, pigs and certain plants to the island. The second, more destructive phase, came with their statue-making and overpopulation. At its peak, the population of 10,000 people was too great for the island's ecosystem to support. Lush palm forests were destroyed for farmland, firewood and for devices to help build and transport the statues. Without the forests, soil nutrients were washed away and many native animals and plants became extinct. The human population shrank as food became scarce, leading to conflicts and even cannibalism.

△ An ancient Moai statue, with its distinctive long nose and deep-set eyes, stands near the coast of Easter Island. Almost 900 of these statues, averaging four metres in height and 14 tonnes in weight, were carved out of rock from the sunken volcanic crater at Rano Raraku.

◁ For thousands of years, humans have reached islands using simple boats, rafts and canoes. The Polynesian peoples travelled thousands of kilometres in canoes with an outrigger, a float which adds stability.

Alien species

New species may reach an island in natural ways, such as flying or floating, or be introduced deliberately by humans – sometimes with a profound impact on ecosystems. The native life of the Hawaiian Islands has suffered in this way. The ancient Polynesians brought with them pigs, chickens and dogs, which both hunted and out-competed certain native animals. The western mosquitofish, introduced more recently to control mosquitoes, has been a major factor in the decline of certain native fishes and damselflies. Feral pigs, related to European wild boars, roam parts of Hawaii, killing plants by crushing them or gnawing at their roots.

Human development

As technology has advanced and populations have risen, humans have transformed many island environments. Mediterranean islands such as Majorca, Ibiza and Malta are now major tourist resorts, housing millions. Native plants and animals have suffered from the resulting pollution and habitat destruction. On some islands, such as New Zealand, humans have cleared large forests to grow crops or rear livestock. Mauritius, in the Indian Ocean, was uninhabited by humans until the 17th century, but is now home to 1.2 million people. Most lowland areas have been cleared to grow crops, and only one percent of native vegetation remains along the island's rivers and volcanic peaks. Mauritius' coral reefs have also suffered, degraded by pollution and by dynamite fishing.

△ The mongoose was introduced to Hawaii by European settlers to kill off rats – also introduced by humans – in sugar cane fields. Instead, the mongoose strayed out of the fields to hunt many species of ground-nesting birds, such as the nene goose.

▽ Human impact at its most extreme saw small coral islands in the Pacific used as sites to test nuclear weapons. This nuclear test, one of the largest ever, completely destroyed Elugelab Island in 1952.

▽ The humid and rainy climate of the island of Mauritius is well suited to growing sugar cane. Almost all of the island's lowland areas – approximately 85 percent of its total area – have been cleared for sugar cane fields.

Human impact
Urban wildlife

Urban ecosystems cover about 4.5 percent of the world's surface. At a time when many biomes are shrinking, urban environments are greatly expanding, as new settlements are created and old ones spread outwards. Cities have always supported far more life than just humans and their domesticated animals. Many creatures migrate to and from cities, or spend all of their lives there. Some have been introduced deliberately by humans while others, such as brown rats, were introduced by accident. Animals which can find food and shelter in a range of ways, known as generalists, are the most likely to flourish in urban areas.

△ The brown rat is one of the greatest pests in urban areas, often living in cellars and sewers. Rats can kill chickens and ducks, destroy underground cables and carry dangerous diseases such as bubonic plague.

△ Marabou storks are African birds. They breed in treetops, where they build large nests, but they like to live near human settlements. Adult marabous get much of their food from scavenging. Carrion from a wild animal kill, ploughed fields and rubbish tips are their main sources of food.

Urban homes

Buildings provide animals with a variety of places to shelter – from attic spaces inhabited by bats and birds such as swifts, to the spaces between walls where mice often live. The high ledges of tall buildings are homes to starlings and sparrows, as well as cliff-nesting birds such as gulls and kestrels. A city's infrastructure – its transport, water, power and sewer systems – provide many opportunities for shelter. Bats may make their homes in ventilation shafts, while underground transport systems and sewers provide shelter for rats, mice and many insects.

▷ The ledges and roofs of tall city buildings make a home for a range of birds, such as this herring gull and its chick.

▷ Many animals seek shelter from the cold or blistering sun inside buildings. Food, in the form of insects, attracts small predators such as these geckos on a ceiling in Southeast Asia.

Heat islands

Many animals are drawn to and flourish in urban environments. One reason is that cities and towns tend to be 'heat islands'. This means they have higher temperatures than the surrounding countryside. Rivers and canals are more likely to be ice-free, which provides extra feeding opportunities for birds.

▽ The green spaces of a town or city provide vital habitats for many different species, such as these common frogs in an urban pond in Britain.

Rubbish

Waste dumps in urban areas give off heat as they decompose. This provides a suitable habitat for some cold-blooded reptiles such as slow-worms and small lizards. Humans generate a vast amount of organic rubbish. Left on city streets, in bins and at dumps, this is a huge food resource for insects, small reptiles, birds such as crows and gulls, as well as foxes, possums, rats and other scavenging mammals.

Challenges to life

An urban environment also poses challenges to life. Food, sunlight and space to live and breed are limited in many cities, while the threat of vehicles and pest controls can restrict population numbers. Pollution, particularly from vehicle exhausts, means that wildlife has to cope with, on average, ten times more dust particles and carbon dioxide, and 25 times more carbon monoxide than in the surrounding countryside. Despite these tough conditions, many cities support a large and quite diverse range of life.

▽ Close to a million alligators live in Florida, many in the Everglades National Park. Occasionally, alligators may stray into urban areas, but they are only dangerous if provoked.

Pests and threats

Many animals which live in towns and cities are seen as pests which must be controlled. Some carry diseases – raccoons, for example, are prone to rabies. Others, such as pigeons, exist in huge numbers due to a lack of natural predators. Some animals lose their natural habitats as cities grow outwards. They have little choice but to try to survive on the fringes of the urban environment. Larger mammals such as coyotes in North America, jackals in Africa and Asia, the opossum in Oceania and the fox in Europe live as scavengers of domestic rubbish and will occasionally attack pets or garden wildlife.

A world transformed

Early humans were controlled by their environment. They hunted wild animals, gathered plants and many lived as nomads, wandering to places where food was available. As people learned to farm, they began to have far more impact on ecosystems. This impact has increased greatly with the growth of cities and large industries, and the advance of technology. Today, much of the world's landscape has been transformed and its natural cycles altered to meet human demands.

Feeding six billion

In 1700, there were approximately 200 million people on the planet. By 1971, the world population had risen to 3.8 billion. Just thirty years later, it broke the six billion mark. With this massive increase in mouths to feed have come radical new farming processes. Many of these generate more food, but also have a major impact on ecosystems. Heavy use of fertilizers has, in places, overloaded the nitrogen cycle, causing nitrates to contaminate groundwater. Massive fields, created by clearing woodlands and ponds, are often used to grow a single species (a monoculture). In response, many people are demanding more organic farming, where foods are grown without heavy chemical use and in a way that allows wild plants and animals to flourish.

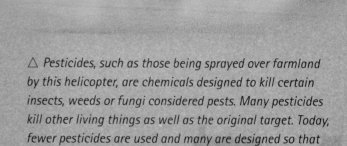

△ Pesticides, such as those being sprayed over farmland by this helicopter, are chemicals designed to kill certain insects, weeds or fungi considered pests. Many pesticides kill other living things as well as the original target. Today, fewer pesticides are used and many are designed so that they will be broken down quickly and naturally.

Shrinking ecosystems

The pressure to feed the growing world population has been a key reason why many ecosystems are shrinking and disappearing. Modern agriculture is often conducted on a large scale, with grasslands and forests destroyed to make room for grazing and crops. Other pressures stem from mining and manufacturing industries which pollute ecosystems, and from towns and cities which have sprawled into countryside, fragmenting what remains of habitats. The combined impact of these human-driven developments is devastating – almost two thirds of Europe's and half of the United States' wetlands have been drained, while around 45 percent of the world's forests have been cut down in the last 40 years.

◁ Large parts of the Amazon rainforest have been destroyed to make room for cattle ranching. The soil can only support the grazing of cattle for a few years.

Controlling nature

Humans use tools and technology to massively change the world around them – from damming rivers and creating artificial lakes and beaches, to reclaiming land from the sea. Recently, scientists have begun to alter the genetic make-up of living things. Genetically modified (GM) species contain genes taken from other species to improve certain characteristics – such as making a plant crop more resistant to frost or pests. Those in favour of genetically modifying foodstuffs believe that it will produce a food boom, with fewer crops lost to disease and bad weather. Some opponents of genetic engineering think that humans shouldn't try to 'play god' by tampering with nature in this way. Others fear that GM crops could spread into the wider environment and introduce their genes into wild plant varieties. This could produce 'superweeds' which are resistant to pesticides.

△ One of the world's biggest construction projects, Hong Kong's Chek Lap Kok airport opened in 1998. It covers 1,248 square kilometres, with a quarter of the site built on existing islands. The other three quarters, equivalent to over 1,200 football fields, consists of land reclaimed from the sea.

◁ Bucardo mountain goats lived in the Pyrenees mountains of northern Spain until the last remaining goat died in 2000. Scientists had taken cells from the goat before its death. Using genetic engineering, they intend to clone the cells and produce an embyro which can be implanted into another species of goat. The hope is that new young can be born and the species brought back from extinction.

Protest

Concerns about the ways in which humans are transforming the planet have led to the rise of environmental pressure groups and organizations. These lobby governments and industry for change. They also raise public awareness of problems – from the plight of endangered species to accelerating global warming – by sponsoring scientific research, publishing reports and, sometimes, protesting. In several countries, particularly in Europe, Green political parties have won many votes. They campaign for bans on poaching, for more sustainable methods of producing energy and food, and for cutbacks in pollution. Certain reforms have taken place. These include greater use of renewable energy, laws to reduce polluting emissions from motor vehicles and the banning of CFCs – types of gas previously used in refrigerators and aerosol cans – which damage the ozone layer and contribute to the greenhouse effect.

▽ Environmental organizations, such as Greenpeace, have campaigned to stop commercial whaling from further reducing the number of whales in the world's oceans. Here, Greenpeace activists make a non-violent protest by confronting a whaling vessel.

Human impact
The future

Earth is naturally dynamic. Its continents shift, its climates change and natural forces – from volcanic activity to shore erosion – reshape the planet. Many species adapt to these natural changes over millions of years while others die out, making room for new species to evolve. However, it is much more difficult for species to adapt to the rapid changes caused by humans in recent centuries. The future may see more and more species become extinct, biological diversity reduced and, possibly, a major climatic shift for the entire planet.

△ At the start of the 20th century, there were an estimated 100,000 tigers in the wild. Habitat loss and poaching by humans has seen that number plummet to below 10,000.

Extinction

Extinction is the end of an evolutionary line with the death of the final member of a species. Many millions of species have become extinct since the Earth first supported life. Extinction is a natural event believed to be vital in the process of evolution – where new species come to prominence and other, older species die out – but the current rate of extinction is worryingly high.

Most of the extinctions which have occurred in the past 300 years have been caused by humans. In North America, for example, over 400 species of plant or animal have become extinct since humans settled there. Thousands more species are in danger of extinction unless their habitats are conserved and the threats to their survival, from pollution to poaching, are removed.

▽ These young spur-tailed tortoises are part of a breeding programme at the Tortoise Village in Gonfaron, France. The centre, home to more than 1,500 animals, was set up in 1988 to study and protect tortoises, turtles and their habitat.

◁ African elephants and impalas gather around a water hole in the relative safety of Chobe National Park in Botswana. The park, 11,700 square kilometres in area, contains over 450 bird species and supports the highest concentration of elephants in Africa.

Biodiversity

Earth is home to at least 14 million species of living thing. This incredible variety supports humankind's own existence by providing foods, fuels, building materials, medicines and raw materials with which to make other products. Biological diversity, or biodiversity for short, also helps buffer ecosystems from sudden change and provides 'natural services' such as clean air, clean water and the removal of decaying matter. With larger numbers of extinctions comes a reduction in biodiversity and the possibility that some of these natural services will not be carried out as efficiently.

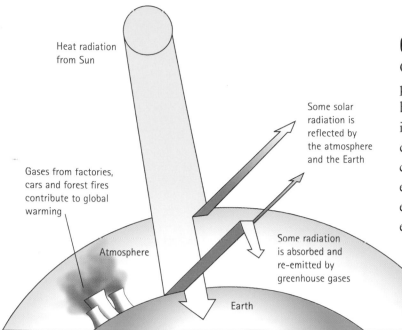

Heat radiation from Sun

Some solar radiation is reflected by the atmosphere and the Earth

Gases from factories, cars and forest fires contribute to global warming

Atmosphere

Some radiation is absorbed and re-emitted by greenhouse gases

Earth

△ *Gases in the atmosphere naturally trap some of the Sun's energy, helping to keep the planet warm. Additional greenhouse gases, emitted by industry, vehicles and other human activities, trap more of the Sun's energy and are believed to be the major reason why the Earth is growing warmer.*

Climate change

One of the biggest threats to the future wellbeing of the planet may come from changes in the climates of many biomes. The world is warming up faster than at any time in the last 10,000 years, with the 1990s being the hottest decade since detailed records were kept. Much of this climate change is believed to be a result of the greenhouse effect, in which more gases which trap the Sun's energy are emitted into Earth's atmosphere. Many experts believe that ecosystems and living things are under threat from global warming. An average temperature rise of 2°C would prevent some farmlands from supporting crops, could lead to an increase in floods, droughts, forest fires and coral decay and see many species of plants and animals disappear from certain habitats.

▽ *One consequence of global temperature rises could be more flooding. This is the swollen Tana river, in Kenya.*

▷ *Scientists predict that the Earth's temperature could rise between about 1°C (the dotted line) and 3°C (the solid line) by 2070. The graph shows this would be a steep rise from 20th-century levels.*

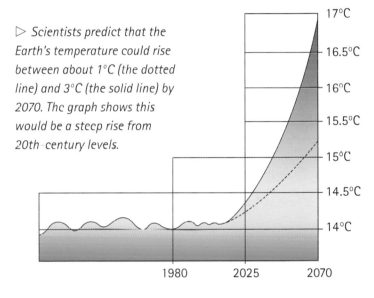

17°C
16.5°C
16°C
15.5°C
15°C
14.5°C
14°C

1980   2025   2070

▷ *Located in a disused china clay pit in Cornwall, the Eden Project houses thousands of plant species in different climatic zones. This is part of the humid tropic biome.*

Conservation

Traditionally, the aim of conservation was to save single species under threat. In some cases, the population of an endangered species is so small that animals are taken out of the wild and into captive breeding programmes. The goal is to increase their numbers in a safe environment before returning the animals to the wild. Today, conservation also aims to preserve habitats and entire ecosystems. As the human population grows and increases its ability to transform environments, the survival of individual species and entire ecosystems will depend more and more on humans finding ways to conserve the planet's resources or use them in a sustainable way.

Classification of living things

Millions of species

There may be more than 14 million different species of life on Earth. Only around 1.75 million have so far been identified. Classification and naming systems allow people to identify and compare different living things. They help scientists around the globe to study and understand the natural world and relate types of living things to species that died out long ago. The first stage of classification divides the millions of species into five kingdoms – animals, plants, fungi, monerans and protists.

▽ *The first stage of classification divides the natural world into five kingdoms.*

Animals (over one million species) Many-celled, usually mobile organisms which are heterotrophic – unable to generate food from direct energy sources. They live by eating plants and other animals.

Monerans (over 4,000 species) Split into two types – true bacteria (or eubacteria) and archaebacteria. Most monerans are single-celled, microscopic organisms. They usually get their energy from substances around them, although some monerans use photosynthesis.

Plants (over 250,000 species) Many-celled organisms which are autotrophic – capable of producing their own food through the process of photosynthesis.

Fungi (over 50,000 species) Organisms which obtain nutrients by absorbing food. Fungi reproduce by making spores.

Protists (over 50,000 species) Mainly single-celled (but sometimes many-celled) organisms, including amoebas and protozoa.

Scientific names

Biologists and naturalists use a naming system invented by the Swedish botanist, Carolus Linnaeus, in which plants and animals are given names in Latin. These names are in two parts. The first word identifies the genus to which the organism belongs, and the second word is the name of its actual species. For example, the grey wolf (*Canis lupus*) is part of the genus *Canis* (which includes jackals, some wolves and the dingo) and its species name is *lupus*.

▽ *Plants can be divided into different groups according to how they reproduce.*

Flowering plants (240,000 species) Monocotyledons (eg tulips) produce seeds containing a single leaf. Dicotyledons (eg sunflowers) have seeds that contain two leaves.

Cone-bearing plants (500 species) Conifers and related plants produce their seeds on woody cones.

Spore-producing plants (26,000 species) Ferns usually reproduce through spores on the underside of their leaves. Mosses and liverworts usually produce their spores in a capsule on a stalk.

From kingdom to species

The differences in the structure of an organism's cells partly determine to which of the five kingdoms the organism belongs. Within each kingdom are a number of phyla (groups of living things which have a similar body plan or organization). Each phylum is divided into one or more classes. Each class is split into orders, which in turn are divided into families and then genera. The smallest complete group is an individual species.

▽ *The scientific name for the honeybee is* Apis mellifera.

Kingdom – Animalia (animals)
▼
Phylum – Arthropoda (joint-footed animals)
▼
Class – Insecta (insects)
▼
Order – Hymenoptera (bees, ants and wasps)
▼
Family – Apidae (bumblebees and honeybees)
▼
Genus – Apis
▼
Species – mellifera

Further resources

Websites

www.bbsr.edu/agcihome/sitelinks/globalchange.html
A large collection of links to webpages concerned with environmental and climate change.

www.biodiversity911.org
Webpages devoted to the issue of biodiversity, with many links to other living world sites.

www.edenproject.com
The website of the giant collection of plants, opened in Cornwall in 2001. The site includes a virtual tour and features on biodiversity and conservation.

www.eelink.net/EndSpp
A website which charts the many endangered species of plants and animals around the world.

www.eppresents.com/VirtualLibrary/Biomes/biomespage.htm
A large, accessible collection of features and images about the world's major biomes.

www.fao.org/desertification
A United Nations' website on the topic of desertification, including maps, images and news.

www.foci.org
Friends of the Earth International is a worldwide collection of groups campaigning for the protection of wildlife and habitats.

www.greenpeace.org
The homepage of Greenpeace International, which runs campaigns and direct action to defend the environment.

www.nationalgeographic.com
The website of *National Geographic* magazine, with features on animals, plants, habitats and regions.

www.noaa.gov
The homepage of the United States National Oceanic and Atmospheric Administration (NOAA), containing information on coastlines, coral reefs and ocean life.

www.nsf.gov/od/opp/wwwsites.htm
A long list of bookmarks and hyperlinks to sites about the Arctic and Antarctic polar regions.

www.panda.org/resources/publications/sustainability/ indigenous/proj_brazil.htm
This Worldwide Fund for Nature (WWF) site examines the challenges facing many indigenous peoples all over the world.

www.pbs.org/tal/costa_rica/rainfacts.html
A website devoted to the science of the rainforest, packed full of interesting facts and features.

www.survival-international.org
Survival International works to protect native tribes and peoples, and the environments in which they live.

www.wildlifer.com/wildlifesites
A large collection of categorized links to websites devoted to all forms of wildlife.

www.worldwildlife.org
The Worldwide Fund for Nature campaigns for animal, plant and habitat protection across the globe.

Books

The Blue Planet, Andrew Byatt et al., BBC Consumer Publishing, 2001.

Deserts, Philip Steele, Zoe Books Limited, 1996.

Facts on File: Environment Atlas, David Wright, Facts on File, 1997.

The Gaia Atlas of Planet Management, Norman Myers (editor) and Gerald Durrell, Oxfam Books, 1994.

The Guinness Book of Amazing Nature, Elizabeth Wyse (managing editor), Guinness Publishing, 1998.

An Introduction to the World's Oceans, Alison B. Duxbury, McGraw-Hill, 1996.

Journey to the Rain Forest, Tim Knight, Oxford, 2002.

The Kingfisher Book of Evolution, Stephen Webster, Kingfisher Publications, 2000.

The Kingfisher Book of Oceans, David Lambert, Kingfisher Publications, 1997.

Landmark Geography: Ecosystems and Human Activity, Julia Woodfield, Collins Educational, 2000.

Nature's Predators, Michael Bright, Barbara Taylor and Robin Kerrod, Southwater, 1991.

World Atlas of Coral Reefs, Mark D. Spalding, Corinna Ravilious and Edmund P. Green, University of California Press, 2001.

Reference
Glossary

Acid rain Rain and snow that contains poisonous or harmful acidic chemicals – such as sulphur dioxide, which is created by burning coal, oil and gas.

Adaptation A change in the structure or behaviour of an organism that makes it better able to live in a particular environment.

Algae Plant-like organisms which contain chlorophyll but have no true leaves or roots.

Atoll A ring-shaped island made of coral reef that surrounds a lagoon.

Bacteria Microscopic, single-celled organisms. Bacteria are the most abundant living things on Earth.

Biodiversity The variety of species in a particular area.

Biome A large, general habitat covering a region of the Earth. Tundra, taiga forest, desert and grasslands are all biomes.

Biosphere The parts of the Earth where living things exist.

Blubber A thick layer of fat which helps keep some animals warm. Polar bears, seals, whales and penguins all have blubber.

Camouflage The way that the colouring and markings of an animal blend with the surroundings, making the animal difficult to see.

Carnivore An animal or plant which eats meat.

Carrion The rotting flesh of dead animals, often eaten by scavengers.

Cartilage A tough, flexible tissue in the skeleton of a vertebrate. It can form parts of the body such as the nose and ears. In cartilaginous fish, such as sharks, it forms the entire skeleton.

Cell A tiny unit of living matter. Cells are the building blocks of all living things.

Chlorophyll The green chemical in a plant which traps the energy in sunlight. Plants use this energy to make food.

Climate The general weather conditions of a region over a long period of time.

Conifer A plant that reproduces by making cones. Conifers are mainly evergreen trees and bushes which keep their leaves all year.

Deciduous Deciduous trees shed their leaves every autumn. This helps them to conserve water through the winter.

Decomposer A living thing that gains nutrients by breaking down dead plant and animal matter. The minerals contained in the dead matter are released into the environment.

Deforestation The cutting down of large numbers of trees for fuel or timber, or to use the land for settlements or farming.

Desertification The way a desert expands and spreads, reducing the land's ability to support life. Desertification is caused by climate change, overfarming, overgrazing and by removing plants which hold soil in place.

Digest To break down food so that it can be absorbed and used by the body.

Domesticated animal An animal that is kept as a pet, a means of transport or for food, rather than one which lives in the wild.

Dormant Inactive, hibernating or not growing.

Ecology The branch of science which studies the relationships between different living things and their environment.

Ecosystem A collection of all the living things and their non-living surroundings in a particular area.

Embryo A tiny bundle of cells that is a young plant or animal in the earliest stage of its development.

Endangered species Species of living thing which are seriously threatened with extinction.

Enzymes A substance which speeds up the processes that take place inside a living thing. For example, digestive enzymes change food into liquids which can enter the blood and travel round the body.

Epiphyte A plant which grows on another plant or a rock instead of in soil. Epiphytes obtain moisture and nutrients directly from the air.

Equator The imaginary line around the centre of the Earth, an equal distance from the North and South Poles.

Evaporation The process by which a liquid changes into a gas. For example, the warming of air by sunlight causes water in plants to evaporate and change into water vapour.

Evolution The long-term process of change in organisms, often taking place over millions of years.

Extinction The permanent disappearance of a species with the death of its last member.

Feral A feral species is one which was once domesticated but has since returned to life in the wild.

Fertilization The process by which a male and female cell join together to form an embryo.

Fertilizer A substance added to soil to make it more fertile.

Food chain A food chain shows the links between different animals that feed on plants and each other. Energy and nutrients pass up through the chain. Large carnivores such as eagles and big cats tend to be at the top of food chains, with plants and decomposers at the bottom.

Food web A diagram showing all the interconnected food chains in an ecosystem.

Gene The part of a cell that passes characteristics – such as eye or hair colour – from an adult to its offspring.

Genetic engineering Changing the genes in a living cell so that the cell can do something it could not do naturally.

Germination The first stage in the growth of a seed or spore into a plant.

Gill The part of an aquatic animal's body which collects oxygen from water and enables the animal to breathe.

Greenhouse effect The build-up of certain gases such as carbon dioxide and methane in Earth's atmosphere. The gases trap the Sun's heat and affect Earth's climate.

Habitat The surroundings that a particular species needs to survive. Habitats include coral reefs, grasslands, lakes and deserts. Some species can live in more than one habitat.

Hemisphere One half of the Earth's sphere, above or below the equator. Seasons in the southern hemisphere are reversed from those in the northern hemisphere.

Herbivore An animal that eats only plants.

Hibernation A deep sleep, usually in winter, which enables some animals to survive when food is hard to find.

Host An animal which a parasite uses as its home and food source.

Humus A substance found in soil, made from dead plant and animal matter. Humus helps to keep soil fertile.

Incubate To keep eggs warm by sitting on them.

Insulation A layer of fur, fat or feathers which reduces the amount of heat lost from an animal's body.

Introduced species A species that people have taken from one part of the world and released into another area. Introduced species can have devastating consequences on the ecosystems into which they are released.

Invertebrate An animal without a backbone, such as an insect, a worm or a snail.

Irrigation A system of watering land by using pipes and ditches to channel water.

Krill Small, shrimp-like animals which exist in their millions in polar seas. They provide food for whales, fish and other animals.

Larva The young form of an insect, which looks very different from an adult. A caterpillar is the larva of a butterfly.

Leaf litter The layer of whole leaves and leaf fragments that carpets the floor of a forest.

Life cycle All the major stages in the life of an organism – from the start of its life, through its growth and breeding, until its death.

Microclimate The climate of a small, defined area, such as a valley.

Migration Round trips made by animals between habitats, in search of food or to reach breeding grounds. Many animals, such as wildebeest and birds, migrate every year.

Mineral A chemical substance, such as iron or magnesium, that occurs naturally in rocks and soil. All plants and animals need to take in certain minerals to survive.

Niche A place that something can fit into. An ecological niche is the way in which a living thing fits into its environment.

Nocturnal Active mainly at night.

Nomad An animal or human which does not have a fixed home and usually keeps on the move, travelling to wherever food can be found.

Nutrient Material taken in by a living thing to help it stay alive.

Omnivore An animal that eats both plants and animals.

Organism Any living thing.

Parasite An organism that feeds on or inside another living thing, which is called the host. Parasites are usually much smaller than their hosts, and don't always harm them.

Permafrost Ground that is permanently frozen, such as the soil below the surface of the tundra.

Pesticide A chemical used by farmers that kills pests – animals that damage crops or livestock.

Photosynthesis The process by which plants use the energy from sunlight to make food from water and carbon dioxide.

Plankton Microscopic living things which drift near the surface of lakes and oceans. Plankton includes algae which collect energy from sunlight, and tiny animals which eat algae or each other.

Pollen A dust-like powder, produced by plants, which contains male sex cells.

Pollination The movement of pollen from the male part of a flower to the female part so that reproduction can occur.

Predator An animal that kills and feeds on another animal, which is known as its prey.

Prehensile Able to grip or grasp an object. Some monkeys have a prehensile tail, which they use to grip branches as they swing through the canopy of a rainforest.

Prey An animal that is hunted and killed for food.

Pupate When an insect larva pupates, it makes a tough case around its body. Protected by the case, the larva changes shape and becomes an adult.

Reproduction The production of a new living thing by an organism.

Respiration Breathing.

Scavenger An animal, such as a vulture or a hyena, which feeds on the dead remains of animals or plants.

Soil erosion The process by which loose soil is washed or blown away.

Species A set of organisms which can be grouped together due to their similarity and their ability to breed with each other.

Symbiosis A close relationship between two organisms of different species. Sometimes, both species benefit, but in many partnerships one species gains much more than the other.

Temperate Neither very hot nor very cold. Temperate zones lie between the tropics and the polar regions.

Territory The area in which an animal lives and finds food. Animals often defend their territory against other members of the same species.

Tributary A stream or river that flows into a larger river or a lake.

Tropics The region around the equator which remains hot all year round.

Vertebrate An animal that has a backbone.

Reference

Index

Acknowledgements

The publishers would like to thank the following for providing photographs:

Front cover Still Pictures/GAYO, *c* National Geographic Society/Annie Griffiths Bell, *cl* www.osf.uk.com/Raymond J. C. Cannon, *t* www.osf.uk.com/Michael Sewell; **back cover** *b* Bruce Coleman Collection/Staffan Widstrand.

Page 6 *c* Still Pictures/Klein/Hubert, *cr* www.osf.uk.com/Paul Kay; **6-7** *br* NHPA/ A.N.T.; **7** *cl* BBC Natural History Unit Picture Library/Sue Flood, *c* Ardea London/Jean-Paul Ferrero; **8** *r* www.osf.uk.com/Neil Bromhall, *bl* Still Pictures/Fritz Polking; **9** *tl* www.osf.uk.com/Satoshi Kuribayashi, *cr* Ardea London/John Clegg, *b* Ardea London/ P. Morris; **10** *tr* www.osf.uk.com/Norbert Wu, *cl* www.osf.uk.com/Paulo De Oliveira; **11** *tr* Frank Lane Picture Agency/Fritz Polking, *cl* www.osf.uk.com/James H. Robinson, *br* BBC Natural History Unit Picture Library/Anup Shah; **12** *bl* Corbis/Alissa Crandall; **13** *cl* NHPA/ B. Jones & M. Shimlock, *c* Still Pictures/Volker Steger, *br* NHPA/Guy Edwards; **14** *c* Ardea London/Pat Morris, *bl* Corbis/Jeffrey L. Rotman; **14-15** *tc* Ardea London/François Gohier, *bc* BBC Natural History Unit Picture Library/David Shale; **15** *tr* Corbis/Ralph White, *br* www.osf.uk.com/ Scripps Inst. Oceanography; **16** *cl* Frank Lane Picture Agency/Silvestris, *bl* NHPA/B. Jones & M. Shimlock, *bc* Bruce Coleman Collection/Pacific Stock; **17** *tc* Ardea London/Ron & Valerie Taylor, *tr* Ardea London/Kurt Amsler, *bl* Bruce Coleman Collection/Natural Selection Inc., *br* Bruce Coleman Collection/Franco Banfi; **18** *tr* Ardea London/Bob Gibbons, *cl* BBC Natural History Unit Picture Library/Niall Benvie, *bc* BBC Natural History Unit Picture Library/Jeff Foott; **18-19** BBC Natural History Unit Picture Library/ T. Andrewartha, *c* Ardea London/Hans D. Dossenbach; **19** *tl* Ardea London/Valerie Taylor, *cl* NHPA/Dr Ivan Polunin; **20** *tr* Ardea London/ John Daniels, *bl* NHPA/Silvestris Fotoservice, *br* www.osf.uk.com/Okapia; **20-21** *c* Ardea London/ Adrian Warren; **21** *tl* Ardea London, *cr* Ardea London/François Gohier, *br* www.osf.uk.com/ Andrew Plumptre; **22** *tr* www.osf.uk.com/NASA, *bl* Corbis/Carl Purcell; **23** *tl* Ardea London/David & Katie Urry, *c* Ardea London/François Gohier, *br* www.osf.uk.com/Mary Plage; **24** *tr* BBC Natural History Unit Picture Library/David Noton, *cl* Still Pictures/Ronald Seitre; **24-25** *b* Still Pictures/Ronald Seitre; **25** *cl* Ardea London/ François Gohier, *br* Ardea London/François Gohier; **26** *cr* www.osf.uk.com/G. I. Bernard, *bl* Bruce Coleman Collection/Natural Selection Inc.; **26-27** *t* Science Photo Library/Gregory Dimijian, *c* Ardea London/Masahiro Lijima;

27 *tr* www.osf.uk.com/Michael Sewell, *cr* Frank Lane Picture Agency/J. Zimmermann, *bl* Science Photo Library/Fletcher & Baylis; **28** *tr* www.osf.uk.com/Mike Linley, *bl* Ardea London/J. P. Ferrero; **29** *tl* Still Pictures/Alain Compost, *tr* Frank Lane Picture Agency, *cl* Ardea London/M. D. England, *br* BBC Natural History Unit Picture Library/Phil Savoie; **30** *tr* Ardea London/Eric Dragesco, *cl* Ardea London/Martin W. Grosnick, *cr* Ardea London/M. Watson; **30-31** *b* BBC Natural History Unit Picture Library/ Andrew Zvoznikov; **31** *tl* Ardea London/J. A. Bailey, *tl* Ardea London/John Swedberg, *cl* Ardea London/Dennis Avon, *cr* NHPA/Stephen Dalton; **32** *tr* NHPA/Stephen Dalton, *cl* Ardea London/ François Gohier, *b* www.osf.uk.com/David M. Dennis; **32-33** Still Pictures/Alex S. Maclean; **33** *tr* Ardea London/J. Swedberg, *cr* NHPA/ A. N. T., *bl* Ardea London/Bob Gibbons; **34** *tr* Ardea London/Bill Coster, *cl* Corbis/Arne Hodalic, *b* www.osf.uk.com/Chris Sharp; **35** *tl* Frank Lane Picture Agency/Silvestris Fotoservice, *c* NHPA/Martin Harvey, *br* Ardea London/ Jean-Paul Ferrero; **36** *tr* Ardea London/Ferrero-Labat, *cl* Ardea London/Ferrero-Labat, *cr* Ardea London/Ferrero-Labat; **36-37** *b* BBC Natural History Unit Picture Library/T. Andrewartha; **37** *tr* www.osf.uk.com/Steve Turner, *cl* www.osf.uk.com/Martyn Colbeck; **38** *cr* BBC Natural History Unit Picture Library/Anup Shah, *b* Bruce Coleman Collection/HPH Photography; **39** *tr* NHPA/Christopher Ratier, *cl* BBC Natural History Unit Picture Library/Anup Shah, *b* BBC Natural History Unit Picture Library/Peter Blackwell; **40** *tr* Bruce Coleman Collection, *cl* Ardea London/François Gohier; **40-41** Bruce Coleman Collection; **41** *tl* BBC Natural History Unit Picture Library/Jeff Foott, *br* BBC Natural History Unit Picture Library/John Downer; **42** *tr* Ardea London/Wendy Shattil/Bob Rozinski, *cl* Ardea London/Adrian Warren, *br* Corbis/ Bettmann; **43** *tl* Frank Lane Picture Agency/ Gerard Lacz, *cr* Corbis/Kit Houghton, *b* BBC Natural History Unit Picture Library/Pete Oxford; **44** *tr* NASA, *br* Corbis; **44-45** *b* Frank Lane Picture Agency/David Hosking; **45** *tr* Ardea London/François Gohier, *cl* NASA, *br* Still Pictures/Frans Lemmens; **46** *tr* www.osf.uk.com/ Michael Fogden, *cl* NHPA/Rod Planck, *br* Ardea London/Peter Steyn; **47** *tr* Ardea London/Peter Steyn, *c* www.osf.uk.com/Michael Fogden, *cr* www.osf.uk.com/Avril Ramage, *br* NHPA/Dave Watts; **48** *tr* Still Pictures/John Cancalosi, *cl* www.osf.uk.com/Tim Jackson, *bl* Corbis; **49** *tr* Corbis, *cl* Frank Lane Picture Agency/L. W. Walker, *br* BBC Natural History Unit Picture Library/Graham Hatherley; **50** *cl* Still Pictures/ UNEP, *cr* Corbis; **50-51** BBC Natural History Unit Picture Library/Pete Oxford; **51** *cl* Corbis,

bl www.osf.uk.com/C. W. Helliwell, *br* NASA; **52** *tr* Still Pictures/Thomas D. Mangelsen, *cr* Still Pictures/Gunter Ziesler, *bl* Still Pictures/ Kim Heacox; **52-53** *b* BBC Natural History Unit Picture Library/Staffan Widstrand; **53** *tl* Ardea London/Andrey Zvoznikov, *tr* Bruce Coleman Collection/Gordon Langsbury, *cr* Still Pictures/ Thomas D. Mangelsen; **54** *cr* Corbis/Amos Nachoum, *b* Ardea London/E. Mickleburgh; **55** *tl* Corbis/Jim Zuckerman, *cr* BBC Natural History Unit Picture Library/Doc White, *bl* BBC Natural History Unit Picture Library/Tom Mangelsen; **56** *cl* BBC Natural History Unit Picture Library/ Doug Allan, *cr* www.osf.uk.com/Rudie H. Kuiter, *br* BBC Natural History Unit Picture Library/ Doc White; **56-57** BBC Natural History Unit Picture Library/Martha Holmes; **57** *tl* NHPA/ Norbert Wu, *tr* Ardea London/C. G. Robertson, *b* www.osf.uk.com/Doug Allan; **58** *tr* Bruce Coleman Collection/Staffan Widstrand, *cl* NHPA/ B. & C. Alexander, *c* Corbis; **59** *cr* The Royal Geographical Society/A. C. Hardy, *bl* The Royal Geographical Society/Charles Swithinbank, *bc* The Royal Geographical Society/Charles Swithinbank; **60** *cl* www.osf.uk.com/John Brown, *br* Ardea London/Jean-Paul Ferrero; **60-61** *tr* Still Pictures/Norbert Wu; **61** *tr* Still Pictures/Fritz Polking, *bl* www.osf.uk.com/John Brown, *br* Frank Lane Picture Agency/Minden Pictures; **62** *tr* Still Pictures/D. Decobecq, *cl* Corbis/Kevin Schafer; **62-63** *b* NHPA/Martin Harvey; **63** *tl* BBC Natural History Unit Picture Library/ John Cancalosi, *cr* www.osf.uk.com/Tui De Roy; **64** *tr* Still Pictures/Ronald Seitre, *cl* Still Pictures/ Ronald Seitre, *br* Still Pictures/Klein/Hubert; **65** *tl* Ardea London/Hans & Judy Beste, *cr* NHPA/ Ann & Steve Toon, *b* Ardea London/Jean-Paul Ferrero; **66** *tr* Clive Gifford, *bl* Getty Images; **66-67** *b* Still Pictures/Sarvottam Rajkoomar; **67** *tr* www.osf.uk.com/Victoria McCormick, *br* Corbis; **68** *tl* NHPA/Nigel J. Dennis, *tr* Ardea London/ Liz & Tony Bomford, *b* Ardea London/J. B. & S. Bottomley; **69** *tr* NHPA/Daniel Heuclin, *cl* NHPA/ John Buckingham, *br* Ardea London/Martin W. Grosnick; **70** *bl* Still Pictures/Mark Edwards; **70-71** Still Pictures/Ray Pfortner; **71** *tr* Corbis/ Michael S. Yamashita, *cl* Ardea London/ M. Watson, *br* Still Pictures/Pierre Gleizes; **72** *c* NHPA/Daryl Balfour, *bl* www.osf.uk.com/Olivier Grunewald; **73** *cl* Still Pictures/G. Griffiths/ Christian Aid, *br* NHPA/Alberto Nardi.

Key: b = bottom, c = centre, l = left, r = right, t = top

Every effort has been made to trace the copyright holders of the photographs. The publishers apologize for any inconvenience caused.